Praise for Rob Mundle

for *Flinders*
'In skilful prose, Mundle vividly stresses the personal costs of Flinders' ambition: shipwrecks, the loss of good friends and crew to a hostile sea, as well as his decade-long absence from home'
The Australian

'Rob Mundle is a master of the maritime narrative' *Sunday Age*

'A drama of adventure and shipwreck' *Sun-Herald*

for *Cook*
'Competitive sailor and accomplished writer Rob Mundle puts readers on the quarterdeck as Cook guides his ship through treacherous reefs and swells to solve the mystery surrounding the existence of Terra Australis' *Courier Mail*

'... a thrilling biography for those who love adventure and the intricacies and challenges of sailing' *sail-world.com.au*

'Rob Mundle brings a wealth of navigational and ship-construction detail to Cook's adventures, and his descriptions of the capricious ocean – having been exposed to Cook's perils himself – lend this biography all the suspense of a good thriller' *Weekend Australian*

for *The First Fleet*
'A colourful, well-researched and fascinating account of the unlikely founding of a great nation' *Australian Women's Weekly*

'Mundle's insight into First Fleet diary and journal descriptions of storms and navigation is enhanced by his personal experience of sailing stretches of ocean traversed by Phillip. But it is his sensitive observation of human frailty that gives his work resonance'
Daily Telegraph

'Wonderful story – useful reading for all Australians' Ian Perkins, *goodreads.com*

'[The author's] seafaring experience, along with his passion for the subject, has produced another extraordinarily compelling book'
Weekend Australian

ALSO BY ROB MUNDLE

Bob Oatley: A Life Story

Bond: Alan Bond

Fatal Storm: The 54th Sydney to Hobart Yacht Race

Hell on High Seas: Amazing Stories of Survival Against the Odds

Learning to Sail

Jack Joel: My Life Story

*Life at the Extreme: The Volvo Ocean Race Round
the World 2005–2006*

*Ocean Warriors: The Thrilling Story of the 2001–2002 Volvo Ocean Race
Round the World*

Sir James Hardy: An Adventurous Life

Sydney to Hobart: The 1995 Golden Anniversary

Bligh: Master Mariner

Flinders: The Man Who Mapped Australia

Cook: From Sailor to Legend

The First Fleet

Great South Land

Under Full Sail

Chasing the Cup: My America's Cup Journey
with Jimmy Spithill

THE SYDNEY HOBART YACHT RACE

ROB MUNDLE

ABC
BOOKS

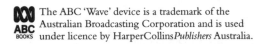 The ABC 'Wave' device is a trademark of the
Australian Broadcasting Corporation and is used
under licence by HarperCollins*Publishers* Australia.

First published in Australia in 2019
by HarperCollins*Publishers* Australia Pty Limited
ABN 36 009 913 517
harpercollins.com.au

HarperCollins*Publishers*
Level 13, 201 Elizabeth Street, Sydney NSW 2000, Australia
Unit D1, 63 Apollo Drive, Rosedale, Auckland 0632, New Zealand
A 53, Sector 57, Noida, UP, India
1 London Bridge Street, London, SE1 9GF, United Kingdom
Bay Adelaide Centre, East Tower, 22 Adelaide Street West, 41st floor, Toronto,
  Ontario M5H 4E3, Canada
195 Broadway, New York NY 10007, USA

A catalogue record for this book is available
from the National Library of Australia

ISBN 978 0 7333 3982 0 (hardback)
ISBN 978 1 4607 1101 9 (ebook)

Cover design by Mark Campbell, HarperCollins Design Studio
Front cover image © Rolex / Daniel Forster
Back cover image: Hurley, Frank. (1910). Sydney Harbour, Hobart yacht race start,
nla.obj-160067477, National Library of Australia
Typeset in Bembo Std by Kirby Jones
Printed and bound in Australia by McPherson's Printing Group The papers used by
HarperCollins in the manufacture of this book are a natural, recyclable product made from
wood grown in sustainable plantation forests. The fibre source and manufacturing processes meet
recognised international environmental standards, and carry certification.

Contents

Introduction

Commodore Paul Billingham

On 7 October 2019, I was at the Royal Yacht Club of Tasmania preparing to launch the 75th Sydney to Hobart Yacht Race. It was the first time the Cruising Yacht Club of Australia had organised a media launch for the race from Hobart, and, perhaps suitably, it was a blustery, moody day in Sandy Bay — the sun occasionally came out, but there was the promise of a storm.

As I prepared to speak I thought about what suitable words I might say to mark the anniversary, and as I did I was drawn to Captain John Illingworth's simple response when asked by founders of the CYCA to join them in a cruise to Hobart in 1945, that first year: 'If you make a race of it, I'll come'.

Of course, they did make a race of it and, ever since the story of the CYCA has been entwined with that of the 'Great Race'.

Over the years, I have realised that the Sydney Hobart race is a story with many different players.

It is a story of yachting evolution — from pre-war wooden classics to carbon fibre supermaxis, and at the same time been, and always will be, a proving ground for boat building innovation.

It is a story of the people who make the race happen, strive to make it as safe as possible, as fair as possible and as exciting as possible.

It is a story of two beautiful cities, 628 nautical miles apart, but tied together in the eyes of the world each Christmas time.

Most importantly though, the Hobart is a story of the characters who sail in the race – some make the pilgrimage annually, while for others it is a once in a lifetime 'bucket list' adventure. But whatever their personal reasons for racing might be, all have been united by the unique challenge which is 'doing a Hobart'. Consequently, they are entitled to join that elite group of sailors who can already make that proud boast.

In this book Rob Mundle tells their stories spanning 75 years – as individuals; as crew, and by being part of a blue water community. Rob does this in a way that helps us understand why people feel that inexorable draw to the challenge of the ocean, year in, year out, and for little more than bragging rights.

At the CYCA we are proud of every one of them and proud of a race that started by a chance conversation and has gone on to become a sporting icon in the eyes of Australia and the World.

Paul Billingham
Commodore
Cruising Yacht Club of Australia
October 2019

Foreword

Sir James Hardy

Rob Mundle has certainly earned the right to author this excellent book celebrating the first 75 years of the Sydney to Hobart Yacht Race.

Rob's early days as a cadet journalist were spent in Canberra and Sydney when Rupert Murdoch launched his great newspaper enterprise, *The Australian*, in 1964.

He has successfully participated in every aspect of sailing, whether afloat or ashore, and over the last 25 years has thoroughly researched and written countless best-selling books, primarily on maritime subjects.

For my own part, I have sailed in twelve Sydney Hobart races. My first, in 1955, was aboard Norm Howard's 42-foot sloop, *Southern Myth*, from the Royal South Australian Yacht Squadron. My last, in the 50th Anniversary race in 1994, was aboard my own yacht, *Nerida*, under the burgee of the Royal Sydney Yacht Squadron.

First impressions are always lasting – and before the start of the Sydney-Hobart race on Boxing Day in 1955, while we were warming up on Sydney Harbour in a building north-easterly breeze, we witnessed the two beautiful, large and historic racing yachts, *Kurrewa IV* (ex-*Morna*) and *Even,* sailing up the harbour, close-hauled and side-by-side on port tack. Both of these classic and majestic yachts had brand new sails made of cream coloured Egyptian cotton, and *Kurrewa's* crew were all wearing white while the crew on *Even* were in red. It was a breathtaking sight to behold – one that has stayed with me ever since.

My experience aboard *Southern Myth* that year taught me one thing that I have never forgotten; the Hobart Race is never lost or won until it is finished. We had been well ahead of that year's eventual winner, *Moonbi,* and runner-up *Cooroyba* all the way across Bass Strait, but after that, they sailed a closer course to the Tasmanian coast and found a favourable wind while we were becalmed with the other yachts well offshore.

Tasman Island, at the entrance to Storm Bay, is often another big hurdle. On many occasions over the years, yachts that appeared destined to be the handicap winner when they rounded the island – including yours truly in 1980 with my yacht *Police Car* – have been all-too-often hobbled by the weather between there and the finish.

Regardless, every yacht receives a grand reception when it reaches Hobart, and there is always great excitement, and eager anticipation, during the long wait for the handicap winner, the recipient of the Tattersall Cup, to be announced.

For me, it is also the camaraderie and sportsmanship among shipmates in ocean racing that is unique. I clearly remember an incident when I was racing my 42-foot yacht, *Nyamba,* during the 1979 Hobart when we were running downwind across Bass

Strait in a fresh north–northeast breeze. Suddenly we lost control of the yacht – bang – our large spinnaker blew out! Not long afterwards we were flattened again when the second spinnaker blew apart. The yacht was knocked flat on its side with the top half around the top of the mast – and we stayed that way for what seemed like ages while we tried to get the yacht back upright.

During this time, I noticed Ray Kirby in his yacht *Patrice*, which was ahead of us, had his crew lower their spinnaker so they could turn back and make sure we were okay. It was a wonderful gesture that I have never forgotten.

The Sydney-Hobart Yacht Race is a unique event that has contributed enormously to the development of the sport of ocean racing in Australia and around the world, especially when it comes to yacht design, construction and materials.

On the safety side, great strides have been made since the 1998 race tragedy. For example, the SOLAS (Safety of Life at Sea) Trust has contributed greatly to this cause through the significant improvement of safety equipment and introduction of mandatory regulations for participating sailors and their yachts.

Each year great credit is due to the many people behind the scenes at the Cruising Yacht Club of Australia who organise the rules for each year's Hobart race – especially when it comes to crew experience, the standard of safety equipment and the inspection and measurement of each yacht.

No matter if I am competing, or ashore and following the race, my hope always is for a fair contest where the winner is a well-prepared and well-sailed yacht.

For me, the great Australian poet Adam Lindsay Gordon probably said it best:

No game was ever yet worth a rap
For a rational man [person] to play
Into which no accident, no mishap
Could possibly find its way.

Sir James (Jim) Hardy
Sydney – September 2019

Prologue

In late December 1998, four long-time mates were standing at the first tee on a picturesque golf course on the Gold Coast, 70 kilometres south of Brisbane. This was the start of their regular weekly round of eighteen holes, an outing where they would laugh a lot, grab every possible opportunity to take the mickey out of each other, then enjoy a few frosty beers in the clubhouse after the game.

When it came time to hit off, the first of the foursome stepped up, placed a ball on the tee, took a couple of practice swings then contemplated driving the small, white sphere on a long and straight trajectory down the fairway.

Another thought flashed through his mind; one which, despite having its origins hundreds of kilometres away, was so distracting it caused him to stop then turn towards his mates and say, 'What about those yachties! They're bloody mad! You'd never get me out there in those conditions. Why on earth do they do it?'

The declaration left his three mates dumbstruck. Here was Alan Jones, Australia's Formula One motor racing world champion in 1980, who had flirted with death on countless

7

occasions as a race-car driver, thinking that participants in an ocean yacht race were insane. Between 1975 and 1986, Jones had guided sleek, low-profile projectiles around race tracks at some 300 km/h, executing daring manoeuvres where he positioned the car just centimetres from the track wall, or a competitor. It was a situation where one small error of judgement could deliver catastrophic, even fatal, consequences.

Regardless of this, from his perspective, the thought of men and women racing yachts, large and small, across a horrendous storm-lashed ocean for little else but bragging rights and the satisfaction that came with completing the course was beyond comprehension; it seemed the element of danger far outweighed the level of pleasure.

Jones's mates shook their heads in disbelief, then got on with the game.

However, there was a cogent reason for Jones's comment. It was the last week of December 1998, and the bulk of the fleet competing in what was the fifty-fourth staging of the 628 nautical mile (nm) (1170 kilometre) Sydney Hobart Yacht Race had been trapped by a *weather bomb* off the south-east corner of the Australian mainland. The heinous nature of the storm brought with it unprecedented carnage and desperate fights for survival by many competitors. The race made headline news across Australia and around the world for all the wrong reasons.

It was the convergence of two extreme weather systems over Bass Strait that detonated the *bomb*, a maelstrom that developed so quickly that it even caught meteorologists by surprise. In a very short period of time the howling south-westerly wind went well beyond cyclone force – 64 knots

(110 km/h). It combined with an opposing, fast-flowing southerly current to generate cresting combers that were peaking and breaking at over 20 metres high.

These were survival conditions so severe that in a matter of hours what would later be recognised as Australia's largest peacetime search and rescue mission was under way.

Forty-eight hours later, when the storm had eased, the alarming toll could be counted: of the 115 yachts in the fleet only 44 reached Hobart; 55 sailors – men and women – had been winched to safety, many in miraculous and heroic circumstances by helicopter rescue crews; and five yachts had sunk.

Most tragically, though, six sailors had perished.

The thoroughness of the official investigations into this tragedy resulted in the Sydney Hobart race in particular, and the sport worldwide, being better organised and made safer. Additionally, international search and rescue procedures were improved.

*

Twenty-one years later, on the eve of the 75th anniversary Sydney Hobart race in 2019, it was estimated that more than 54,000 competitors – men and women, young and old – had participated in the classic since its inception in 1945, and a total of 6198 yachts had crossed the start line on Sydney's magnificent harbour.

Today the Hobart race remains one of the world's three premier offshore racing events, the others being the Fastnet

Race (603 nm) out of England, and America's Newport (Rhode Island) to Bermuda Race (635 nm). The one significant difference between the Hobart race and the others is that it is an annual event while the Fastnet and Bermuda races are staged biennially. Also, the Hobart is the only major ocean race in the world that starts on a harbour and finishes on a river. Beyond that, when it comes to status on the international scene, there is a credo that stands among many sailors worldwide that puts the Australian event as the greatest race of all: 'You haven't done an ocean race until you've done a Hobart.'

One significant difference that sets the Hobart apart is that it is a lot more than a great sporting challenge just for 'yachties'. While the Fastnet and Bermuda races go virtually unnoticed outside the sport, the Hobart is a highpoint of interest during the Australian summer festive season for sailors and the public alike. From the moment the starting cannon booms out its signal amid a cloud of white smoke at 1pm on Boxing Day (26 December) until the yachts reach the finish line in Hobart, landlubbers and sailors alike pursue news of the race via television, newspapers, radio and social media. Indications are that the national television audience in Australia exceeds 1.6 million while the international broadcast reaches an estimated 16 million subscribers across 43 countries.

For the spectators it is as if nature created Sydney Harbour with the sole purpose of accommodating the amazingly colourful scene that comes with the start of the race. The harbour is arguably the world's most magnificent natural amphitheatre – from beachfront to clifftop. In the many thousands of residences and apartments in between, an inordinate number of people gather on Boxing Day to party and absorb the excitement of the scene. On the cobalt blue water of the harbour there is always a logjam of craft, ranging from superyachts and large ferries to tiny dinghies, every one of them crammed with enthusiastic onlookers. Overhead, a flock of helicopters whirl around with television camera operators and photographers on board, all eager to capture every aspect of the colourful kaleidoscope below.

For the racing sailors, this spectacle is one of the many reasons that the Hobart stands as the world's premier ocean race. Between the unmatched scene at the start and the spontaneously warm welcome each yacht receives on reaching Hobart (no matter the hour), there is a complete, four-stage, round-the-clock test of yacht and crew from start to finish.

After clearing Sydney Heads and turning south, the fleet is on a 240 nm coastal leg down the western edge of the sometimes volatile Tasman Sea to Cape Howe, located on the border between New South Wales and Victoria. The next stage is 'across the paddock', a 240 nm stretch across the relatively shallow Bass Strait to St Helens on the north-east corner of the Tasmanian coast. The strait is known for its many, often hostile, moods: some years it can be glassy and smooth; at other times at the opposite end of the spectrum – like in the tragic 1998 race.

With Bass Strait in their wake the crews experience what can often be a scenic 100 nm coastal leg to Tasman Island, the major turning point on the course, at the entrance to the often appropriately named Storm Bay. Should it be daylight when rounding the island then the crews get to see one of Tasmania's many spectacular natural assets, the 300-metre-high pillars of rock known as The Organ Pipes at Cape Pillar. These are the tallest such rock formations in the Southern Hemisphere.

From that point it is a 28 nm direct course across Storm Bay to a tiny islet named The Iron Pot. It marks the entrance to the Derwent River, and the start of the 11 nm home stretch to the finish line which is sited on the city's historic waterfront, at the foot of the mighty 1200-metre-high Mount Wellington.

For the spectators in Hobart everything about the finish is like being ringside; so each year there will be between a hundred and more than a thousand locals and visitors gathered around the waterfront and on the docks to welcome the yachts as they arrive. There have also been times, especially when the supermaxis are locked into a battle for line honours, that ten thousand or more have been on the riverfront or aboard boats to watch the duel and welcome the crews.

But it is what happens over that 628 nm between the start and finish that really matters. The fact is that unless everything goes your way – particularly with the weather – you are not likely to achieve your goal, be it finishing first (line honours), winning the ultimate prize (first place in fleet on corrected time), winning your division on corrected time, or simply beating friends on a rival yacht.

Put simply, this race demands multiple skills: it's like combining football, flying and surfing then coupling that with the endurance of a marathon runner. Add to that the luck of the draw that comes with playing poker, and the skill of a chess player in planning a forward strategy, and you have the formula.

This race is an around-the-clock challenge from the harbour to Hobart, even over the final 11 nm from The Iron

Pot to the finish line. Across the decades there have been many occasions when the race for either handicap or line honours has been won or lost on the Derwent – due on most occasions to the whim of the weather and the flow of the tide. Also, there have been times when a bitterly cold gale of 50 plus knots has roared up the Derwent from the south and hammered race yachts, shredding sails, damaging rigs and even driving yachts aground – all when the finish line was in sight. At other times yachts have gone backwards towards the river entrance due to there being no wind and an ebb tide – an agonising experience where, instead of taking 45 minutes to get to the line, it can take a horribly frustrating number of hours.

Out on the ocean the competitors can be confronted by numerous unpredictable elements: swirling coastal currents; calms; gales; and seas that can vary from table-top smooth to horrendously high. There is also an invisible component, the wind. It can range from nothing to nightmarish.

For the sailors who are serious about their position in the fleet, no stage of the contest can be deemed easy. In light winds or strong, the level of concentration and energy the crew needs to apply to keep the yacht moving at maximum speed can be physically and mentally exhausting. As a result, fatigue is always a factor. To counter this problem the crew is split into watches, with each watch having a helmsman, and the appropriate number of sail trimmers to ensure the yacht performs to its best. Crews are generally off watch for 3 to 4 hours, but can be called on deck to attend a problem at any time.

When it comes to the make-up of crew, the navigator and tactician are the 'chess players'; they must do their best to anticipate what moves the wind and coastal currents might make, then set a course for the yacht so that it gains the maximum benefit from any anticipated changes. It is an unrelenting challenge, as are the roles of the helmsperson and sail trimmers. If the person steering is too aggressive when handling the helm then the rudder can become a brake as much as a control mechanism, and similarly, in most conditions, the sail trimmers must constantly ease the sails out or winch them in so the wind flowing across them delivers maximum speed. The value of being on top of these challenges is clearly evident when it is realised that a yacht being sailed at half a knot below its optimum will lose 12 nm in 24 hours. That's expensive!

A fine example of how every second can count came in the 1982 race when, after sailing for more than three days, the maxi yacht *Condor of Bermuda* snatched line honours over the Sydney yacht, *Apollo*, by a mere 7 seconds!

Despite this level of intensity there are many plusses. Nature sometimes delivers magical moments – like high-speed surfing down powerful waves, or simple scenes of natural beauty on the land, across the sea or in the sky, all of which provide memories that can last a lifetime.

The late Roger Hickman, a Sydney Hobart legend who won in 2014 with his yacht *Wild Rose*, once commented:

> Ocean racing takes place in the arena of life. It's not as
> though you're inside some artificially heated and lit
> stadium. It's got all the elements of 'why do people climb
> mountains?' It's something you just have to do and it
> happens in one of the most romantic environments in the

world. You get the benefits of the wind, the sea, the sun,
the moon and stars, plus the spectacle of marine life, all
rolled into something that is competitive.

Even so, because this world is in the hands of the weather gods,
a blissful scene can go from millpond to minefield in a very
short time. All it takes is for an infamous southerly buster,
packing a bitterly cold, 40-knot plus headwind with its origins
in Antarctic waters south of Tasmania, to come over the
horizon and turn a sleigh ride into a rollercoaster. From the
moment the weather front hits, the seas increase in height and
soon become capped with foaming crests.

The approach of such a change is always forecast to the fleet,
but if it arrives at night, crews can be caught unawares as there
is no sound or sight to warn of its approach. Regardless, day or
night, the crew must scramble and reconfigure the sail plan
from light weather sails to a reefed mainsail and a small, heavy
weather jib that is suitable for sailing upwind in a blow. From
that moment the yacht is heeled over – leaning over at a
dramatic angle – while crashing and bashing its way to
windward. This change also impacts the crews' rigs; they go
from casual shorts and T-shirt sailing to being lashed by bullet-
like spray while wearing thermals, wet weather gear with hoods
and seaboots.

Such changes don't always come from the south; sometimes
gale-force winds come from behind – from the north-west or
north-east. These conditions generally call for small spinnakers
and, sometimes, reefed mainsails to be set. More often than not
the ensuing scenario, where the yachts become sailing surfboats

set on a rollicking downwind ride, is something to remember forever.

All these elements create the adrenalin moments that have contributed to the Hobart race retaining its appeal over the decades. It takes the men and women in the crew out of their shore-bound comfort zones and into another world. The majority enjoy it. However, it must be said that there have been those who, on reaching Hobart, have declared never again, and have stuck by that vow.

*

Over the decades, the competing yachts have been representative of the full spectrum of monohull, offshore-capable yachts, ranging from around 9 metres in overall length and comparable in cost to a comfortable motorhome, through to 30-metre supermaxis – pure racing machines that are designed and built using the latest space-age technology, and costing at least $20 million. Also, some yachts built specifically for the race have been experimental in design and construction.

Yet, despite this remarkable contrast in concept and cost, it is quite possible for the smallest yacht to be declared the all-important outright winner of the race through the application of a complex rating (handicap) system. That result matters most to the competitors, but as far as the vast majority of the public is concerned, it is the battle for line honours between the gladiators – the supermaxis – that holds the most interest.

*

As for the men and women who compete in the Hobart, the vast majority have come up through the ranks over the years; they learned to sail either in small dinghies or on yachts in Australia or overseas and graduated towards their ultimate goal – to race to Hobart. Some have become so hooked on the adventure that they have started many times: 132 yachtsmen and yachtswomen have competed at least twenty-five times, ten have done forty races and another four have reached the fifty mark.

One of those who reached the forty mark was the late Richard 'Sighty' Hammond, a world class ocean racing navigator. His induction into the classic in 1952 would have been enough to deter most people forever, but not Hammond. He was aboard the Tasmanian schooner *Wanderer*, in the era when foul weather gear generally comprised heavy oilskin jackets, sou'wester hats and greasy, cable-knit woollen sweaters that tended to absorb more water than they repelled. Seaboots were then unknown, so bare feet were the order of the day.

His most vivid recollection when he first stepped aboard *Wanderer* was that its owner, Eric Massey, and many of the crew were very old.

'I went for the adventure,' Hammond recalled. 'To race to Hobart was something just about every young sailor wanted to do. I was one of the lucky few to secure a ride.'

By the time *Wanderer* reached mid-Bass Strait, Hammond thought his Hobart race initiation was complete: they had sailed through a howling southerly gale that delivered a 40-knot headwind and big seas. Within an hour of that storm arriving *Wanderer* was being impacted so severely by wind and waves that Massey ordered all sails to be lowered. The yacht rode out the storm under bare poles.

Worse was to come. After *Wanderer* had resumed racing and rounded Tasman Island another equally harrowing south-westerly gale blasted onto the scene. Hammond recalled the experience:

> It was blowing 60 knots, the seas were raging and the
> spray was near horizontal. To say it was bitterly cold was
> an understatement – there was bloody ice on the mast –
> in high summer! Without doubt it was the most
> memorable and miserable Hobart race I ever did, partly
> because it was my first and partly because it was so
> rugged and cold.

*

In recent times some crewmembers in the Hobart race have been first-timers because they held star status in other sports, or were high-profile community leaders in Australia.

Quite often these individuals were invited to be part of the crew to help raise the profile of a project or product associated with a yacht, while others were aboard simply to enjoy the ride – hopefully. Among those who have been part of this guest category are: Gerard Healy, Nathan Buckley and Jude Bolton (Australian rules football); Phil Kearns, Phil Waugh, Kurtley Beale, Paddy Ryan and Jeremy Tilse (rugby union); Anthony Minichiello (rugby league); Danny Green (boxing); Sally Fitzgibbons and Layne Beachley (surfing); Kurt Fearnley (paralympian); Geoff Huegill (swimming); Larry Emdur (TV host), and Michael Clarke (cricket).

Their experiences were many and varied. Gerard Healy is an all-time great Australian rules football player who retired from the game in 1990. In 1999 he accepted an invitation from Melbourne yachtsman Grant Wharington to be part of the Hobart race crew aboard the maxi yacht *Wild Thing*. With it being the year following the tragic race, Healy was somewhat apprehensive about the challenge he would face – he had heard the stories but he still didn't know quite what to expect. He need not have worried. The 1999 Hobart race, especially for the crews aboard the big boats like *Wild Thing*, was a sleigh ride. It was downwind most of the way and the fast and easy sailing conditions led to the Danish entry, *Nokia,* lopping a whopping 18 hours and 19 minutes off the race record time.

'The race was so fast and easy that Healy wondered why it had the reputation for being one of the toughest sporting challenges to be had,' Wharington said.

With those pleasant memories still fresh in his mind, Healy enthusiastically accepted the invitation to join the *Wild Thing* crew the following year. It, too, was a relatively easy race except for one particular moment, which he had no hesitation in detailing when he was greeted by the news-hungry media on the dock in Hobart after the finish. Healy related how a powerful squall had struck *Wild Thing* while rounding Tasman Island, 44 nm from the finish. The blast was so severe that it almost knocked the shuddering and shaking yacht flat on its side – a situation that led to him declaring he was 'terrified'. Healy said,

It was just pure skill, courage and determination by the crew that got us through. If something had gone wrong we were gone. I saw more courage during this race than in a lifetime on the football field. For a start, there were no fresh reserves to run on whenever anyone got tired; everyone just had to keep pulling their weight. It is a pity the people at home can't see what goes on out there.

*

As many Hobart race sailors will declare, when it comes to challenges within the many spheres of nature, competing in the Sydney Hobart race could be likened to scaling Mount Everest: both have inherent elements of danger – usually weather related – but if you prepare well, carry the right safety equipment, and have a capable team around you, the chances are you will achieve your goal. Hong Kong-based Karl Kwok, a successful department store owner and world champion offshore yachtsman, certainly agrees, adding that the Hobart race is something that all yachtsmen should do at least once. However once was obviously not enough for Kwok. He won the race in 1997 with his yacht *Beau Geste* and has subsequently contested another two Hobart races.

The unique challenge the Hobart presents is one of the reasons it has attracted so many high-profile and competitive individuals from Australia and around the world – mega wealthy businessmen, politicians and celebrities among them. This extensive list includes: American computer mogul Larry Ellison; Australia's Rupert and Lachlan Murdoch; American billionaire Jim Clark, and wife Kristy Hinze-Clark; CNN founder Ted Turner, American shipping magnate Huey Long, and British conservative politician Edward Heath, who won the race in 1969 with his little sloop, *Morning Cloud*, and was elected as Britain's Prime Minister the following year.

It is an undeniable fact that offshore events, and in particular the Sydney Hobart race, always establish a strong bond between crews. Most importantly though, no matter if you are a prince, pauper or millionaire, you are only as good as the person next to you when it comes to racing offshore. The sport is a great equaliser, and that is why it has such widespread appeal.

Those same people will tell you that one of the more appealing attributes of the Sydney Hobart race is that it transfers you from one great party to another. Some of those post-race parties, in particular 'The Quiet Little Drink', have gone into yachting folklore in Australia and around the world. So too have some of the salty characters who brought unbridled shore-side colour and humour to the classic.

CHAPTER 1

If you make it a race I will come

It is somewhat incongruous that a yacht club formed on a foundation of coastal cruising and not racing stands today as one of the world's premier ocean racing yacht clubs, which hosts what many would say is the most celebrated offshore race on the international calendar.

However, that is the case when it comes to the Cruising Yacht Club of Australia (CYCA).

Making the circumstance even more intriguing is the fact that two completely separate events provided the impetus that led to the establishment of the organisation and subsequently what has become a Boxing Day sporting tradition in Australia – the Hobart race.

It was on a Sunday in March 1944 when Peter Luke and Charlie Cooper literally crossed tacks while sailing their respective yachts on Pittwater, a picturesque, hilly and heavily-timbered waterway located 17 nm to the north of Sydney Harbour. It was Luke's home turf and one of his favourite cruising grounds. On this particular day he was aboard his

11.6-metre-long yacht, *Wayfarer*, when Cooper's similarly designed sloop, *Asgard*, appeared on the scene. The pair chatted as they sailed the yachts along side-by-side, then Luke, who was a professional photographer, took a photograph of *Asgard*, a copy of which he subsequently sent to Cooper. Cooper, a fruiterer (whose actual name was Alfred Edwin Charles Cooper), reciprocated by sending Luke a case of fruit.

This encounter led to the two men enjoying telephone conversations on a regular basis where cruising was the principal topic, and it was during one of these casual chats that Cooper suggested to Luke that, as neither of them was interested to any great degree in racing around buoys on Saturday afternoons, they should look to forming a club that embraced cruising. The thought was that the club could organise cruises-in-company and casual races out of Sydney to destinations along the coast of New South Wales.

The pair agreed that they should pursue the idea, so they set about contacting a few like-minded cruising enthusiasts and asked if they would like to meet and discuss the concept. Within a matter of days they had enticed six other yacht owners to join them for an informal meeting in the city in June 1944. The venue was a photographic studio in Castlereagh Street in Sydney, owned by Luke's father, Monty, who, like his son, was a successful commercial photographer and also a keen yachtsman.

The gathering was an easy-going affair, so much so that no minutes were taken. However some years later Luke gave an insight into what happened:

A motion was passed that it be called the Cruising Yacht Club and that was agreed. I was made Honorary Secretary, a position where my main objective was to recruit more members. Also, a sum of £1 was donated by each member to defray administrative costs. At this stage stamps were two pence each!

Luke also confirmed that Tasmanian Bert Walker, being the most senior person at the meeting, was elected President, while noted marine artist and yachtsman Jack Earl, who was the second Australian yachtsman to circumnavigate the world under sail, designed the club's unique sail identification for registered yachts, 'cYc'.

More information on the club's origins surfaced in an interview in 1983, when Charlie Cooper provided his recollections of that inaugural meeting, in particular as to the name of the organisation and whether Bert Walker should have the title of President or Commodore.

There was a controversy as to whether it was to be an association or a club. Initially some of those present thought it would be an association, hence the term President. But there were ideas that, one day, the club might obtain a Royal Charter. The name put up originally was The Cruising Yachts Association, but some members wanted the Cruising Yacht Club of Australia.

When the dust settled it was agreed among the nine original members that the organisation would be called the latter and

Bert Walker would become Commodore. This decision also meant that flag officers could be appointed.

Cooper added that once the club was established its membership grew rapidly: 'We used to have very good meetings, quite heated meetings at times, because the interest was intense. Everybody had different ideas as to how things should be run.'

*

While the fledgling group came together under the banner of cruising, the club's first event, staged on 1 October 1944, was actually a near-20 nm race from Sydney to Broken Bay, at the entrance to Pittwater. An item announcing the event, published in Sydney's *The Sun* newspaper on 27 September, read:

> The first ocean yacht race since the war [began] will take
> place on Sunday. Twenty yachts will leave Sydney at 10am
> on a 20-mile course to Broken Bay. The race is intended
> to be the first of a series arranged by a group of yachtsmen
> who recently formed a cruising club.
>
> Entry fee proceeds will go to the Red Cross. Any
> yacht owner interested should ring the Hon Organiser,
> Mr AC Cooper (MA 2625).

The race was declared a great success both as a contest and socially. The fact that there were nineteen starters confirmed there was strong support among sailors for the CYCA and its agenda. It was obvious that, like Luke and Cooper, many other sailing enthusiasts had grown tired of racing around buoys in enclosed waters; they wanted the excitement and adventure that came with passage racing on the open sea and cruising to different destinations. Consequently, applications for membership continued to climb at an impressive rate.

Peter Luke's endeavours to help grow the membership extended beyond the harbour shoreline. The late Jeanette York, who would become a CYCA Life Member, recalled that whenever Luke was sailing *Wayfarer* on the harbour and saw a yacht that was obviously a potential entrant for races, he would pull up alongside and shout to the owner: 'What a nice looking yacht! We've just formed a cruising club; why don't you come along to our next meeting?' It was an approach that obviously worked because one of the people he did recruit while sailing on Sydney Harbour was Mervyn Davey (who was Jeanette York's father), a yachting enthusiast who became a driving force within the club for more than 50 years.

*

Like so many Australians who loved the freedom and adventure that came with offshore sailing, Jack Earl was eager to go cruising once the war was over. He and his wife, Kathleen, had been living with their children, Mick and Maris, aboard their classic 13.4-metre-long ketch, *Kathleen Gillett* (later abbreviated to *Kathleen*) since it was launched in 1939. At times, the yacht and others on the CYCA register became part of the war effort when the Royal Australian Navy assigned them to voluntary coastal and harbour patrol duties.

When their yacht was not on patrol, Jack, Kathleen and the children would sail as often as possible to their favourite anchorage, a secluded and peaceful location named Quarantine Beach, just inside the entrance to Sydney Harbour at North Head. In April 1945, when the Earls were enjoying a weekend of seclusion just off the beach, another yacht known well to them sailed into the bay and anchored nearby. It was *Saltair*, the 14.6-metre-long raised-deck ketch owned by Commodore Bert Walker and his brother Russ.

During the preceding months Jack and Kathleen had been planning a Christmas cruise to Tasmania which they wanted to take with the children when the war was done. With the end of hostilities likely in months, and with Christmas not long away, they began to expand their plans in a more positive fashion.

For Jack, the fact that the Walker brothers, who hailed from Hobart, had anchored *Saltair* nearby, presented him with an opportunity to visit them and garner information for *Kathleen*'s proposed cruise south.

As soon as practicable Jack jumped into his dinghy and rowed across to *Saltair* with the intention of sitting down with the brothers and picking their brains about cruising in their home waters, in particular along the east coast of Tasmania and on the Derwent River.

Jack recalled: 'Bert pulled out some charts for me to look at, and as we pored over them he became increasingly excited by the cruise we were planning, so much so that he soon asked me if it might be possible to join us with *Saltair* – it would be a cruise in company.'

Jack thought that was an excellent idea so had no hesitation in saying 'Yes'. Then, just a few days later, Peter Luke heard what was planned, and he also asked if he could join in with his yacht, *Wayfarer*.

Jack's answer was a very definite 'Yes'.

*

The anxiously awaited VP Day (Victory in the Pacific) came on 15 August 1945 – just days after nuclear bombs were detonated above Hiroshima and Nagasaki in Japan. After some 6 years of heinous slaughter, the war was finally over and the long road back to normality was open.

Earlier in the year, when it became apparent that Germany was facing defeat in Europe, the Allies had seen an opportunity to direct more assets towards regaining the regions in the Pacific, where the Japanese were still occupying what had previously been significant British, French and Dutch territories.

Consequently, the Allies formed one of the mightiest armadas ever assembled in the southern hemisphere; a Pacific taskforce designed purely to challenge the Japanese. This fleet eventually comprised four battleships, seventeen aircraft carriers, ten cruisers, forty destroyers, thirty-one frigates, thirty-eight minesweepers, twenty-nine submarines, 100 escort vessels, 1200 aircraft and two amphibious divisions.

The manpower required to support this massive mission was almost incomprehensible and involved tens of thousands of men and women.

With Sydney boasting one of the world's finest deep water harbours, it was inevitable many vessels associated with the armada would be docked there at some stage during the campaign. As a result, there was a requirement for a significant number of naval personnel, in particular British, to be based in Sydney just to maintain the ships and their equipment.

In May 1945, Peter Luke learned that the Royal Navy's Chief Engineer Officer, Captain John Illingworth, was stationed at the fleet base at Garden Island at Woolloomooloo, on Sydney Harbour, for this very reason. Most importantly for Luke, this was the same John Illingworth who was recognised as the greatest international ocean racing yachtsman of the era. His knowledge of yacht design, seamanship and offshore racing was second-to-none. Also, he was a Past Commodore of the pre-eminent Royal Ocean Racing Club in London and the Royal Naval Sailing Association.

On realising this, Luke took it upon himself to invite Illingworth to be guest speaker at one of the club's dinners, and he accepted most willingly.

This was an exceptional coup for Luke and the CYCA.

A feature article in a CYCA Hobart race program that profiled Illingworth read:

Here was a man whose reputation preceded him:
experienced sailors who had raced with him offshore
described him as being the best skipper with whom they
had ever sailed.

Asked why, and they invariably replied: 'First, because
he knows what he's doing, and second because he gives

the orders. There's no back-chat and no mucking about when he's on board!' Friends described him as a tall and well-built man with a voice that could be heard all over an anchorage. He was seen as being informal in attire and manner, so much so that he was often seen at formal receptions dressed in coarse-woven shirt and trousers, like a Breton fisherman.

*

For some time after the club was formed, and in the absence of its own premises, Monty Luke's studio had continued to be the venue for CYCA meetings. Those gatherings were described as very informal and low-key. On some occasions, members would get together over dinner, usually at Sue's Café near Wynyard train station in the heart of the city. As a venue it was very convenient, but that was about all there was going in its favour. As Peter Luke explained, 'The food they served was sufficiently bad for us to always refer to it as the Greasy Spoon.'

For the Illingworth dinner which was held on 28 May 1945, there was only one venue deemed suitable: the plush, multi-storeyed, stone and brick Usher's Hotel, which was next door to Monty Luke's studio.

An impressive number of CYCA members attended the function, which proved to be a great success. When it came to Captain Illingworth's address, the audience was captivated by his vivid stories of offshore racing in England and the success he had enjoyed.

With the formalities complete and Illingworth thanked appropriately with a rousing round of applause, those present relaxed over after-dinner drinks, primarily port, in the superbly comfortable lounge and an atmosphere filled with the rich aroma of cigars.

At this time Peter Luke and Bert Walker, who were sitting with Illingworth, began to talk all things sailing with the guest, and this prompted Luke to mention to Illingworth that he and some other members of the club were planning a cruise to Hobart at Christmas and suggested that he might like to join them. Luke explained later: 'At that point Illingworth said, "I will if you make it a race".'

With that, a cruise to Tasmania became a race from Sydney to Hobart.

*

Until then the only offshore yacht race of any significance to be sailed out of Sydney was over a 120 nm course from the harbour, north to Newcastle and return. Staged in 1864 by the newly founded Royal Sydney Yacht Squadron, it was a showdown between two of the largest privately owned yachts ever to be on the register of the club – the 70 ton schooner *Xarif*, owned by the Squadron's foundation Commodore, William Walker, and the similar-sized *Chance*, raced by Charles Parbury. Interest in the race spread rapidly, so much so that thousands of people lined the shore to watch the start off Fort Denison at 1pm. Hundreds of pounds had been wagered on the result – and that didn't include the considerable side-wager between the owners.

A forty-knot southerly gale was blasting across the harbour when the race started and it lasted for the duration of the challenge. After turning at Newcastle, *Chance* thrashed its way down the coast and entered the harbour the following afternoon with the crew confident they had 'donkey-licked' their rival, *Xarif*, which they had not sighted since clearing Sydney Heads. Happy with that thought, bottles of chilled champagne appeared on deck and corks were soon arcing through the air. It was a wonderful celebration ... until *Chance* rounded Bradleys Head and the crew saw *Xarif* riding at anchor near Fort Denison, the winner by several hours.

*

Only days after a race to Hobart became a reality, CYCA members met to outline plans for the event. Fortunately, the club had money in the bank to cover initial costs – it was reported to members that at the end of the financial year in 1945 the club, which at this time had forty members, showed a credit balance at the bank of £34/9/9. This resulted from the club having a joining fee of 10s 6d, and an annual subscription fee of £1/10/0.

The most pressing need was to announce a starting date for the race to Hobart. The decision was 26 December 1945 – Boxing Day – because it meant competitors could enjoy Christmas Day with their families prior to setting sail. That time of the year was also high summer, the season when it was most probable that the best sailing conditions would prevail. Even so, there were no guarantees: it was quite possible for the tempestuous Tasman Sea to throw a tantrum, as was the case for Bass Strait.

While the preliminary plans for the race generated eager anticipation for those closely associated with it, three people were disappointed, Jack Earl's wife, Kathleen, and their two children. The long desired port-hopping cruise to Hobart was now a race, and that meant there was no place for them aboard the family yacht.

News of the seemingly daring and dangerous ocean challenge was spreading around the waterfront rapidly and went public via *The Sydney Morning Herald* on 16 June 1945. It was a brief note that reported: 'Plans for a race from Sydney to Hobart ... are being made by the Cruising Yacht Club ... five possible entries have already been received.' Interestingly though, the more conservative and long-standing yacht clubs in Sydney greeted this same news with disdain, members declaring that the race was a foolhardy stunt. It was a sentiment the CYCA members ignored.

Five months out from the start of the Hobart race, some competitors were under considerable pressure to be ready, none more so than Illingworth. He was starting from scratch: first up he needed to purchase a suitable yacht then prepare it for racing, and while doing so, select and train a crew. Adding pressure to that schedule was the fact that his position within the Royal Navy meant he also had to deal with a considerable workload. Fortunately, his crew selection procedure was made easy when he realised there were sufficient experienced naval officers within his staff and many enthusiastic local amateurs capable of manning the yacht.

Being the great offshore sailor and seafarer that he was, Illingworth knew he faced one additional challenge; he was a stranger to Australian waters so had no existing data to work with that related to the 630 nm course.

Illingworth's search for a suitable yacht on Sydney Harbour and Pittwater to the north was soon rewarded. He found his ideal sloop anchored on Pittwater; a sturdy, 10.7-metre-long, canoe-stern cutter, the lines of which he later said 'represented a brilliant design; a very easily driven hull that was fast and sea-kindly under all conditions.' It had taken its then name, *Maharani*, from a Hindu queen. However, in a matter of days after the purchase was complete it became obvious that Illingworth did not like such a lengthy name as he abbreviated it to *Rani*.

The yacht was built in 1936 by the highly regarded shipwright Les Steel, at Speers Point, on Lake Macquarie, at a cost of £616. It had been commissioned by a Dr Rowland Pittar, of Newcastle, and named for his wife, Doris.

On 18 December 1936, the *Newcastle Morning Herald* ran a short story about the yacht:

Dr R. Pittar's new yacht will be launched to-morrow afternoon, at 3.30. The yacht is of the flush-deck type, and has a spoon bow and canoe stern. It is of the most modern design, and will carry 900lb of trimming ballast.
Propelling power is installed under the bridge deck, with a folding propeller on the portside. Accommodation below deck is a feature of the craft. A comfortable saloon extends from the companion way to the bulkhead situated forward

of the mast. A large galley has been provided, and there is considerable cupboard space, interior fittings are of Queensland maple. The yacht has an overall length of 35ft., with a beam of 9ft., and will float easily in 5ft. 8in.

Once Illingworth had completed the purchase he wasted no time when it came to getting the yacht suitably prepared for racing because, in the October edition of *Australian Power Boat and Yachting Monthly* magazine, it was reported that the CYCA's race from Sydney to Broken Bay had been won by Captain J. Illingworth in his new vessel.

This same edition of the magazine also announced plans for the Hobart race. Details were in an item so small that it could easily have gone unnoticed. It read:

> Yacht Race to Tasmania; it is expected that an Ocean Yacht Race may take place from Sydney to Hobart probably starting on 26 December 1945. Yachtsmen desirous of competing should contact Vice President Mr P. Luke, 62 Castlereagh Street, Sydney, for information. Entries close 1 December 1945.

With the race to Broken Bay behind him, Illingworth could put his mind to selecting a capable crew for the Hobart. One of the Royal Navy personnel he chose was Ray Richmond, a 25-year-old lieutenant engineer who was working as an assistant to him. The young lieutenant eagerly accepted the invitation to join the team and soon after was seen scrubbing the bottom of the yacht's hull and generally getting it ready for the race. He later recalled: 'There were no anti-fouling products available at that time so we used Johnsons Wax Polish applied by hand.'

Ironically, while Richmond was very enthusiastic about this adventure, it would prove to be the only long distance offshore yacht race in which he would participate over his long lifetime.

Illingworth's 'find' for his crew was a local, Norm Hudson, a well-seasoned sailor with many offshore miles under sail to his credit. He took up the position of mate aboard *Rani*, second in charge.

Being a stranger to these waters, Illingworth knew all too well that the key to success in any ocean race was preparation, and never more so than in this one. He held little to no knowledge about the coastal currents, weather patterns, sea conditions and the local anomalies and vagaries of Storm Bay and the Derwent River. So, considering the short timeframe before the start of the race, there was only one solution – self-education.

As soon as it was possible he drove down the coast to the south of Sydney, stopping in many ports so he could talk to trawler skippers about the east coast current – better known to mariners as the southerly set – and the likelihood of there being swirling eddies associated with that current. Then, back in Sydney, he met with staff at the Weather Bureau so he could learn about weather patterns over the entire course, including Tasmania's east coast and Storm Bay. He also spent countless hours at night studying navigation charts, his desire being that, 'When he came to the various landmarks, they were like old friends, appearing much as expected.' It was a remarkable effort on his part, so much so that it was distinctly possible the Englishman Illingworth knew more about the weather and current than any other competitor.

Due to the war there were numerous obstacles all yacht owners had to overcome before being race ready. Canvas sail fabric was in short supply, and what was available was very expensive, so most yachts carried well-used and baggy old sails that should have been retired years earlier. It was the same scenario when it came to much-needed rope; the preferred manila rope, which was used for halyards and as sheets for the trimming of sails, was near impossible to buy. So the only real alternative was sisal, which was described as rope with needles sticking out of it.

As part of the preparation for the race, Peter Luke wrote to the Secretary of the Royal Yacht Club of Tasmania (RYCT) on 26 July 1945, and advised him: 'Several of our members who intend cruising to your state early next year have requested us to organise a race for them terminating at Hobart.' He enquired if RYCT would co-operate by managing the finish of the race in Hobart.

This concept for a 600-plus nautical-mile race from Sydney met with instant approval from the RYCT hierarchy, so much so that the Commodore replied almost immediately. His letter, dated 1 August 1945, read in part:

This news gladdens our hearts and we will be most happy to co-operate in any way desired. We will certainly take care of the ships and their people upon arrival and will arrange a suitable racing program for them … We look forward to the event with great interest.

For the RYCT, hosting the finish of this race was seen as a significant seal of approval. The club had survived a stuttering start at its inception in 1859, but it wasn't until 1880 that an influx of members and vessels brought some level of certainty regarding its future. It grew from there, and by 1908 the club's stature was seen to be sufficient for it to be granted a Royal Warrant.

*

In some ways it could be said that the Sydney Hobart race was a bridge between the two towns that had pioneered leisure sailboat racing in the latter half of the 1800s. But, when it came to actual offshore racing, it was the state of Victoria that had shown the way. In early 1907 the editor of the American magazine *Rudder*, Thomas Fleming Day, wrote to his friend, Mr T.A. Dickson, Commodore of the Royal Geelong Yacht Club, with the suggestion that to promote the sport of offshore yachting in Australia, he should consider establishing an annual 198 nm race across Bass Strait to Tasmania, with the finish line at the entrance to Launceston's Tamar River. He also offered a trophy, *The Rudder Cup*, as an appropriate prize.

Dickson pursued the idea, and when the start gun sounded in December 1907, the four competing yachts set off for what would prove to be an extremely rough race. It was won by Mr Edgar Newland's 14.6-metre-long yawl, *Thistle,* the crew of which included Mrs Newland and their daughter. When it came time to plan the race for the following year, Mrs Newland refused to relinquish *The Rudder Cup*, the reason being that she was adamant no yachtsman should ever again be tempted to compete in such a dangerous sporting endeavour.

*

As is the case to this day, the yacht that is first to finish in the Sydney Hobart race, and almost every other offshore race in the world, is not necessarily the winner. Instead, that yacht is initially recognised only as the winner of line honours. From the time a competing yacht completes the course, it usually becomes a waiting game for the crew – a wait to see which yacht has the best corrected time for the course. Corrected time is achieved by multiplying the yacht's elapsed time by its time correction factor (TCF), the yacht's handicap figure. On most occasions, it is not until a significant number of yachts have crossed the finish line that the actual winner can be declared. That winner – the yacht with the lowest corrected time – can be the largest and fastest yacht, the smallest and slowest, or anything in between. The handicap rule is designed to equalise the chances of yachts of widely differing designs and sizes. Today, the handicap rule takes into consideration a myriad of factors relating to the yacht's design before it calculates a four-decimal-point number, and that becomes the time correction factor. It is a lengthy and complex formula that is informed by such things as the yacht's waterline length, sail area, stability, overall weight (displacement) and hull shape to come up with the final figure. Obviously, if it wasn't for a handicap system there would be very few yachts competing in the Hobart race, or any other offshore event, as it would be purely a battle between the largest and fastest yachts – for example modern day supermaxis. In today's offshore racing arena the Grand Prix level racers compete under the International Racing Certificate (IRC) rule, while the slower and more cruising oriented yachts are measured under the simpler Performance Handicap System (PHS) rule.

Understandably then, when it came to handicapping the yachts in the inaugural Hobart race, having Illingworth in Sydney was like striking gold – especially when he provided organisers with an actual copy of the Royal Ocean Racing Club's handicap rule.

*

When dealing with safety regulations, the organisers of the Sydney Hobart Yacht Race have, from the very first event, attempted to establish and maintain the highest safety standards. The yachts contesting this inaugural race were all considered to be sturdy, seaworthy craft. The skippers and crews took pride in their seamanship, sailing skills and the seaworthiness of their yachts for one very simple reason: once they cleared Sydney Harbour and turned south they had to accept the fact that they were on their own. Few yachts, if any, carried two-way radios. In the event of a crisis, there was no way to call for assistance. They could not expect the crew of another race yacht, or any other vessel, to come to their aid. Still, the Cruising Yacht Club of Australia created a list of safety equipment to be carried by all competing yachts. It included: a lifebuoy with attached waterproof light; life vests for each crew member; at least six red distress flares; white flares (for crossing the finishing line in Hobart at night); navigation lights as required by the Regulations for Prevention of Collisions at Sea (these were usually kerosene lanterns that frequently blew out in windy conditions); a first-aid kit; and a St John's Ambulance Manual (a requirement that was not uniformly adhered to).

Further safety requirements included: 'Life rails fitted along both sides of the vessel, not less than 20 inches above the deck and running from within 6 feet of the stem (bow) to a position abaft (astern) of the cockpit.' However, compliance with this particular regulation appears to have been overlooked by many competing yacht owners. Instead, some yachts were fitted with a fixed line stretching along the centreline from the bow to the stern so safety harnesses could be clipped onto it, although safety harnesses were not a requirement for the race!

Another race regulation was for each yacht to carry a heaving line, an emergency lifeline of ¾ inch (19 millimetres) rope, or more, and not less than 75 feet (23 metres) in length. Its purpose was to assist in any man–overboard emergency, so it had to be carried on deck at all times with one end attached to the yacht and the other end heavily knotted.

Another requirement read 'All yachts must carry a dinghy securely lashed on deck. Serviceable collapsible boats are allowed.'

Auxiliary motors were not to be used for propulsion from 10 minutes before the start until after crossing the finish line.

However, yacht owners were not required to seal their engines so as to prove that the propeller had not been engaged during the race. This requirement, or lack of it, would lead to considerable debate among competitors in years to come.

In keeping with the cruising philosophy that formed the foundation of the club, and the fact that sailcloth was in short supply due to the war, competitors were reminded in the Sailing Directions that the setting of spinnakers (should a yacht have one) was not permitted. However, to facilitate maximum sail area when sailing in a following wind, headsails could be boomed out to windward so they could capture more wind.

The course for the race was seemingly straightforward: start on Sydney Harbour; turn south; cross Bass Strait; cross Storm Bay; enter the Derwent River; and finish off the Hobart waterfront. As a precaution, just in case a competitor decided – as dangerous as it might be – to take a 30 nm short-cut through the East Bay Neck Canal (today commonly referred to as the Dunalley Canal) and sail from there directly to the entrance of the Derwent River, the Sailing Directions declared that passage was illegal. Also, while competing yachts were allowed to stop and anchor in ports along the way, the yacht owner was required to go ashore and advise the yacht's location via urgent telegram to either *The Mercury* newspaper in Hobart or the ABC radio network in Sydney.

Meanwhile, Charlie Cooper, an enthusiastic amateur radio operator and excellent communicator, contacted his brother, Eric, a Royal Australian Air Force wing commander based in Sydney, and subsequently the Secretary of the Air Board in Melbourne, regarding the race. He successfully negotiated for

RAAF flying boats to schedule flying exercises over the course area in the hope they would report back the identity and location of any race yachts that were sighted.

This act was only a small indication of Charlie's enthusiasm for the race, and the club in general over many years. At various times between 1945 and 1949 he filled the roles of Secretary, Rear Commodore and Vice Commodore. It was much the same when it came to Peter Luke; he was the club's Secretary, Vice President, Vice Commodore and Commodore over a similar period.

*

As Boxing Day drew near, there was ever-increasing interest from the media, both print and radio, and the public in general in this seemingly hazardous race across an often hostile and unpredictable stretch of ocean. Men and women putting their lives on the line in defence of one's country was understandable, but to put your life in peril in the name of sport was near incomprehensible.

For the competitors, there was one particular problem they had to contend with before the start – a beer shortage in Sydney. Post-war power rationing had had a significant impact on beer production, so much so that, almost unimaginably, hotels were shut because they could not get supplies. The sailors were struggling to get enough of the amber fluid to last them for the duration of the race.

Initially, ten yachts were entered; an impressive number considering the short lead-up time to the start and the fact that this was an event without precedent in Australia. Unfortunately, though, the Livingston brothers were forced to withdraw *Warana*, the sole entry from Melbourne, because it was not able to reach Sydney in time for the Boxing Day start. It was a disappointing outcome for the brothers, Frank and John, but as race history reveals, they went on to make an indelible mark on the classic. They also donated a perpetual trophy, the *F. & J. Livingston Trophy*, for the first yacht to be positioned south of Tasman Island at the entrance to Tasmania's Storm Bay in each year's race.

The competing yachts were:

Ambermerle (Sydney) John Colquhoun & Clarrie Kiel –
    34 feet (10.36 metres)
Archina II (Sydney) Phil Goldstein – 52 feet (15.85 metres)
Horizon (Sydney) J.R. Bartlett – 40 feet (12.19 metres)
Kathleen (Sydney) Jack Earl – 44 feet (13.4 metres)
Mistral II (Sydney) R.F. Evans – 63 feet (19.2 metres)
Rani (United Kingdom) John Illingworth – 35 feet
    (10.67 metres)
Saltair (Sydney) Bert & Russ Walker – 43 feet (13.11
    metres)
Wayfarer (Sydney) Peter Luke – 40 feet (12.19 metres)
Winston Churchill (Hobart) Percy Coverdale – 51 feet
    (15.54 metres)

Because the WWII anti-submarine boom gates were still in place between Bradleys Head and Rose Bay at this time, the club set the starting line in the northern part of the harbour.

This imaginary line stretched from the western-most headland on North Head – Flagstaff Point, now Cannae Point – to the start boat, which was anchored to the west, 200 metres offshore. The boat was identified by the fact that it carried a large white flag featuring the letters 'cYc', a custom that has carried through to today.

CHAPTER 2

Rabbits, Crayfish and a Keg of Beer

Wednesday, 26 December 1945 was a typically warm Sydney summer day: a clear blue sky and a gentle north-east sea breeze was on the make, and the harbour's turquoise waters shimmered in the morning sun – a sea of dancing diamonds.

A noticeable air of excitement prevailed along much of the waterfront and around the city. It was the start day for the first Sydney to Hobart.

Apart from the celebrated annual horse race, the Melbourne Cup – which had been won a few weeks earlier by *Rainbird* – and the post-war 'Victory' cricket tests between Australia and England being played in England, sporting events had been all but unknown during the war years. Now, with hostilities having come to an end, the Hobart race was generating its own unique level of excitement. Here was a home-grown and refreshingly new sporting event that had the potential to be a panacea for war-weary locals, especially in New South Wales and Tasmania. Much of the interest, both locally and across

Australia, could be attributed to media stories which had, over preceding weeks, reported on the countdown to the start of what was seen by many to be an extremely testing and daring escapade, Australia's first long-distance ocean yacht race. But no one realised they were experiencing sporting history, the embryonic days of an event that would gain worldwide acclaim as a great maritime challenge.

While the start time was scheduled for 11am, the crews of the nine competing yachts were on board in the early hours so they could complete final preparations and make sure everything was in readiness. Eventually, when the last of the fresh food supplies had been put aboard and stowed, and a checklist confirmed everything else was done, it was time to depart.

Depending on circumstance, each yacht was eased away from its dock or mooring and steered towards North Head. Some of the crews were farewelled with rousing cheers and shouts of good luck while men raised their wide-brimmed felt hats in salute. For others it was a more casual farewell; hauling up the yacht's anchor then simply waving to family and friends onshore. From that time there was one common sound; the puttering of auxiliary motors as the yachts made their way down the harbour.

For all but Illingworth, this was going to be an adventure as much as a race. The Englishman was the only competitor who had taken part in long-distance, overnight offshore races. For the others, many of whom had just returned from the war, this would be a baptism by fire. They did not know what to expect, so they looked forward to the start and what would follow, with eager anticipation and some trepidation.

At this time none of the competing crews or race organisers from the Cruising Yacht Club of Australia knew what to expect as far as public interest in the race was concerned, but an answer was soon forthcoming. The race yachts were becoming increasingly easy to identify as they progressed towards the starting area, simply because they were being escorted by a growing number of small boats, all carrying enthusiastic supporters who were waving and shouting words of encouragement.

Meanwhile onshore, countless equally keen families and individuals, all of whom had had their appetite for this adventure whetted by the media, were either driving or walking to vantage points on North or South Head or around the harbour just to watch the sea-going daredevils set sail.

If there was a wish-list for perfect conditions for the start of the race then this day would top it: the prevailing north-east wind, which would no doubt strengthen during the afternoon, meant that the small fleet would make an easy exit from the harbour then head south on the face of a refreshing following wind that would continue into the night. It would be a dream run downwind. But how long would it last?

Each yacht carried between six and eight crew members, depending on its size, and they were busy from the outset. During the time it took to reach the starting area, the men had hauled heavy cotton sails up onto the deck from below and readied them for being hoisted aloft and set. It was hard work, but nowhere near as hard as it would be once they were at sea and in rough weather.

Winches – or more specifically, ratchet-handled snubbing winches, which were designed to assist with the hoisting and trimming of sails – were a luxury in this era, so few, if any, of the competing yachts had them fitted. Instead, it came down to sheer manpower and block-and-tackle purchase systems to get the sails set and trimmed efficiently.

The easiest competitor for the spectators to identify once the fleet moved into the starting area was the largest entry, the 19.2-metre-long *Mistral II*. A classic design built in 1922, this yacht featured a towering two-masted schooner rig that carried a cloud of sail. The favourite with the bookmakers and knowledgeable yachtsmen for winning the race on handicap, and possibly taking line honours by being first to finish was, however, the 15.5-metre-long *Winston Churchill* out of Hobart. It had been launched just 3 years earlier for the express purpose of servicing the remote lighthouses that were dotted along Tasmania's rugged 1500 nm coastline. However, while designed to be a work boat, owner Percy Coverdale (who had to get special permission from the then British Prime Minister for the yacht to carry his name) soon realised his yacht was one of the fastest sailing vessels on the Derwent River, and that fact was enough for him to decide to enter the inaugural Sydney Hobart race. Bringing further reinforcement to the yacht's favouritism for a win on corrected time was the knowledge that *Winston Churchill* had, only weeks earlier, established a record of 4 days and 8 hours for the passage between Hobart and Sydney. However, Coverdale was starting the Hobart race with his own handicap – a broken wrist from being struck by the handle of an out-of-control windlass when *Winston Churchill* was being relaunched for the voyage to Sydney. Coverdale had to delay the yacht's departure from Hobart for a couple of days so his broken wrist could be set in plaster.

Included in *Winston Churchill*'s crew was eighteen-year-old John Gordon. Fifty years later he recalled how he came to be a last-minute addition to the *Winston Churchill* crew, and in doing so, became one of the youngest participants in the race that year.

'Captain "Perc" had busted his wrist and needed someone who could operate a sextant because he couldn't,' Gordon explained. 'I grabbed the opportunity, but if the yacht had sunk I would have disappeared without trace because I wasn't on the crew list so no one would have known I was on board.'

*

Apart from the excitement and visual impact of the yachts lining up for the start, and the firing of the start signal (a flare gun, otherwise known as a Very pistol) it was obvious that this was not going to be a spectator sport for long. Once the yachts cleared Sydney Heads and disappeared over the southern horizon there was no way of knowing when they might be seen or heard from again. With two-way radios not being mandatory for the race, some ship-to-shore position reports were hoped for, but not expected. A few yachts were fitted with a radio receiver and transmitter. In 1924, *Mistral II* was one of the first offshore yachts in Australia to be equipped with a receiver, but cost and unreliability caused only a few other yacht owners to follow that lead and carry them for this race.

The crew of *Rani* was in that category; good naval sailors that they were, they recognised the importance of radio communications, so they managed to borrow a two-way radio from a Royal Navy aircraft carrier that was in port at the time. Unfortunately though, the unreliability factor came into play very early – two of its valves burned out before the start and rendered it useless. 'We set sail with no ship-to-shore communications whatsoever,' crew member Ray Richmond reminisced much later in life. 'No one on board cared anyway ... no life rafts, rescue ships, or helicopters in those days to take you off, or guide you if you got lost.'

Radio communications were also ruled out for the crew of *Horizon* for one very exasperating reason. Just days before the start, some thieving individual went on board at night and stole the yacht's radio set and battery charger.

When it came to electrical systems, on the majority of the yachts they were either non-existent or generally unreliable. The crews of those yachts with limited or no battery power had to make do with kerosene lanterns and the like, usually with great difficulty.

While today's Grand Prix level offshore racer has cockpit instrumentation to rival a commercial jet, in the 1940s, offshore racing was primarily seat-of-the-pants sailing. Usually there was just one instrument: a compass mounted on a binnacle which was often so dimly lit at night that it was almost impossible to read. The only other instrument was a Walker Log, a torpedo-shaped spinning drogue that was towed behind the yacht to measure its approximate speed and distance sailed. When possible, day or night, the navigator would use a sextant to take sun or star sights so the yacht's position could be plotted on a chart, but in adverse weather they could only rely on dead reckoning.

Refrigeration was a little-known luxury found primarily on large yachts in this era, but some of those racing to Hobart were fitted with an icebox. However, there was little chance of ice lasting anywhere between six and eleven days, the anticipated duration of the event. Thus, salt-cured meat – sometimes referred to as 'salt-horse' or 'junk' – was the dominant feature of most main meals, which were usually taken in the middle of the day. This repast was sometimes enhanced with uninspiring and relatively tasteless tinned food.

*

It was mid-morning when the start boat, manned by CYCA members, was on station and anchored off Cannae Point, near the Quarantine Station at North Head, so that the start line – the imaginary line between the boat and the point – could be established. It was a rule of the race that no competing yacht could be to the south of this line prior to the 11am start time, but it appeared there would be no danger of that occurring. While this was a designated race, there was very much an air of cruising casualness about it; after all, these were primarily cumbersome cruising yachts, not race boats ... something akin to draught horses contesting the Melbourne Cup. Additionally, of the more than fifty-odd sailors aboard the nine yachts, only Illingworth could be considered an offshore racing yachtsman.

So, unlike the intensely exciting and sometimes near shambolic starts of the Sydney to Hobart seen in modern times (where every second counts for the majority of the fleet), this historic moment back in 1945 was almost gentlemanly in procedure. Still, there was a powerful air of adventure sensed by the sailors and spectators alike. There was also an incentive to sail at their best: the owners of the first four yachts on corrected time would be awarded a trophy in recognition of their achievement.

There is no known report relating to the actual start of the race, but it is safe to assume that the highly experienced Illingworth would have had *Rani* – the second-smallest yacht in the fleet – at or near the head of the pack. Most of the others would have just ambled towards the start line after the gun had been fired and the last of the countdown flags lowered.

An hour later almost the entire fleet was out of sight. Those that could still be seen from North Head were small and somewhat fuzzy grey triangular shapes off Bondi, some 5 nm south of the harbour entrance. No crew could have wanted for a better way to settle into the adventure – it was a relaxed and cheerful ride downwind in ideal conditions where the power of the billowing sails was sufficient to propel the yachts down the face of waves amid a mass of surging white water.

The yachts sailed into the night, and soon after darkness fell the crew of *Wayfarer* had a memorable moment. As Peter Luke recalled:

The first day was uneventful, although Fred Harris, our helmsman on the first night, gave us a scare. I was woken by Fred's shouts that a boat was going to ram us. We rushed onto deck, only to discover 'the boat' was the crescent of the moon rising above the horizon. It was an understandable mistake. Everything looks different when you are out there alone in the darkness.

The north-easterly wind continued into the next day, which was another hot one, but when the leading yachts were approaching Montague Island, 150 nm south from Sydney, there was an ominous indication on the horizon ahead that a significant change in the weather was developing. The atmosphere across the entire southern sky was turning grey, and the long, low, cigar-shaped clouds capping that band of grey were obviously charging north towards the fleet at a rapid rate of knots. This was a local weather phenomenon – a southerly buster – a summertime weather event on Australia's east coast where a powerful and cool change roars in from the south and brings instant relief from the searing heat of a summer day. However, as well as bringing a much desired drop in the temperature, a buster's storm-like force can cause considerable damage on land and sea.

The official pre-race weather forecast indicated that this change could be expected, but the strength of the wind was completely underestimated – the anticipated 30-knot southerly wind turned out to be closer to 50 knots. Also, with that much wind opposing a fast-running south-flowing current, sea conditions were expected to deteriorate – and they did. Before long, the waves were averaging around 5 metres in height and breaking, but within a few hours of the storm arriving, there came the occasional monster. Ray Richmond would later recall that one wave which burst over *Rani* towered above its 16-metre-high mast. It was an avalanche of turbulent white water so large that it completely submerged the yacht, but, as Richmond revealed, *Rani* burst through it like a surfacing submarine.

When the storm was at its worst it was an extremely perilous time for those crew members on watch on deck, especially when a sail had to be reefed, lowered or changed. All too often the need to change a jib was literally a death-defying experience. The yacht would be bucked and tossed like a wild steer and sometimes semi-submerged as it speared through the near vertical wall of an approaching wave. In this era many yachts were not fitted with safety rails around the side of the yacht, nor safety harnesses as we know them today, so when the need came for a crewman to go to the bow he would tie a rope around his waist before leaving the cockpit, then lie on his belly on the deck and slide himself to the bow, hanging on tight to whatever fitting there was to cling to. Worse still, the closer he got to the bow the more violent the pitching motion of the yacht became. Then, when a fellow crew member released the halyard so the jib could be pulled down to the deck, the canvas fabric of the wildly flogging sail would tear at the tips of his cold and numb fingers as if it was sandpaper.

Once the sail change was complete and the crewman had slid all the way back to the cockpit, his crewmates, knowing how difficult the task had been, would drag him into the cockpit, slap him on the back and congratulate him on a bloody good effort.

For those on watch on deck in any storm, the wet weather clothing of the day was no match for the conditions. The only thing this apparel provided was a reduction in the wind chill factor – but only marginally. Life below deck was equally miserable. On some yachts the caulking used as a sealant in the gaps between the deck planks began to fail, so the experience for those below was like water torture. Each time a wave broke across the deck, water would teem through the cracks, saturating everything in the cabin. The crew of *Wayfarer* described the experience as like being in a chamber of horrors.

The most miserable experience for the crew came when they were trying to sleep. One sailor recalled how, when he lay down in a bunk, he could feel the water in the soaking wet kapok mattress rising up around his body. He said it was like sleeping in a swamp.

Some 40 hours after the race started, the ageing crew aboard Phil Goldstein's *Archina* agreed the conditions had become too challenging for them, so the decision was made to head to the coast and anchor in the hope the storm would abate and they could continue racing the following day. Goldstein was able to make radio contact with shore stations and advised the operators of this plan. Somehow, though, there was a misunderstanding in the communication: it was assumed that *Archina* was in difficulty, so in response a ship that was in the vicinity was diverted to go to the yacht's aid. On hearing this, Goldstein advised the shore stations the yacht was not in need of assistance. However there was a change of plan: with everybody on board horribly seasick, *Archina* retired from the race and returned to Sydney.

Meanwhile, the ferocity of the storm provided the crew of *Saltair* with the opportunity to replenish supplies. They opted to anchor in a sheltered cove on the coast near Montague Island — almost certainly Narooma — so they could escape the wrath of the weather. They rowed to shore and went rabbit hunting. The story goes that they were successful: they shot two rabbits and got to enjoy rabbit stew on board that evening. Sydney Hobart race folklore also suggests that this crew took the time to go to the pictures, probably at the historic Narooma Kinema (cinema).

Aboard *Wayfarer*, Peter Luke also decided to take shelter, but not before suffering serious sail damage. Crewman Geoff Ruggles, who at the age of 18 was one of the two youngest competitors in the race, recalled what happened in an interview with the ABC when he was aged 90:

> It knocked us about very badly and the sails were all torn. We had second-hand, worn-out cotton sails which had no life in them at all. Everything flapped, and when old sails flap, they tear. And that's what they did all the time. It was a mess-up. Lots of it was unexpected.

With the yacht unable to set sail, Luke initially chose to ride out the storm under bare poles, but when he realised how rapidly *Wayfarer* was being blown to the north, and that the majority of his crew was very seasick, he changed his mind. The yacht's log read: 'Dec 28: 4.30pm. Anchored behind Broulee Island …. after a good meal went ashore to phone. Tricky surf to land in and get off.' The storm abated overnight, so, with everyone having had a feed and a sleep *Wayfarer* resumed racing at first light.

The radio news that morning confirmed that *Wayfarer* had lost 70 nm on the leaders as a result of the storm, but Luke was not overly concerned:

> That radio news taught me a salutary lesson. It told me there was no room for compassion in ocean racing. While my first thoughts were for the preservation of the boat and the well-being of the crew, the other skippers were hell-bent for Tasmania.
>
> That did not worry me unduly. We were still cruiser-racing and enjoying ourselves.

While some boats took shelter, the remainder of the fleet pushed ahead, most with some level of difficulty. Jack Earl, aboard his double-ended ketch, *Kathleen,* was no doubt pleased that he had chosen the Colin Archer design of a stout, 1901 vintage Norwegian coastal patrol vessel to build and become *Kathleen* as it was handling the conditions very well. 'We reefed down and nursed our ship along in a very conservative fashion, and hove to through that gale,' Earl said in his biography.

The severity of this storm also caused Earl – who was unaware that *Rani*'s two-way radio was not operational – to be certain that Illingworth's yacht could not have survived such a severe storm:

> We were sure *Rani* had copped it. We thought they had sunk. We became very melancholy about it all as news

filtered through that *Rani* was still not sighted. We kept saying things like 'So-and-so was a nice bloke. We'll miss him'.

However, it was the Englishman's superior ocean racing experience that enabled *Rani* to continue racing during the gale with all possible sails set. Subsequently, the skipper explained he had decided to not take sail down because 'we would only have to put it back on again'.

Ray Richmond later explained what happened aboard *Rani*: 'We had our storm — 36 hours of it. Before the storm broke Illingworth tried his best to make every mile that he could. But he held on to the mainsail just a few minutes too long and it blew out.'

Even after the storm broke, Illingworth's strategy was to drive the yacht hard, but it wasn't without incident. In a situation which a crewman later described as being 'desperate', crew on deck had to be lashed to the mast or other fixtures so they weren't washed overboard. And, at the height of the storm, some of *Rani*'s sails were blown apart. But instead of taking all sail down and riding out the storm, Illingworth elected to set the storm trysail in place of the mainsail, plus the storm jib, and press on.

Twenty-four hours later the mainsail was back in one piece and ready to be reset, due in no small way to a monumental effort by Norm Hudson. Then came more dramas — this time below deck. The yacht had sprung a leak and water was entering the hull at a considerable rate. A frantic search through the cabin and up into the bow finally found the problem. At some stage when *Rani* had speared off the top of a wave and pounded into the trough that followed, the caulking had come out from between some of the deck planks, just as had happened aboard *Wayfarer*. Consequently, with waves continually crashing over the deck, water was cascading into the cabin. The quickest and most effective solution was to grab a blanket, tear it to pieces and force those remnants into the gaps.

That endeavour stemmed the flow to a degree, but there was still a lot of water to get out of the bilge. More problems were to come: the pumps fitted in the cabin to pump out the bilge failed – they had become clogged with paper labels which, because they were so wet, had parted company from the tins of food to which they had been attached. So, with the pumps not working, the only way the sloshing water could be removed was by bailing it out using pots and saucepans. One crewman became so exhausted from bailing that he collapsed in the bilge and fell asleep with six inches of seawater sloshing around him. Eventually, his crewmates woke him and helped him into an already wet bunk.

Illingworth later explained that while water came aboard during the gale, they managed to keep the primus stove going and got meals of a kind. On that note, one crewmember commented after the yacht reached Hobart, 'We had some strange meals on the way down!' Due to the absence of labels, no one knew what was in the cans they were opening. As if that wasn't enough, even making a cup of tea presented problems as five of the seven cups which they had on board had been smashed.

Subsequently, in his highly acclaimed book, *Offshore*, Illingworth wrote of his experience with the clogged pumps, advising sailors heading to sea to remove the labels from all tins carried on board and identify the contents with an indelible ink pen.

When it came to plotting the yacht's position in these extreme conditions, it was as much *guesstimation* as navigation because getting an accurate sun sight using a sextant was extremely difficult, if not impossible. However, here again, Illingworth's ability as a navigator via his application of dead reckoning impressed his crew: 'Illingworth was a master tactician,' Ray Richmond recalled. 'We plotted every mile of the way. Every half hour of every watch we had to put down our estimated position, which Illingworth checked on the course.'

This gale, which packed pelting rain, ferocious winds and at times disturbingly powerful seas, lasted for 36 hours. Then, as if begging forgiveness, the weather gods delivered near ideal sailing conditions. At that stage the eight remaining yachts were scattered over a wide expanse of ocean. Because there was no radio communications with shore stations, it could only be speculated which yacht was leading the race and where the others were placed.

Still, newspapers required headlines, but it was only pure speculation by shore-bound sailing 'experts' that provided any news angles for the then ravenous reporters. However there was one thing everyone agreed on – the tiny *Rani*, if it had survived the gale, would definitely not be leading the race.

As soon as the weather cleared, the Royal Australian Air Force (RAAF) resumed flying operations over the Tasman Sea, and while these were officially referred to as training missions, the flight crews were also eyes in the sky looking out for the fleet. But as expansive as these missions were, four days into the race, two yachts had still not been sighted – *Rani*, with its crew of six and the 12.2-metre-long ketch, *Horizon*. However, while there was concern for both vessels, there was no great alarm.

Not surprisingly, the dramas associated with the storm were causing the race to get headline status in newspapers and on radio stations Australia-wide. The next report in *The Sun* newspaper announced that *Winston Churchill* held a convincing lead over the rest of the fleet:

> The Tasmanian cutter, *Winston Churchill*, which has headed the field throughout, was ploughing her way across Bass Strait tonight well clear of her rivals, and only some unexpected piece of bad luck can prevent her from being first across the line.

At the same time, a newspaper in Melbourne reported that *Winston Churchill* was about 120 miles ahead of the fleet: 'Now half-way across the Strait, the *Winston Churchill* has good weather ahead and should win easily.'

Then *The Sydney Morning Herald* published the following race update on the morning of Monday, 31 December under the headline, 'Exciting Finish Likely':

> A *Sydney Morning Herald* reporter, who flew over the route of the yacht race to Tasmania in an RAAF Catalina at the weekend, wrote yesterday:
> The Tasmanian cutter, *Winston Churchill*, had a 78 mile lead over the Sydney boat, *Kathleen*.

Progress of the 635-mile race suggests an exciting finish tomorrow night between *Winston Churchill* and *Kathleen*.

We did not see *Horizon*, which might be in serious difficulties between 20 and 30 miles offshore, and it is felt that a search should be made for her tomorrow.

From the Catalina we estimated that nearly 170 miles separated *Churchill* and the last yacht, the Bermudan ketch, *Wayfarer*. The remaining six yachts and their crews appeared none the worse for their two days' fight with head-on southerlies that sometimes reached gale force, and the heavy seas.

The crews waved cheerily to the Catalina as we flew alongside them at 150 feet. The Catalina was engaged on a meteorological flight over the southern Tasman.

The yachts were shipshape and appeared to have withstood the buffeting well. Their sails and paintwork glistened in the sun as they gracefully rode the moderating seas.

Meanwhile, the 31 December afternoon edition of *The Sun* newspaper in Sydney carried a headline: 'No Sign of Lost Yachts – Catalina is Combing Wide Sea Area'. The story continued:

No trace of two yachts missing for four days in the Sydney–Tasmania race has yet been found by the RAAF Catalina today making an intensive 1600 square mile search along the coast.

The missing boats are the 35-foot Bermudan cutter, *Rani*, with a crew of six, and the 40-foot Bermuda ketch, *Horizon*, with a crew of five.

CATALINA TO SEARCH FARTHER OUT

The Catalina ... turned back off Cape Barren (50 miles NE of Tasmania) at 3pm and will extend its search further out to sea on the way back [to Sydney].

Though seasoned yachtsmen anticipate that the yachts, both of which are manned by experienced crews, may have weathered the harsh winds and heavy seas, anxiety is growing for them.

The Catalina left Rose Bay at 8:15am today and will sweep 10 miles out to sea along the NSW and Victorian coasts to the northern shores of Tasmania.

It is doing a 'square search', which means every section of the sea can be closely observed.

It is reporting by radio to Rose Bay [in Sydney] every half-hour.

An unconfirmed report [from a ground station] to the Catalina at noon stated that a boat was awash near Jervis Bay. An intensified search failed to reveal any vessel.

Expert yachtsmen in Sydney today expressed the hope that the vessels may be sheltering.

BIG LEAD

Meanwhile, the *Winston Churchill* (P. Coverdale) today will be sailing down the east coast of Tasmania and approaching Hobart waters.

Yesterday she was leading *Kathleen* (J. Earl) by about 100 miles with *Mistral* (R.S. Evans) 10 miles further back and another 12 miles to *Ambermerle* (J.R. Colquhoun).

About 6 miles farther back was *Saltair* (R.M. Walker), sailing about 4 miles due east of Cape Howe at 12.20pm. *The Wayfarer* (P.N. Luke) was another few miles back sailing due east of Green Cape at 12.12pm.

The first of the yachts is not expected to enter the Derwent until sometime tomorrow, a Tasmanian message states.

Because of his knowledge of the Tasmanian coastline, and his big lead, P. Coverdale, in the *Winston Churchill*, is expected to win.

GOOD SEA BOAT

A special forecast gave 'north-west winds, 15 to 20 knots, and slight seas north of Flinders Island, soon changing south-west to south 15 to 20 knots with a moderate sea'.

Ernie Messenger, of Double Bay, who once owned *Horizon*, described her as a wonderful sea-boat.

The crew, he said, were all experienced men. 'Boy' Messenger is his 21-year-old son and had been sailing boats all his life.

J. Bartlett bought *Horizon* only 10 days before competing in the race.

He was in business in India for 25 years and arrived in Australia on November 11.

Captain Illingworth purchased *Rani* from Capt. H.W.B. Livesay in October.

Yachtsmen say the missing boats may have sailed well off the coast in order to pick up favourable winds which would bring them into Tasmania.

However, damage to the well-built Tasmanian cutter, *Winston Churchill*, during a storm shows the severity of the seas. *Winston Churchill* had part of her starboard planking stove-in just above the waterline when she hit floating debris.

The rest of the yachts in the 630-mile race, which started at 11am on Boxing Day, have been battling for most of the time against gales and heavy seas.

In fact though, the majority of these reports were based on speculation. The whereabouts of *Rani* and *Horizon* remained unknown. On 1 January 1946, the Sydney *Daily Telegraph* carried a headline: 'Search for Yachts Fails. Boats May Have Been Dismasted. Plane Out Again Today'.

However, just a few hours later, the mystery surrounding the whereabouts of all eight yachts began to be solved, albeit not accurately in the first instance. In the early afternoon on the same day, the passengers aboard a light plane that had flown out from Hobart to look for the fleet reported back that they had seen a yacht some distance away from Tasman Island, at the entrance to Storm Bay. It was immediately assumed this was *Winston Churchill*, and it was calculated that if the existing weather pattern held, it should arrive in Hobart overnight.

Back in Sydney, a *Sun* newspaper reporter delivered his own 'scoop' in the afternoon edition of the paper:

The ketch *Horizon*, with a crew of five, missing since last Thursday in the Sydney Hobart race, was sighted safe 80 miles from Hobart by the RAAF's searching Catalina today and should run second.

'I'm so happy, I can't talk,' said Mrs E. Messenger, mother of 'Boy' Messenger, one of *Horizon*'s crew, when told the news, 'though we never really had any fears.'

Relatives of other members of *Horizon*'s crew also expressed their relief at the news.

Mrs S.A. Payne, mother of Alan Payne, said: 'It's excellent news. Although we didn't really expect to hear anything until today, we couldn't help sharing the general anxiety.

'News of the yacht's safe arrival is improved by the fact that it will gain second place.'

Mrs Bartlett, wife of *Horizon*'s skipper, was still indisposed today. On her behalf it was stated she was very relieved by the news, although she had felt confident her husband would arrive safely.

Mrs J. Forsythe, mother of a member of the crew, was overjoyed when she heard the news. Her married daughter, Mrs Bidwell, said: 'We're tickled to bits.'

Alan Payne, who at age 23 was another young member of the *Horizon* crew, would, in later years, go on to become a highly acclaimed yacht designer, locally and internationally. Coincidentally, his younger brother, Bill, who had flown RAAF bombers over Europe during the war, was a spotter aboard the Catalina that located *Horizon*. The aircraft flew out of Rathmines, near Newcastle, for that mission, and having located *Horizon* and other race yachts off the coast of Tasmania, the aircraft flew on to Hobart to refuel. When it took off on the return flight to Rathmines, the crew was all smiles: as well as savouring the satisfaction they felt with locating *Horizon*, they knew there was a reward for their efforts on board the Catalina. A crate of fresh crayfish was in the cargo hold for them to share when they got home.

The information regarding the sighting of *Horizon* caused a CYCA spokesman to announce that the yacht was in second place behind *Winston Churchill* in the race for line honours, but the distance between them was unknown.

However, later in the day the Tasman Island lighthouse keeper, who was perched 300 metres above sea level, radioed race organisers in Hobart with the news that he had sighted a yacht on approach to the island. It was immediately assumed by officials that he had been looking at *Winston Churchill* through his telescope, but that thought lasted only a few seconds as the lighthouse keeper was adamant that he could see the number 44 on the mainsail – *Rani*'s sail number. This brought about another assumption: that two yachts, *Winston Churchill* and *Rani*, were then on approach to the finish, with *Winston Churchill* in the lead. Consequently, while *Horizon* had been located, its position in the fleet could not be confirmed.

This misinformation was then telephoned through to members of the CYCA in Sydney, and within a very short time the Sydney *Sun* newspaper was running a stop press headline: 'Yacht *Rani* Turns Up Running Second in Race'.

But *Rani* was the bolter. She was actually leading, but no one knew it.

Fifty years later, on 2 January 1995, seventy-five-year-old Ray Richmond was guest speaker at a dinner in Hobart celebrating the 50th anniversary race. During his address he gave a colourful insight into the closing stages of *Rani*'s race:

Coming into Storm Bay we were very despondent. The winds were light. It had taken us six days to get there. We were the smallest boat in the race so we expected the bigger boats to have tramped through the storm and be well ahead.

When we were in the bay we were spotted by a small aircraft which, it would appear, reported to the RAAF that they had seen a yacht that might have been *Rani*. A short time later a RAAF plane came out and found us. They circled us while we continued to sail as fast as we could, even though we were certain we were tail-end Charlie. Never mind, we told ourselves.

Illingworth was still very much in racing mode and wanted to get there in the best time possible. Next thing, in came a Catalina flying boat, obviously having a very good look at us as it was on approach – in fact it was so low when it flew over us it blew what little wind there was out of our sails. Our next thought was, yes, we had probably been posted as missing, which, as it turned out, was right. We had been declared missing for four days.

After a while the Catalina headed off towards land, leaving us more despondent.

As we were sailing into the entrance of the Derwent we got a change of weather, a very strong wind – too strong for the genoa. Illingworth immediately gave us the order to douse the sail, but it was too late – it blew apart into rags. Ah, old canvas sails ... they do that sort of thing! This was the saddest moment of the trip as far as we were concerned.

Once we were settled and sailing properly again we noticed motor car headlights on the shore were flashing out a message in Morse code: 'Are you *Rani*?'

We replied using our signal lamp: 'Yes, we're *Rani*.'

'*Rani* from Sydney?'

'Yes, we're *Rani* from Sydney.'

'Thank God you're safe.'

The news that we were in the river had got through to the Royal Yacht Club of Tasmania's small motor launch, which was out on the water, and it dashed back to the club with the news that *Rani* was coming in. Then the launch came back out and came up close to us. As it did someone on board shouted: 'Are you well?'

'Yes, we are well.'

'No injury?'

'No.'

'We will tell Sydney – they've been worried about you.'

That was enough to convince us we were definitely tail-end Charlie.

Those aboard the launch then told us where the finish line was located and how to get to it, information which we thanked them for. The launch then headed off into the darkness.

Our morale was then very low.

It was New Year's Day, and around 10pm another small launch loaded with an inebriated group – probably remnants from New Year's Eve celebrations – came up close to welcome us.

Someone shouted: 'Anything you want to know?'

'Yes' said Illingworth. 'How are we doing?'

The inebriated group, obviously assuming we knew we were leading, replied with raucous laughter.

With that our morale fell even further – until someone shouted, 'You are winning!'

There was disbelief aboard *Rani*: 'Did we hear right?'

Illingworth then asked: 'How many boats are in?'

There was more raucous laughter, then came the reply: 'You are the first.'

Unbelievable!

Someone on the launch then shouted a question: 'Are you a dry ship?'

'Yes', we replied. The launch then closed in and a bottle of whisky was passed across to us.

Yes, we must be leading, we thought!

Soon after, as we continued to make our way up the river towards Hobart, two small yachts took up station just ahead of us, one either side of our bow. It was a welcome escort that was silently indicating when to tack. They pulled off near Sandy Bay, leaving us to cross the line to a tumultuous welcome. The jetty was packed. This was

1.22am on 2 January 1946. In my scrapbook I noted about 500 people were there. In Illingworth's writings, and who am I to doubt his veracity, he says there were 5000. Regardless, Hobart did us proud.

*

Even when *Rani* was in the river and approaching the finish the news was spreading across Hobart's population of some 70,000 that *Winston Churchill* was nearing the finish and set to claim line honours. However, with communications being what they were in those days, it was possible few knew it was *Rani* until just before the little yacht reached the line.

It was a long wait. *Rani* was not in sight of the line until after midnight, but even so, spectators were crowded along Castray Esplanade at Battery Point to welcome the yacht they still assumed was *Winston Churchill* into port. Little did they know as they peered into the darkness across the Derwent, that the faint port and starboard navigation lights they could see out on the river were aboard *Rani* and not the local hope, *Winston Churchill*. Apparently not even the race officials – who were struggling to have the finishing cannon in place and loaded in time for the historic moment – would have believed that. But as the ghostly outline of the yacht closed on the line, which extended from the shore to a buoy anchored some 300 metres out in the river, the spectators began to realise that what they were looking at in the darkness was too small to be *Winston Churchill*. Immediately, the word spread like wildfire through the crowd: it could only be *Rani*.

The frantic efforts by race officials to have the cannon loaded and ready to go were successful, but only just. Within minutes the fuse had been lit and seconds later an almighty boom thundered across the river. Simultaneously rapturous applause, cheering and clapping filled the air along with a cacophony of car horns.

At that time, *Winston Churchill* was lying becalmed some 100 nm from the finish.

*

News-hungry reporters and an excited crowd rushed along the few hundred metres from Battery Point to the waterfront near the century-old Constitution Dock, to welcome the unlikely victors. As the yacht pulled alongside the dock, the crowd broke into a rousing rendition of 'For He's a Jolly Good Fellow'.

When questioned by reporters, one of the unshaven and unkempt crewmembers described things as being 'desperate' for 12 hours. However, Illingworth, being the ever-modest Englishman, downplayed the impact the gale had on their race.

'*Rani* is a good boat in rough weather and we never had any anxiety,' he said. 'We had a fine and safe trip. It's funny to hear we were thought lost.'

He added that he could not understand how crew aboard RAAF Catalinas flying over the fleet had not sighted his yacht. The only explanation might have been that *Rani* was missed because it was so small.

'At no time was *Rani* more than 20 miles from the coast and at times only a mile out,' he explained. He added that he had sailed his yacht on a direct course from Gabo Island, at the entrance to Bass Strait, to the north-east corner of Tasmania, then paralleled the coast south to Tasman Island and Storm Bay. However, the stretch down the coast was not without incident – the mainsail had split in half yet again, and yet again the crew had gone on deck with large sail-making needles and thick thread and had sewed it back together.

Considering the size of the yacht and the storm it endured, this remarkable achievement further confirmed Illingworth's status as the world's pre-eminent offshore-racing yachtsman.

However, while paying due respect to the talents of their captain, the crew also heaped praise on Norm Hudson:

Norm won the race for us because he just would not accept what we believed to be the inevitable. We had burst our only big mainsail in the southerly blow that hit us the second night out, and had stowed the sail below as scrap, to be repaired if possible by tradesmen when we got to Hobart.

For the next 38 hours Norm stood his usual watches during the blow, but also worked almost incessantly on the sail. He squatted on his bunk for hour after hour, stitching. We were able to reset the repaired sail a few hours after the spite had gone out of the wind. By then Norm, whose only previous experience in needlework had been on felt dolls while in an RAAF hospital during the war, had hand-sewn 175 feet of canvas seams.

If there was a bonus for Illingworth on his arrival, it came via the fact that Tasmania's newly appointed Governor, Sir Hugh Binney, had taken a more than casual interest in the race – for good reason. Illingworth had served under him aboard the flagship of Britain's Mediterranean battle squadron, HMS *Malaya*, in 1937–38. So, soon after *Rani* docked, an emissary from Government House arrived with an invitation from the Governor for Illingworth to stay at Government House. In a further coincidence, when Illingworth arrived at the Governor's impressive residence overlooking the Derwent River, he realised that Sir Hugh's Aide-de-camp was none other than his brother-in-law, Captain Gold.

*

The challenging and dangerous nature of this race, coupled with the courage of the competitors who had put their lives on the line in the name of sport, along with nature's unpredictable temperament, had made this more than a yacht race. It was a sporting contest that had held a surprising level of public interest across Australia, from the backblocks to the Big Smoke. The day after the mighty little *Rani* claimed line honours, the impact this daring sailing adventure had nationwide was all too evident. Apart from newspapers in the capital cities running it as front page news, papers in outlying towns were doing likewise. *The Evening Advocate*, published in Innisfail, the centre of a small community of less than 2000 people, some 1600 kilometres north of Brisbane, ran a prominent story under the headline '*Rani* Wins Yacht Race'. It read in part:

HOBART — After being 'missing' for five days the cutter *Rani* has won the Sydney to Hobart yacht race.

Rani crossed the finishing line at 1:23 AM today and looked certain to win both the scratch and handicap events when she was sighted off Cape Raoul about 30 miles from Hobart.

Rani was last seen just before a violent southerly arose near Port Kembla last Wednesday.

The cutter put well out to sea. Widespread searches by RAAF reconnaissance Catalinas failed to locate her.

Captain J.H. Illingworth, owner and captain of *Rani*, said he could not believe that the vessel was considered lost for five days.

'We had a fine and safe trip,' he said. 'It's funny to say we were lost.

'The crew never lost one hot meal.'

On Friday two Catalinas passed high over *Rani* but obviously did not see her.

The Bermuda-rigged *Winston Churchill*, which had been reported as leading and looked a certain winner, was becalmed yesterday about 100 miles north-east of Hobart.

There is still no news of the Bermudan ketch *Horizon*, which has been missing for five days, but the crew of the *Rani* believe that it is not yet necessary to fear for her safety.

'I think that the *Horizon* has been missed in an aerial survey,' said Captain Illingworth of the *Rani*.

'She has experienced men aboard and is a good craft.'

The Miner newspaper published in Kalgoorlie, 600 kilometres from Perth in the Western Australian outback — where the locals knew more about kangaroos than ketches and cutters — ran the same story.

The press also took pleasure in reporting that *Rani* had taken the double — line and handicap honours — and consequently that 'Captain J. Illingworth, owner and skipper of the *Rani* will have to present himself with a cup that he had donated for the owner of the first yacht to cross the finishing line.'

Winston Churchill reached Hobart more than 17 hours behind *Rani* while *Kathleen* was almost a day in arrears in third place. On handicap, *Rani* was victorious by a margin of 29 hours over *Ambermerle*.

Once docked in Hobart, Jack Earl told how *Kathleen* had been hammered by a gale in the Derwent when just a few nautical miles from the finish:

> When we got right up into the Derwent there was a tremendous north-westerly gale. It blew 74 knots and really knocked the fleet about. We had a triple-reefed main, a jib and a mizzen. But within a quarter of a mile of the line the breeze suddenly dropped and the Derwent was as flat as a millpond. It wasn't worth putting all that gear back on again so we just concentrated on getting across the finish.

A crew member of *Saltair* told a fascinating story about the yacht running before a real blow near Tasman Island. For 4 hours *Saltair* rode down the face of tremendous seas like a surfboat at up to 15 knots. He then topped that with a fishing story: they were trailing a log-line off the stern to measure the yacht's speed (for dead-reckoning navigation) when a very large barracouta surfaced and – thinking it had found that day's meal – bit off the bottle-sized, torpedo-shaped metal spinner on the end of the line. The story went that they got their revenge by catching two barracouta and eating them for breakfast the following morning. *Ambermerle* was another yacht that copped a hiding soon after entering the Derwent. Savage squalls descending from lofty Mount Wellington – which stands as Hobart's backdrop – were so strong that both the mainsail and the jib blew apart. The crew lowered the torn sails and replaced them with what they had left – the tiny storm trysail and a grossly unsuitable balloon jib. With that jury rig set, *Ambermerle* made slow progress up the river towards the finish, only to encounter more problems less than a nautical mile from the line by running aground on Red Chapel Beach in Sandy Bay.

The crew tried desperately to lever the yacht off the beach using the spinnaker pole, but when that effort was unsuccessful, they accepted a tow back into deep water. *Ambermerle* crossed the finishing line at 7.17pm, an hour after running aground. However, a controversy ensued: some competitors claimed that *Ambermerle* should have been disqualified for accepting a tow, but in the true spirit of the inaugural race, this claim was ignored by officials and it was placed second on handicap.

The schooner, *Mistral II,* was another entry that ran aground when closing on the finishing line, primarily because it could barely make headway to windward and tack in the same north-westerly gale. With the line in sight it became essential that the yacht be tacked and change course towards Battery Point. But a savage squall at that time made that change impossible to complete. Instead, *Mistral II* continued sailing across the river until it came to an abrupt halt on the beach at Bellerive, directly opposite Battery Point. The owner, Robert Evans, was then forced to start the yacht's engine and reverse back into deep water. However, when that manoeuvre was complete, it was obvious that the yacht would still not be able to reach the finish line under sail in those conditions, so Evans chose to retreat. *Mistral II* was sailed 11 nm downstream to Tinderbox Bay at the entrance to the Derwent, where it was anchored alongside *Horizon,* which was already sheltering there. When the gale abated later in the day and conditions became more favourable, Evans and crew were able to sail *Mistral II* to the finish, crossing the line at 11:55pm.

Saltair was the next yacht into Hobart, but in confusing circumstances. A large number of the cars parked at the finishing line had their headlights on and this was enough to bamboozle *Saltair*'s crew as to the actual location of the line. Convinced they had reached the finish, the crew commenced celebrations with a round of drinks, while the owner started the engine so he could guide the yacht into the dock, only to then realise they hadn't crossed the line at all. This incident and the *Mistral II* grounding brought more controversy: the headline in the *Hobart Mercury* on 5 January trumpeted: 'Official Denies Sydney Yachts Disqualified'.

This story came from hearsay around the dock. It was suggested that both *Saltair* and *Mistral II* should be disqualified for using their engines while still racing. But the Race Committee had no such intention. Both finishing times were recorded as being official and let stand in the true spirit of a gentleman's game.

Saltair's average speed over the entire course was a leisurely three knots, but there was still one yacht yet to reach the finish, its whereabouts unknown. It was Peter Luke's *Wayfarer*, who was obviously cruising more than racing towards Hobart. The yacht was still in Bass Strait on 1 January and battling a westerly gale that delivered squalls of up to 45 knots. The environment on board was nothing short of miserable: when on deck the crew had to contend with spray that came at them like buckshot, while in the cabin, the water torture continued due to the deck leaks.

When *Wayfarer* was about halfway down Tasmania's east coast, the exhausted crew was desperately in need of some respite, so Luke decided to shelter in the lee of Schouten Island. Within 24 hours, conditions had eased considerably, so the sails were raised, the anchor brought aboard and the yacht set on a course for the next turning point – Tasman Island. Unfortunately though, Storm Bay lived up to its name in the form of another westerly gale, which meant *Wayfarer* was confronted by a punishing upwind stretch in big seas before reaching the entrance to the Derwent River. The situation was like belting one's head against a wall in the most miserable of circumstances, conditions so bad that after tacking 18 times over 12 hours, the navigator declared they had made no headway. In fact, they had probably lost ground towards Cape Raoul, a rocky lee shore famous for its pillars of stone known as The Organ Pipes.

Luke quickly took stock of the situation and decided he and his crew had had enough for the time being, so he made the call to drop the sails and motor to safe sanctuary at historic Port Arthur, located in a sheltered bay some 10 nm to the north. When first settled in 1830, Port Arthur was a tiny timber-gathering community but within 20 years it had become the destination for the worst of the English convicts being transported to Australia.

By mid-afternoon, *Wayfarer* was at anchor off The Isle of The Dead adjacent to the small settlement. The crew then launched the yacht's dinghy, rowed ashore and headed for the little local pub, the Arthur Hotel. Luke did as required under race rules and called organisers to advise of *Wayfarer*'s whereabouts. He then did the same with family in Sydney, telling them that the plan was to continue on to the finish when the weather improved.

With those obligations complete, Luke and his crew found themselves being treated like heroes: the publican, Tasman Pitman, tapped into a new keg of the now famous local beer, Cascade, then put on the table a feast of the equally famous local delicacy, freshly caught crayfish, and some roasted pork.

The beers and the food flowed on into the evening. Unfortunately, though, for crewmate Fred Harris, he became the focus of much ragging. Legend has it that he was on a liquid diet, unable to eat solids because he had lost his false teeth overboard during a sail change earlier the previous day.

Hobart race folklore also refers to another entertaining moment that night involving the *Wayfarer* crew. This occurred when they decided it was time to return to the yacht. As they made their way along the wooden pier to the dinghy, one unnamed member of the crew literally disappeared straight over the side of the dock and into the water. Dark as it was, his crew mates were able to fish him out and get him into the dinghy.

Next morning, *Wayfarer* was under way in far more favourable conditions and making good speed towards the Derwent River and the finish line. News of the yacht's approach spread quickly through the town and, as a result, a large crowd was on hand to welcome the persistent *Wayfarer* into port at 5.20 pm. There were rousing cheers, applause and car horns honking in recognition of what would become an historic moment. Later, when looking back on *Wayfarer's* participation in the inaugural Sydney Hobart race, Luke said: 'The purpose was to arrive, not necessarily to win it.'

Wayfarer's elapsed time for the race, 11 days, 6 hours and 20 minutes, still stands as the slowest time in the history of the classic. Peter Luke and his crew didn't care; the reception they received made every mile worthwhile: 'I reckon half the city of Hobart was there to greet us,' Luke said.

*

Elapsed times:

Rani (United Kingdom) John Illingworth – 6 days 14
    hours 22 minutes
Winston Churchill (Hobart) Percy Coverdale – 7 days 7
    hours 38 minutes
Kathleen (Sydney) Jack Earl – 8 days 6 hours 20 minutes

Horizon (Sydney) R. Bartlett – 8 days 7 hours 47 minutes

Ambermerle (Sydney) John Colquhoun & Clarrie Kiel – 8 days 8 hours 18 minutes

Mistral II (Sydney) Robert Evans – 8 days 12 hours 55 minutes

Saltair (Sydney) Bert & Russ Walker – 8 days 13 hours 48 minutes

Wayfarer (Sydney) Peter Luke – 11 days 6 hours 20 minutes

Archina II (Sydney) Phil Goldstein – Did Not Finish

FOOTNOTE: To put 75 years of the Hobart race into perspective, when the official race record holder, the 30-metre supermaxi *LDV Comanche,* reached Hobart in the 2017 race, the leading yachts in the inaugural race in 1945 would have been more than 500 nm astern – somewhere near Batemans Bay on the south coast of New South Wales.

CHAPTER 3

Home are the Heroes

With all eight yachts docked safely in Hobart, there was an air of celebration and salutation around the historic waterfront. A constant throng of local residents, many from outlying districts, crowded around the docks to see the yachts and to welcome the crews who had undertaken – and survived – such a daring challenge. No doubt, they were seen as maritime heroes.

Many of the locals also opened up their hearts and homes to the weather-beaten sailors, hosting them with home-cooked meals and even a dry bunk for an overnight stay. The remarkable level of community support was also stirred by the fact that in the matter of a few days the race had delivered more national headlines and column inches of reporting for Hobart, and Tasmania, than any other event – ever. And, it was continuing.

Understandably, there were many parties and official functions for them to attend, the most important of which was a civic reception at the Hobart Town Hall on 8 January 1946. It was hosted by the Lord Mayor, Mr John Soundy, with the Governor, Admiral Sir Hugh Binney, also in attendance. They made glowing speeches welcoming the sailors and both mentioned the hope – widely held within the community – that the race would become an annual event.

In response, Illingworth lent support to that wish. He said that he and his crew were 'deeply impressed by the welcome given us in Hobart, which is an ideal place to end an ocean race'. Then, in the true spirit of sportsmanship and encouragement, he suggested that congratulations should also go to all competing crews, not just the crew of *Rani*.

Unfortunately though an undercurrent of controversy and doubt was emerging among a section of the local community, experienced sailors or otherwise. Many struggled to believe that a yacht so small could beat considerably larger and potentially faster vessels in such a storm-ravaged race. Consequently, the whisper on the waterfront was that Illingworth must have used *Rani*'s engine during the race for his little yacht to be first home. Obviously those naysayers gave no consideration to the fact that the English yachtsman's reputation in the world of offshore racing was second to none, and that his determined crew – who would never have entertained the thought of cheating – did not give up, even in the roughest weather.

However, as no official protest against *Rani* was lodged, these dockside whispers were not dealt with in a formal fashion, so they persisted. In fact it wasn't until after the second Hobart race, a year later, that they were laid to rest. This opportunity came when CYCA member Bob Bull, a Sydney dentist who had skippered his yacht, *Christina*, in that race, realised with some level of disgust that the *Rani* rumours were still circulating in Hobart.

On his return to Sydney, Bull was given the opportunity to address CYCA members about his victory in the race, and while doing so he used the occasion to defend Illingworth to the hilt. Subsequently, on 20 February 1947, the *Daily Telegraph* in Sydney carried a report on Bull's speech.

RANI SKIPPER SEALED ENGINE BEFORE RACE

Rani's skipper, Captain Illingworth, RN, sealed his motor before taking part in the 1945 Sydney Hobart yacht race, said Mr Bob Bull last night.

Mr Bull, who is skipper of *Christina*, was addressing members of the Cruising Yacht Club, which organised the race.

He said rumour-mongers in Tasmania had conducted a whispering campaign against Captain Illingworth.

'In Hobart last month I was astonished to hear responsible Tasmanian yachtsmen say they believed Captain Illingworth won the race by using his motor,' Mr Bull said.

'These yachtsmen, if they had desired, could have scotched the report.

'Although he did not make a fuss about it, Captain Illingworth sealed his motor and wired his propeller before the race.

'The seals and propeller were still intact when *Rani* was slipped in Hobart after the race, as anyone sufficiently interested could have seen.'

*

The *Australian Power Boat and Yachting Monthly*'s report on the inaugural race detailed what its writer saw as 'a uniquely Australian sailing event that could match the best in the world'. It was suggested that the Hobart race should be declared an annual event and, after that, an Australian assault on the best of British ocean racing yachts should follow: 'An Australian yacht should visit Great Britain and take the Ashes away. Every other branch of Australian sport had been represented in contests in Britain.'

The report continued: 'The Cruising Yacht Club at Sydney and the Royal Yacht Club of Tasmania had launched the sport of ocean racing on a firm basis. As for the future, the president of the CYC, Mr Bert Walker, was quoted as suggesting that when the next race was held it was likely to attract between thirty and forty boats.'

An exultant Walker went on to declare: 'At no far distant time Australia should challenge the USA. We have the men in Hobart now who can steer a boat as well as, and better than, Mr Vanderbilt [the USA's famed *America's Cup* defender].'

The same report in *Australian Power Boat and Yachting Monthly* justified why the Hobart race, which had only been sailed once, could be compared more than favourably with the world's two most prominent ocean races, the Fastnet Race and the Newport (Rhode Island) to Bermuda Race. Ironically, while each of these races was of a distance near identical to the Hobart race, the author of the article added '... the Sydney to Hobart is perhaps the greatest of them all.'

Meanwhile, support for the race to be staged annually was snowballing, but many of the suggestions were somewhat off-beam. The *Hobart Mercury* had already published an editorial declaring that the race should be run at a time that would allow the competing yachts to participate in the Royal Hobart Regatta (held in mid-February each year). Illingworth then chimed in with the thought that it might be 'a fine thing' to vary the course by making Hobart the starting point and Sydney the destination. Bert Walker then ventured his opinion: after declaring his support for an annual race, he suggested Melbourne might be considered as a stopover port, while other buffs went to the extreme of proposing that thought should be given to including Brisbane in the course.

Back in Sydney, the small membership of the CYCA was having to deal with a dilemma that would have a far-reaching influence on the club's destiny: just a matter of months after being formed on the foundation of cruising and not racing, they had to deal with the possibility of staging an annual offshore race which had the potential to become one of the world's classics. Fortunately, common sense prevailed: the club hierarchy had the wisdom to not rush a decision, and instead stepped back and carefully assessed the situation over some two months. The decision came in March 1946: what had originally been planned as a casual cruise to Hobart for a few mates would become an annual ocean race.

It was the unexpected and vast media coverage (due in part to the dramatic impact of the horrendous storm that pummelled the fleet), and the astonishing reception the crews received in Hobart, that had forced the CYCA's hand, and in turn brought about a dramatic change of direction for the fledgling 'cruising' club. On that note, at the same time as the decision regarding the future of the race was confirmed, the membership formally agreed that the title of the club would be the Cruising Yacht Club of Australia.

*

Speculation as to how many yachts might be on the start line for the second Hobart race varied dramatically. Bert Walker's prediction that between thirty and forty yachts would be on the line was considered by many to be optimistic, but when the extent and impact of the media coverage of the 1945 race was considered, a fleet more than four times that of the inaugural event had to be deemed possible. Buoying this thought was the fact that public interest in the amazing race had hardly waned since the yachts reached Hobart. Newspapers and yachting magazines across the nation were publishing every snippet of information they could find. For example, on Tuesday, 19 March, just after the CYCA made its announcement about the future of the race, a story in the *Newcastle Sun* confirmed for readers that the Hobart race would be staged annually, and then added a local angle to the story by suggesting a feeder race from Newcastle to Sydney was planned:

> The first Sydney Hobart race was a thrilling affair. Two yachts, *Rani* and *Horizon*, were reported missing but finished the event, the former being placed first in the race.
>
> In addition to the Sydney Hobart race, races from New Zealand, Brisbane, Newcastle and Melbourne to

Sydney will act as 'feeder' races to the main event, which will start from Sydney on December 26, 1946.

It is hoped to have all competing yachts in Sydney by December 18, so that arrangements can be made for some harbour races prior to the start of the Sydney Hobart event.

Illingworth's crushing victory, and the storm that was encountered on the way south, could easily have been enough to cause many CYCA members to want to revert to the club's initial manifesto – comfortable and casual cruising in company. Instead, it had a consolidating effect towards racing, and in particular the exciting and already high-profile Sydney Hobart.

The fact is that the two-week period of the race, and the elements of danger it contained inspired sailors and the public across the nation: for them, there was no major offshore race in the world that could be compared with the Hobart – and it had only been staged once! Consequently, ocean racing as a sport then had its equivalent of the Melbourne Cup and cricket's Ashes series.

Little wonder then, with the club having achieved so much in the short time since it was founded, that there was talk all over town of it being likely the CYCA was in line to receive a Royal Charter – if so it would become the Royal Cruising Yacht Club of Australia. But this theory proved to be rumour, not reality.

*

In a matter of weeks the club without a clubhouse had gone from obscurity to being the talk of the town, much to the chagrin of many members of the well-established clubs around the harbour. This might explain why, some months later, the CYCA's application to affiliate with the Sydney Yacht Racing Association was rejected, apparently due to there being opposition from another club. But that rejection only galvanised the CYCA membership. It was soon decided that the club would concentrate its sailing activities on racing offshore, rather than smooth-water contests around buoys in the harbour. That done, it took only a few weeks for a schedule to be drawn up for a season comprising eleven ocean races over offshore courses to the north and south of Sydney. Apart from being innovative, these races would provide members, and anyone else who might be interested, with the opportunity to gain blue-water racing experience and be better prepared for the next Hobart, should they wish to compete. The events also provided club officials with the opportunity to become more proficient in race management, and to develop improved safety requirements for competing yachts.

Not surprisingly, with the success of the Hobart race creating an unimagined public profile for the CYCA, growing pains emerged: the club became difficult to manage effectively due to a sizeable growth in membership and yacht numbers. There was only one solution: employ someone who could oversee its administration. Enter Erling Greve Le Brun – otherwise known as Earl Le Brun – a popular individual and keen sailor with all the qualifications needed for the job. In February 1946 the CYCA committee appointed him to the position of General Secretary on an annual retainer of £100. It was a deal that also had a direct benefit for the club as Le Brun decided the CYCA should use the offices of his accountancy practice in the heart of Sydney as its headquarters.

As the club's status in the yachting community grew under Le Brun's stewardship, members looked on with a great degree of satisfaction and pride. Most gratifying was the fact that yacht clubs across Australia were following the CYCA's lead and planning their own ocean races. In the west, the Royal Freshwater Bay Yacht Club staged an 80 nm race from Perth to Bunbury in 1948, while that same year the Queensland Cruising Yacht Club sent a small fleet away in the inaugural 308 nm Brisbane to Gladstone race. Two years later saw the commencement of the 160 nm Adelaide to Port Lincoln race. Like the Hobart race, these events have continued to this day.

*

As the months ticked by and 26 December 1946 drew nearer, interest in the second Sydney Hobart began to escalate, so it wasn't surprising that in a very short period of time the number of entries exceeded that of the inaugural line-up. This fact sat comfortably alongside a prediction published in a Sydney newspaper earlier in the year: 'John Illingworth set a pace which will gain in momentum yearly as crews and boats improve.' However, while enthusiasm for the race was on a rapid rise, the controversy that centred on *Rani* would not go away.

Consequently, the debate relating to the sealing of engines in the Hobart race came to a head at the club's annual general meeting in September 1946, but still could not be resolved. This led to the club's Rear-Commodore, Charlie Cooper, being directed to contact the Royal Ocean Racing Club in London and seek their advice on the matter. The reply that came by cable a few days later was both terse and direct: ENGINES NOT REPEAT NOT SEALED HERE.

They were six words that set a rule in stone: the official documentation relating to the regulations for the 1946 race did not refer to the sealing of engines. Instead it was stated that auxiliary motors must not be used for propelling from 10 minutes before the start until the finish line was crossed. Motors could be used only for the charging of batteries.

It was a ruling that caused considerable angst for the CYCA's Commodore, Bert Walker, so much so that he announced he would not compete in the race that year. It was his prerogative to decide on whether or not to race, yet it was how he went about announcing his decision that did not sit well with the club's committee.

On Saturday, 30 November 1946 the *Daily Telegraph*, in Sydney, carried a story written by noted yachting journalist of the time, Lou d'Alpuget, under the headline, 'Won't Sail in Ocean Race'.

In the story Commodore Walker declared that he would not be part of the race with his 44-foot ketch, *Saltair*, because the club '... will not order owners to seal engines'. He went on to say, 'I believe the committee's decision will militate against the success of the race. The club is accepting the guidance of the Royal Ocean Racing Club of Great Britain, which does not seal engines. However, I believe that certain people are so keen to win this year's event they will do so at any cost.'

The CYCA committee was not impressed and within days Walker found himself under censure and ordered to appear before the committee. His response was prompt: he resigned as CYCA Commodore.

Meanwhile, there were two interesting developments that took some of the heat out of that controversy – the race's first female participants, Jane (Jenny) Tate, from Hobart, who shared the helm with her husband, Horrie, aboard their yacht, *Active*, and Dagmar O'Brien, who sailed with her husband, Brian (aka Mick), aboard *Connella*. Also, the first entry from New Zealand had been received: Mr N.W. Thomas would sail his yacht, *Ilex*, across the Tasman Sea from Wellington to compete.

The entries being lodged for the second race represented a remarkable cross-section of yacht designs from that era. One of the more interesting was the classic Eight Metre class sloop, *Defiance*, a sleek, narrow and low-profile design intended more for bay and harbour racing than dealing with the might of the monstrous waves that could be encountered on the Tasman Sea. But the thought of his yacht thrashing its way upwind in rough weather and spearing through gigantic waves did not deter the owner, Frank Bullock.

Legendary English sailor and author, Uffa Fox, wrote of the beauty and appeal of the elegant Eight Metre class in a publication he released in 1934. He said sailing a yacht of this class

> ... would give owners the two most sought things in life,
> health and happiness, for without doubt sailing at sea
> brings peace to the mind, and the clean salt-laden air

health to the body; which are both needed by all in this mechanical age of irritating noise and poisonous fumes. The Eight Metres are very popular, for in the cabin the owner can live, or simply change his wet clothes after a hard race and eat his lunch in comfort according to his ideas of pleasure. Added to this there is the protection the cabin gives in bad weather.

As eloquent as the words appeared, Uffa Fox had obviously given no thought to the possibility that an Eight-Metre might one day take on the challenge of the notorious Tasman.

Defiance was launched in Melbourne in 1935 after being designed and built by the highly respected Victorian yachtsman and shipwright, Ernest Olney Digby, better known as 'Old Dig'. It was the time of the Great Depression and with there being few employment opportunities for a man of his considerable talent, he took the project on as a personal undertaking and applied himself to every aspect of the build.

After designing the yacht, Old Dig began construction in the backyard of the small property at Williamstown, in Melbourne, where he lived with his wife and eight children. It would prove to be a labour of love as he handcrafted almost every part of the beautifully proportioned 14.78-metre-long design, from the Queensland kauri used for hull planking through to moulding the lead keel, making the bronze keel bolts and shaping the mast and spars.

Once in the water it was Digby's talent as a competitive yachtsman coupled with the sleek lines of *Defiance* that saw it become the gun boat on Port Phillip. Old Dig enjoyed this success for a decade then sold the yacht to Sydneysider Bullock, whose primary desire was to race *Defiance* to Hobart in 1946 under the burgee of the CYCA.

After preparing the yacht for the delivery voyage to Sydney, Bullock decided he should make an assault on the fastest time recorded for the passage from the entrance to Port Phillip to Sydney Heads. All was going well until *Defiance* was east of Wollongong, 45 nm from Sydney, and the wind evaporated. The yacht lay becalmed on a glassy sea for more than a day, a situation that soon came to the attention of newspaper reporters in Sydney who had been monitoring its progress. The following day there were reports in the city's papers suggesting that if the wind did not reappear soon the crew might starve. Fortunately, the wind returned and *Defiance* went on to reach Sydney with a very hungry crew on board. A member of that crew was a young sailing enthusiast named Neville Wran, a future Premier of New South Wales.

Within a few days of arriving in Sydney, Bullock had a team of shipwrights working feverishly to convert his bay yacht into an ocean racer. As a safety precaution, the cockpit was reduced in size to minimise its capacity to hold water, and a second hatch was fitted in the foredeck. He also added some modern equipment for the benefit of the crew – a gimballed stove and an icebox. *Defiance* has recently been restored close to its original glory. And it can still be seen racing on Sydney Harbour with considerable success.

*

Much to the satisfaction of the hierarchy and membership of the CYCA, twenty-two yachts had nominated for the start of the second Hobart race – thirteen more than the inaugural fleet a year earlier. Disappointingly though, three of these yachts were forced to withdraw before the start on Boxing Day as they were not ready to compete. Still, it was obvious the race had far-reaching appeal as the fleet included yachts from New South Wales, Victoria, Tasmania and New Zealand.

After the experiences of the previous year, where it was feared that both *Rani* and *Horizon* might have foundered and their crews perished, some new safety regulations were introduced for the 1946 event, including regular aerial observations and weather forecasts which were created specifically for the fleet to be broadcast each day in nominated radio news bulletins at 6.45am and 7pm.

The air cover would be provided by an RAAF Liberator heavy bomber which was scheduled to fly over the fleet each day. To make this as efficient as possible, skippers were briefed pre-race on the use of radar equipment and radar reflecting beacons (supplied by the RAAF) which would be carried by all yachts.

However, as explained in a pre-race report in *The Sun* newspaper in Sydney, it was still going to be a tough task for the crew of the Liberator when it came to locating and identifying the yachts:

> The RAAF radar operator will pick up the 'blip' on his radar screen and direct his captain to the yacht. As all radar sets carried [by the yachts] will transmit the same

type of blip, the RAAF crew will have to identify each craft as it is picked up — no easy task from the window of an aircraft moving at 170 mph.

The fact was though, this carefully planned aerial observation of the fleet did not deliver the desired results, as was reported post-race in *Australian Powerboat and Yachting Monthly* magazine:

> No reliable information became available until the boats came within view of Mt Nelson Signal Station, which is situated high up on the slopes of the River Derwent. The air reconnaissance provided by a Liberator was a complete failure, many of the boats not being sighted after leaving Sydney Heads.

It is apparent that the pleasure that came with being part of the inaugural Hobart race outweighed the pain as many of the sailors who competed in that event returned for the second year, as did three of the yachts that were in the original fleet. Bob Bull, who sailed as mate with Jack Earl aboard *Kathleen* in 1945, decided to race his own yacht, *Christina*, a design based on a double-ended Colin Archer concept which was built in Sydney by Lars Halvorsen. Bull had his great sailing mate, Jack Earl, join him for the race while Norm Hudson, who had tasted victory aboard *Rani*, stepped up to be skipper of the mighty schooner, *Mistral II*.

Weighing in at 50 tons and manned by a crew of fifteen, the 19.7-metre-long *Mistral II* was the heavyweight of the fleet by a small margin over the similar-sized cutter, *Morna*, at 19.5

metres. Designed by Scottish naval architect William Fife and launched in 1913, *Morna* had been purchased by Claude Plowman from newspaper publisher Sir Frank Packer in the early 1940s. Plowman was a Tasmanian-born, Sydney-based industrialist who had been involved in negotiations between the CYCA and the Royal Yacht Club of Tasmania regarding the establishment of the Hobart race.

After moving to Sydney, Plowman dominated racing on the harbour for many years until the concept for the Hobart race presented him with the opportunity to seek new pleasures under sail by competing offshore. To that end he spared no effort preparing the yacht for the challenge; it was re-rigged as a far more efficient Bermudan cutter, then he created a crew selection process under the guidance of his sailing master, the highly respected local yachting legend, 'Rubber' Kellaway. There were forty-six applications, and fourteen of the most experienced applicants were chosen to join *Morna*'s team.

The owner and his sailing master obviously placed great emphasis on navigation for this race as five of *Morna*'s crew were capable navigators. They were led by Royal Navy Captain Harry Livesay and were under instructions to pinpoint the yacht's position over the entire distance to Hobart.

As is often the case when it comes to yachting, the media loves talking money, and it was no different in 1946. Sydney's *Daily Telegraph* ran a story that declared the value of the nineteen yachts competing that year was around £80,000 with the replacement value of Mr R.F. Evans's palatial schooner, *Mistral II*, the biggest vessel in the race, £18,000. The other competitors ranged in value down to £2000 for Bjarne

Halvorsen's 34-footer, *Saga*, one of the smallest in the big fleet. The story then went on to detail the impact the arduous race would have on crews:

> The strain on the vessels before the punishing course is covered will take an average of a couple of years off their lives.
>
> The strain on the 160 men who will crew the yachts will cause each to lose an average of 7 lb in weight. A sprinkling of these will have 'had it' by the time they reach Hobart, and will not want to sail back in the yachts. A few, no doubt, will also lose their nerve.
>
> The ideal ocean-racing yacht-hand who never 'packs up' has the strength of a bullock, the enthusiasm of a dervish, and the nerves of Superman. He knows that the pretty boating scenes of Sydney Harbour weekends have no relation to the grim business of 'driving' a small vessel under sail at sea.

To make the start of the second Sydney Hobart race a greater public spectacle, the CYCA's planning committee decided to relocate the start line from North Head to a location abeam of Clark Island, just 3 kilometres to the east of the Sydney Harbour Bridge and within sight of the city.

Here again former Commodore Bert Walker did not agree with the actions of the CYCA's committee:

> I do not agree ... with the committee's decision to start the race on the short line, off Clark Island, in the

Harbour. Such a restricted line will hamper the big boats and may cause serious collisions. The race should be started at the Heads. This would give all competitors an even chance and would also allow the public a fair view.

However, the media liked the change, as did the public. It meant that the fleet would race on the sheltered waters of the harbour for 3 nautical miles from the start line to South Head, where they would turn to starboard and make for the wide open waters of the Tasman Sea.

Consequently, the ten headlands, blocks of flats and homes that the fleet would pass while sailing from the start to the Heads would form a huge natural grandstand from where many thousands of people could share in the colour, drama and excitement of the start.

The Sydney Morning Herald put the vision of the race into somewhat flowery words in its Christmas Day preview:

No other sporting event of the Christmas holiday season will stir the imagination of Australians in quite the same way as the ocean yacht race from Sydney to Hobart. The thrills of a contest fought out under the eyes of an applauding multitude will be absent, but in all other respects the race will lack nothing of drama and interest.

The spirit is with us still that moved Bass and Flinders in their early exploratory voyages, in boats far less pretentious and well-equipped than most of those that will engage in the ocean race tomorrow; and whatever nurtures and develops it is for the lasting good of Australia.

The fleet was reduced to nineteen at the last minute when the Tasmanian entry, *Wanderer*, which had been battling light winds for much of the delivery voyage from Hobart to Sydney, was snared by an oily calm off Jervis Bay, 80 nm south from Sydney, and was unable to make headway. That meant the final fleet comprised twelve yachts from New South Wales, three from Victoria, six from Tasmania and one from New Zealand.

*

As the official timekeeper's clock ticked away towards the 11am start time on Boxing Day 1946, it was estimated that some 250 boats of widely varying sizes were milling around the starting area off Clark Island. It was impossible to estimate how many thousands of people were lining the shore on both sides of the harbour to savour the same spectacle.

Meanwhile, on board the CYCA's start boat, the official timekeeper was shouting out the countdown minute by minute, then second by second, so everyone would be ready for the firing of the starting cannon.

There was a light south-westerly wind blowing as the yachts manoeuvred into position for the start, and already some crews were showing the benefit they had gained from competing in lead-up races over the preceding months. Those with the experience had their start perfectly timed, while others of the cruising ilk opted to keep clear of the congestion and amble across the line when the rush to get away had abated.

Morna was the favourite for line honours, but as Plowman revealed in the personal log he kept for the duration of the race, he and his crew were casual in approach but determined to do well:

> Thursday, 26 December:
> The weather the day of the race was glorious and from early morning Rose Bay was a scene of great activity with the Yacht Pier crowded with people.
> Just prior to leaving for the start, a very nicely chilled bottle of champagne was produced and we all drank good luck to *Morna*.
> We managed a perfect start. The yacht *Saga* broke the line ahead of us, but we immediately took the lead ...

And lead they did: at Sydney Heads *Morna* was 10 minutes ahead of the Melbourne-based, Bermudan-rigged cutter *Merlan*, with the similarly-rigged Tasmanian entry, *Active*, another 3 minutes astern. However, with these positions coming after only 3 nm had been completed in such a long race, it was anyone's guess as to which yacht would be first home.

Regardless, *Morna* was staking an early claim for line honours. After sailing for just 11 hours, reports back to the CYCA indicated that *Morna* was then leading by at least 30 minutes over *Merlan*.

The weather conditions for this first stage of the race were in complete contrast to that experienced in the inaugural event 12 months earlier: meteorologists were predicting light variable winds for the 230 nm stretch from Sydney to Gabo Island at the entrance to Bass Strait.

If there was one indelible mark Captain Illingworth had left etched in the minds of all sailors wanting to do well in the second Hobart race, it was that there was no running away from bad weather – no seeking shelter. As it turned out, the 1946 race proved him correct: it was a gruelling test of the qualities of every craft. Nature threw everything at them, from flat calms and light winds through to punishing gales and breaking seas of a size no sailor wished to see. The larger and faster yachts had a relatively easy race but the majority of the mid-sized yachts were hammered.

The skipper of *Defiance*, Vaughan Jones, reported the gale that blasted across Bass Strait had forced him to heave-to for almost 14 hours. In that time *Defiance* was blown 30 nm off course. He estimated that at the height of the storm the seas were near 8 metres high and, when conditions were at their worst, he had 'only one man on deck, and he was lashed to the tiller'.

Meanwhile *Morna*, which continued to show the way, experienced far more favourable conditions. It was storming down Tasmania's east coast at a great rate of knots for much of the time with a big bowsprit spinnaker set. Only misfortune or a flat calm in the Derwent could rob the yacht of line honours.

Plowman wrote in his log:

Tuesday, 31 December 1946:
Shortly after 8pm the wind started to come in from the WSW and this time it looked like lasting. We sighted Tasman Light, the turning point, at 9.45pm and it was abeam at 3.17am next morning.

Having entered the Bay, the wind came from ahead so we had to beat up to Hobart. We crossed the line at

7 minutes to 2 that afternoon having taken 5 days 2 hours, 53 minutes for the trip.

An incredible crowd of some 7,000 people were at the waterfront to welcome Claude Plowman and the crew of *Morna*, with many of them – because of his origins – seeing it as a hometown victory.

Plowman wrote:

> The reception we received in Hobart was amazing. The whole town appeared to be waiting for us and as we crossed the finishing line, the firing of the finish gun was the signal for an outburst of cheering and the blowing of whistles.
>
> On tying up [at the dock] we were boarded by hundreds of people, amongst whom were movie cameramen, press photographers and reporters.
>
> The facilities of the town were more or less at our disposal – in short, we were granted the Freedom of the City.

In the depths of darkness the following night – some 16 hours after *Morna* had claimed line honours – the schooner, *Mistral II*, cruised into Hobart to claim second place across the line. However, at that stage the primary interest for race officials and spectators related to which yacht would be recognised as the all-important winner on handicap. This answer came 40 hours after mighty *Morna* cruised into Hobart when the smallest yacht in the fleet, the stoutly built and pleasantly proportioned,

10-metre-long cutter, *Christina*, appeared on the Derwent after racing for 6 days and 18 hours – undoubtedly the winner on corrected time.

It was not long after first light when *Christina* arrived, but even at that early hour there was an enthusiastic crowd lining the shore and along the docks, all wanting to be part of the celebrations and to welcome the crew, especially the legendary skipper Bob Bull and mate Jack Earl.

At that stage, *Morna* was calculated to be third on handicap, but then the party atmosphere around the docks turned sour when it became known that Plowman had lodged a protest over the measurement of his yacht. He claimed that *Morna*'s spinnaker pole had been measured incorrectly and, because of this, his yacht's handicap was higher than it should be. If this was the case then the chances were that *Morna* would finish higher up the result sheet, possibly even win on corrected time. But his protest was dismissed – the results would stand, and the celebrations aboard *Christina* resumed.

'We were a very happy crew on *Christina*,' Bull told the waiting media at the dock.

We knew we had to try a lot harder than we did the previous year if we wanted to win, so we were ready for that.

It was a good race until we reached Bass Strait, and there we copped a caning. It was a 70 miles an hour south-westerly gale, and whereas we would have slowed down or stopped aboard *Kathleen Gillett*, this time we pushed on. The yacht was taking quite a bit of water and one of the blokes, who was forever in his bunk being seasick, must have thought it was the end. He kept asking when we would pump the yacht out, and that annoyed us so much we told him that the only way to keep the yacht afloat was for him to pump it. That worked wonders.

The other memorable thing in the race was the creation of a new dish, which we called 'train smash', because that's what it reminded us of. Bob Sloman just threw everything you could imagine into a pot and mixed it up. We never bothered to ask what was in it.

Encountering the full force of the gale, *Christina* was able to work her way through it under shortened canvas while other competing yachts hove-to.

After explaining this, Bull gave away one of the secrets relating to *Christina*'s success: 'Throughout this ordeal the crew maintained stamina and determination on frequent rations of rum and egg flips, made from egg powder.'

Having raced his yacht, *Kathleen Gillett*, and seeing first-hand the great ocean racing skills exhibited by Captain John Illingworth, Jack Earl brought to light another reason for their victory aboard *Christina*:

We learned a lot from the race a year ago. That time, by comparison, we knew little. This time there was no 'get lucky' way about it for us; we were out to win. Captain Illingworth set a terrific pace to win with *Rani* last year. We realised that this time we would have to abandon common sense, even good seamanship, and take risks if we were to win. Also, we knew the boat could take it. She is small and easy to handle.

*

In years to come it was realised that the second place on corrected time achieved by Bjarne Halvorsen's little 10.3-metre sloop, *Saga*, signalled the start of an era in the Sydney Hobart. The name Halvorsen would soon become legendary within the race and the world over.

In 2001 Magnus Halvorsen reminisced about how he and brother Trygve (pronounced Trig) garnered such a famous reputation within the marine industry through being associated with the Sydney Hobart over the decades, and how close their little yacht went to winning the 1946 race.

I left school as soon as I reached the leaving age of fourteen in 1932 and became a boatbuilder working for my father, Lars Halvorsen. On hearing about the Sydney Hobart race in 1945, Trygve and I thought we should give it a go the following year. To my hull design we built a 10.5-metre sloop, *Saga*, at the family boatshed. She had no engine, no radio communications and no self-inflating liferaft, and none of the crew of five had been out of sight of Sydney Heads.

The 1946 Hobart race produced storm conditions not seen again until the disastrous 1998 race. It lasted 3 days, more than twice as long as in 1998. We had a problem with [the hull] pounding when sailing upwind, so we developed the technique of sailing up the face of the wave and falling away on its crest … a zig-zag course, but very effective.

Saga very nearly won the 1946 Hobart. We were becalmed for 12 hours at the mouth of the Derwent River just 11 miles from the finish. The sea breeze, which usually arrives before midday, didn't kick in until dusk. We took second place on handicap – just 1 hour behind the winner, *Christina*.

*

Eight of the fleet of nineteen starters failed to complete the course that year, the majority of those casualties coming as a result of the storm in Bass Strait. Much to everyone's surprise was that, even after having the mainsail blown to shreds during that storm, the low-profile gaff cutter, *Defiance*, managed to finish and register a time that resulted in it being fourth on corrected time – an impressive effort.

One of the yachts forced out was *Connella*, with Dagmar O'Brien in the crew. However, Jenny Tate, who steered *Active* for much of the race, did reach the finish. Thus, Jenny became recognised as the first woman to helm a yacht in the Sydney Hobart and complete the course – but it was an experience she certainly didn't enjoy. The severity of the storm in Bass Strait caused her to be seasick for the first time in her life, so sick in fact she told a newspaper reporter in Hobart: 'I will never sail in that race again.' However, her name lives on for posterity – the *Jenny Tate Memorial Trophy* is awarded each year (if warranted) to the first female skipper to reach the finish.

As is always the case at the end of a Sydney Hobart race, the news-hungry media was looking for a scoop, or interesting angle, to separate their story from the rest. Such was the case for this race when the *Pittsworth Sentinel* – Pittsworth being a tiny town of a few hundred people situated amid cattle country 170 kilometres west of Brisbane – published a story on 10 January 1947 under the headline 'A Kid and a Cat in the Hobart Yacht Race':

A kid and a cat were among the crews who took part in the second annual Sydney Hobart 680 nautical mile yacht race held during the Christmas holidays. The kid in the race — one of the world's three longest ocean yacht races — was 14-year-old Roydon Thomas, son of N.W. Thomas, owner of New Zealand's only entrant, the *Ilex*. The cat in the crew belonged to Mr and Mrs Brian O'Brien, of the gaff ketch, *Connella*.

Neither kid nor cat brought winning luck to the two contestants in the race, which was won on handicap by J.R. Bull's 34-foot cutter, *Christina*.

This Sydney Hobart race is a good example of sport for sport's sake. The prize money is small — £100 cash given by the Tasmanian Government — and that, of course, only goes to the winner. But every contesting yacht costs something like £200 to prepare for such a race — what with overhaul, replacement of gear, purchase of food, and the purchase, perhaps, of new sails.

*

Exactly 100 years before the 1946 race, a quaint little stone pub was opened adjacent to where the race yachts docked in Hobart. It was named the Customs House Hotel and its proximity to the docks, coupled with its convivial atmosphere, made it a favourite haunt for thirsty, salt-encrusted yachties. It's a tradition that remains to this day. Almost inevitably, if you couldn't find someone from one of the race yachts on the dock you would find them at the Customs House pub.

The presentation of trophies in Hobart for the second race had a historic element to it; this was the first time the superbly crafted *Tattersall Cup* was presented as the perpetual trophy to the winner on corrected time.

The magnificent trophy had been donated to the CYCA a year earlier by the Estate of George Adams, the founder of Tattersall Lotteries in Australia. He had passed away in 1904, and some years later, his great-nephew, William Adams, set himself the task of finding a suitably impressive trophy that would match the prestige associated with being the winner of the Sydney Hobart race on corrected time. His search took him to Prouds Jewellers in Sydney where he was shown an ornate trophy that was originally commissioned by Mr Proud and struck by silversmiths in 1913. It was to have been the major award for a trans-Tasman yacht race which, because of the outbreak of World War I, never eventuated. The trophy was considered to be 'the finest piece of workmanship in silver to have been done in Australia'. Official documentation described it as a 'hand-wrought 288 ounces sterling silver cup and plinth — 25 inches high under a glass dome. Decorations of mermaids, grapevine and seahorses at base. Lid surmounted with mermaid on crest of wave calling up winner.'

After being presented to *Christina*'s owner, Bob Bull, in a formal ceremony in Hobart, the trophy was sent to the engravers who first inscribed *Rani*, sailed by Captain Illingworth, in recognition of that yacht being the winner of the inaugural race the previous year.

Bernie Case

SAILING BIO

I started sailing at thirteen, joining a 12-foot cadet dinghy fleet. I was promoted to helmsman at fifteen. Later I was invited to join *Larntarni* as a helmsman in the 1962 Sydney Hobart – my first. Subsequently I participated in forty Sydney Hobarts, on twenty-five different yachts, becoming the fifth Australian to gain the forty-race award. Other highlights include being a member of two different Australian *America's Cup* teams, competing as a helmsman in seven successive *Admiral's Cup* regattas, eight Fastnet races (including a handicap win in 1989), seven *Clipper Cups*, winning Hamilton Island Race Week three times and representing Australia with Jock Sturrock in the One Ton Cup and then winning the Australian Three-Quarter Ton Championship aboard *B195*.

WHAT WAS YOUR BEST DAY SAILING IN THE SYDNEY HOBART?

Rounding Tasman Island first and heading into Storm Bay on *Condor* in the 1986 Hobart race, then be awarded line honours.

WHAT DAY OR EXPERIENCE WAS THE TOUGHEST OR MOST CHALLENGING?

It was aboard *Four Winds II* in the 1963 race. We were south of Eden when the weather began to deteriorate. The wind reached 70 knots+ and stayed there for more than 50 hours. The waves were over 30 feet high. We progressively down-sized the sails until we were hove-to with only the storm jib up and the helm lashed to leeward. The entire crew was enclosed below deck. During this period, the waves rolled the yacht more than 90 degrees seven times. The owner then decided that we should take down the jib, steer the yacht downwind and trail drogues over the stern to slow the yacht. A young RAN cadet midshipman was nominated to take down the jib while my job was to organise and set the drogue over the stern in the hope this would prevent the yacht being rolled over by a breaking wave. That done, we continued downwind somewhat more comfortably for another 48 hours before the conditions improved enough for the owner to then decide 'to continue to Hobart'. Not all the crew agreed with that decision, but we did agree to steer the course he had nominated. When we finally reached land, it was Eden, not Hobart. Once there, I left the yacht and hitch-hiked back to Melbourne.

The young midshipman who took down the jib single-handed eventually became known as Rear Admiral Chris Oxenbould, Head of the Royal Australian Navy! He also became Chairman of the CYCA National Safety Committee.

WHAT KEEPS YOU GOING BACK TO THE HOBART RACE?

We usually had a large family Christmas lunch which meant there was a big pile of dish washing and drying to be done by mid-afternoon. I always managed to book a mid-afternoon flight to Sydney on Christmas Day so I had an excuse for not having time to help do the dishes. The Sydney Hobart race was my excuse for forty years!

WHAT ARE SOME OF THE BIG CHANGES THAT YOU'VE WITNESSED IN YOUR YEARS ASSOCIATED WITH THE RACE?

The original entrants were cruising yachts, but that changed to cruising-racing yachts, then progressed to racing yachts. A comparison of the time it took to complete the course in those early years to what we are seeing now is quite amazing. The development of canting keels has introduced some additional issues – the effect of an involuntary tack or gybe in severe weather conditions can cause a major drama! When it comes to sails, asymmetrical downwind sails associated with lighter and wider hull designs have changed downwind tactics.

CHAPTER 4

Pigeons, Protests, Pain and Pleasure

More than 2 years after being founded, the Cruising Yacht Club of Australia was still a club without a clubhouse, due primarily to there being insufficient funds in the coffers to secure a waterfront property – not that many suitable sites were being offered for sale.

Still, the club had one significant asset that was building in profile and value every year – the Sydney Hobart Yacht Race. This was evident when the invitation went out for the club's Annual Dinner Dance and Presentation of Prizes in April 1947 where none other than His Excellency, the Governor of New South Wales, Lieutenant-General Northcott (CB, MVO) had accepted the Commodore's invitation to be the guest of honour.

The sell-out gala evening, held at the new, luxuriously appointed Wentworth Hotel in the city centre, was full of glamour, charm, revelry, and what was an impressive surprise for many. The primary purpose of the evening was to recognise the winners from the 1946 Hobart race and present the yacht owners, once again, with their trophies. It was this latter point which created what was no doubt a world first for a trophy presentation for a major offshore yachting event.

A few months earlier the Royal Ocean Racing Club in London had donated to the CYCA a special trophy which was to be awarded each year, along with the *Tattersall Cup*, to the winner on corrected time. With there being no RORC hierarchy in Sydney to make the presentation on that club's behalf, CYCA and RORC officials came up with a unique format for the ceremony. With the assistance of the BBC, a radiophone link was established between London and Sydney so that the RORC's Rear Commodore, Mr E.W.R. Peterson, could speak on behalf of his club. He spoke of the little-realised contribution offshore racing sailors made to the British war effort, and of the erroneous image problem the sport then held – and still does to some degree to this day:

> I do not have to preach to you about the joys of ocean
> racing, or about its value as a school of seamanship ... but
> remind you of the vital part played by members of our
> club, and other yacht clubs, who had learned by sailing in
> small boats how to remain at sea day and night out of sight
> of land, and were able in the autumn of 1939 and winter
> of 1940, to take their places as watch-keeping officers in
> trawlers and minesweepers, and to lay the foundation of
> coastal forces. But for their help it is not too much to say
> that Dunkirk might never have happened, for the U-boat
> war might have been lost in the first winter. When some
> idiot politician talks then of yachting being a pastime of
> the idle rich, you will know how to answer him.

With the Rear Commodore's speech complete, the State Governor presented the RORC trophy to Mr J.R. Bull, owner of *Christina*. Then, with that presentation done, the CYCA Vice Commodore, Peter Luke, replied to Rear Commodore Peterson on behalf of the club.

The significance of both the Rear Commodore's address from London, and the presentation of the RORC trophy, was not lost on the guests that evening. This could only signal that, after little more than 2 years since being founded, the CYCA was already being recognised on the international ocean racing scene as a club of high standing.

This function was also sufficiently newsworthy for *The Sydney Morning Herald* to publish a report on the morning of 25 April 1947:

Model Yachts At CYC Dance

Miniature copies of racing yachts made of flowers were among the attractive table decorations at the dinner dance held at the Wentworth Ballroom last night by members of the Cruising Yacht Club of Australia. More than 300 guests were present to watch the presentation of the trophies to the winners of the 1946 Sydney Hobart ocean yacht race by Vice Commodore PM Luke.

*

While the start of the 1947 dash south was still eight months away, the level of interest was already impressive. As it would turn out, that year's classic would leave no doubt that the

Sydney Hobart had become a sporting event of national importance. The amount of ink the race was getting in newspapers Australia-wide during the lead-up period was testament to that.

This circumstance was made more remarkable by the fact that the vast majority of the readership knew very little about ocean yacht racing, apart from the fact that it was a sport. Maybe the race was a post-war panacea for Australians, or maybe it was because so many of the sailors, who had survived active participation in the war, were now seen to be putting their lives on the line in the name of sport. Whatever it was, the race's profile was escalating.

It was not surprising then that newspaper editors across Australia, in towns large and small, realised they had an obligation to explain to their readers what it took to be part of the Hobart race, and what it was like to be challenged around-the-clock for up to six days in conditions that ranged from raging storms to flat calms. In essence the public wanted know, 'Why do they do it, and where is the pleasure?'

On 20 December 1947 – just six days before the start of the third race south – *The Sydney Morning Herald* did its best to explain ocean racing and the event in general. The story, which appeared under the headline, 'Blue-Water Men Ready For Sydney Hobart Race', appeared concurrently in other newspapers around Australia.

In a smart move by the editor, instead of having a reporter with no knowledge of ocean racing trying to explain its appeal, he went to the coalface. Norm Hudson, a member of the victorious crew aboard *Rani* in the inaugural race, and who was sailing in 1947 as skipper of the large schooner, *Mistral II*, was commissioned to write the copy and did a damn fine job.

This is an excerpt from that story:

With cracking sails and the chattering of winches, 30 yachts will pour over the line and out of Sydney Harbour – Hobart bound.

The Hobart race … who will win? What are each boat's chances in the overall picture? What is the big factor… the boat, the skipper, the navigator, or the crew as a whole?

Any blue-water man will tell you that there is more to it than just sailing a boat hard all the way to Hobart, the boat's turn of speed, the weather, or the capabilities of the crew. It is the sum total of work and planning put into the initial stages of pre-race preparations, perhaps weeks or even months ahead of the starting day, that counts.

Past experiences have taught skippers that attention to the minor details aboard a boat will mar or make a successful passage. They realise that the sea is no respecter of ships or persons; that their very lives may hang on the breaking strain of a small iron shackle, or some innocent looking piece of equipment that in reality plays such a major part; that, in fact, everything aboard a ship must be just right before she sets sail in turbulent waters.

Take No Chances

The good practical seaman is a distrustful person. He distrusts almost everything aboard his vessel, always tries to anticipate the unexpected, and takes nothing for granted. The skipper of any ocean-going yacht, apart from seamanship and sailing experience, must necessarily be a versatile person with a knowledge of, and able to adapt himself in a reasonably satisfactory way, to the wide range of trades involved in boat-building, carpentry, rigging, ropes and cordage, plumbing, engineering, electrical work, painting, navigation, weather-lore, cooking, first aid, and if I might mention it here, tact and psychology.

Make a study of the men that go to make up an ocean racing crew and you will find they have been selected because they are also very versatile individuals.

First Hobart Race

Anyone who has sailed in offshore races knows how important it is to have a dry boat below decks. Perhaps nobody has experienced a wetter trip than we had in the little 34-foot cutter, *Rani*, in the first Hobart race of 1945. I can recall how those decks poured forth water like a perpetual shower: the moral of it is, however, that had the little things – such as recaulking – been done before we put to sea, we might even have had a pleasant journey.

Battened Down

With hatches and skylights battened down, ventilation becomes an important factor for the crew below. Accommodation is restricted and in all boats the crews live in very confined quarters. Manoeuvring the human frame with ease in the smaller boats becomes an art not very quickly accomplished. The larger craft will have temporary pipe berths [canvas cots] fitted and every man has his own appointed sleeping place; but in the smaller craft many of the crews will sleep feet to feet, with two men in the same berth.

An interesting fact is that in any sort of seaway or 'blow' two-thirds of the crew usually succumb to seasickness. Sometimes this number is less, but more often it is greater. This means that the remaining few must stay on deck to keep the ship afloat and moving, as the others are usually lethargic and, if bad cases, no use whatsoever.

Dangers

It cannot be denied that ocean racing has its moments of direct danger. Fire, collision and rushing water – these three constitute the ever-present hazards, with falling overboard the greatest of them all. On *Mistral*, as on most boats, every man will wear a specially designed safety belt from which hangs a line capable of being clipped or tied to the nearest rigging or support. Life rings, smoke buoys, and water lights are now standard safety fittings on every craft. All are located within easy reach of the helmsmen.

Thousands of men have defied the sea, tempted and cheated it, in more than 50 years of ocean racing overseas. Yet, from all these voyages the sea has taken in forfeit only 14 lives. A great deal of green water has swept the decks of small craft since the first great race to Hobart. It has purged them, speeded them up, and inculcated in increasing numbers of yachtsmen the conviction that there is no sport like ocean racing – none!

Understandably, Norm Hudson's words locked in with the CYCA's ideology: 'The ethos of ocean-going yachting is seamanship, self-reliance and survival'.

Two days before the start, the *Melbourne Herald* gave its readers a more personal insight into the Hobart race:

SYDNEY, Wednesday — Thousands of pounds worth of blue-water craft in the form of 29 ocean-going yachts will swing out of Sydney Heads soon after 11am on Boxing Day when Australia's greatest ocean-racing classic, the Sydney Hobart race, will begin.

Behind this array of aquatic splendour lies the story of months of hard work by crews and owners, and the expenditure of many thousands of pounds in fitting out and victualling the vessels. For the 650-mile tussle with the always uncertain Tasman even the smallest screw and nut on every one of the craft must be just right.

From the lessons of the two previous races the skippers this year have given minute attention to equipment. Only the best-equipped boats have reached the finishing line under sail in the previous races, and last year only 12 of the 19 starters completed the race. Even the fastest yachts will be four or five days on the wave — the slower ones from nine to 10 days, mostly out of sight of land.

The 221 members of the 29 crews include professionals and businessmen, university students and schoolboys.

They will live in cramped and stuffy quarters and of every 6 hours of the time they are afloat, will spend two on wave-washed decks and four below — if they are not called on deck in an emergency.

Washing is restricted and shaving forbidden because of the limited amount of water carried on each craft, but the general feeling of crew members can be summed up by the remark today of middle-aged Cec O'Dea, who will navigate the 54ft schooner *Sirius*: 'It's uncomfortable, but I wouldn't miss it for worlds.'

Skippers plan to serve each man with two hot meals and a bottle of beer a day and a nip of rum in coffee after bad weather. Stores aboard the *Christina* include 30 dozen eggs, a bag of potatoes for each man and a gross of tinned food.

*

The fleet of twenty-eight yachts for the third Hobart race was believed to be a record for any major ocean race within the British empire. The number of people crowding vantage points in the harbour and on the seaward side of South Head was estimated to be around 30,000 and there was no disputing that the spectator fleet was the largest so far – an armada that would escort the race yachts over the three nautical miles from the start to the harbour entrance. There was an electric air of excitement for the sailors and the spectators as the start time of 11am approached. However, a shadow was hanging over the final countdown which was known only to a few club officials and sailors. The start line had been relocated to the western side of Rose Bay where, at the time,

Sydney's 'international airport', the Rose Bay flying boat base, was located. The CYCA secretary, Earl Le Brun, had earlier written to base officials seeking confirmation that it was okay to start the race at that location. The simple reply was along the lines of: 'Contact the Duty Air Traffic Control Officer on the morning and he will tell you if any flying boats are likely to be on final approach to Rose Bay'. Fortunately, no flying boats were scheduled, so the race got under way as planned.

Apart from being the centre of attention through sheer size, the crews of the larger yachts knew that to be first out of the harbour would deliver great recognition from the public and the media, but most importantly, they would hold an early psychological advantage over their rivals. The first step towards achieving this goal involved winning the start and heading the fleet from the outset. But there was an inherent risk in going all out to accomplish this: the fight for a good start can be fraught with danger – and that soon became apparent.

The charge towards the line began to unfold some 5 minutes prior to a flare being fired skywards, the signal that the race was under way. At this time the experienced sailors had recognised that there was a slight advantage to be gained by starting as close as possible to the start boat – an RAAF crash boat (which unfortunately became one). The problem was that the skippers of three yachts all had the same idea.

Even before the start gun was fired and a signal flare sent skywards, crews were bellowing at each other, all claiming that their respective yachts held right of way. In the final couple of minutes before the race began, three yachts – the previous year's winner, *Christina*, the sleek *Defiance* and the mighty

Morna – emerged from the pack and accelerated towards the line (an imaginary line between the flag mast on the start boat and a buoy moored about 500 metres away). Due to either over-enthusiasm or poor judgement, the trio came together in a wedge formation – *Defiance* struck *Morna*, which in turn collided beam-on with *Christina*. Consequently, *Morna* pushed *Defiance* onto a course from where there was no escape; the 7.8 tonne *Defiance*, which was sailing at three knots, struck the start boat and subsequently left a swathe of its hull paint along its topside – clear evidence of impact. The cacophony of sounds that accompanied the collision between the three yachts and the start boat was almost louder than the on-going bellowing between the crews. There was also significant background noise – cheering and jeering emanated from the spectators aboard nearby boats as they watched the crews aboard the three race yachts do their best to get clear and get on with the race.

All three were damaged in some form, none seriously. However, it appeared that *Christina* had suffered the most as a crewman immediately climbed the mast to make repairs to a damaged mast spreader and the backstay. At this time the yacht's owner, Bob Bull, was fuming, as was evident when he shouted to spectators aboard a nearby launch that it was his intention to lodge a protest against his rivals as soon as *Christina* reached Hobart.

When the drama dissipated and all crews got down to racing, spectators afloat and onshore were treated to a spectacular sight: twenty-eight yachts sailing down the harbour leaving behind them white wakes that resembled vapour trails. *Defiance* led the fleet out and on to the open waters where a gentle east-nor'easterly breeze and relatively smooth seas prevailed; ideal conditions for an easy, sun-drenched reach down the coast under large headsails and a full mainsail. Also prominent was the Livingston brothers' 15.2-metre ketch, *Kurrewa III* (*Kurrewa* being an Aboriginal word meaning 'fast swimming fish'). The brothers, Frank and John, were successful pastoralists from Western Victoria who had an affinity with the sea. Over the ensuing years they became well recognised for their endeavours in the Hobart race and across yachting in general.

The following morning *The Sydney Morning Herald* set the scene at the start with these words:

Gay Send-Off

Sydney went down to the Harbour in force yesterday morning to watch the 28 yachts set out on the 680-mile race to Hobart.

For more than half an hour before the start, the yachts cruised around leisurely, testing gear and getting the 'feel' of the light wind. Scores of motley craft followed the yachts as they wheeled, one by one to the starting point off Clark Island, near Double Bay. With the firing of the first Very pistol, the excitement became more intense. Two minutes later the lowering of the third flag on the starter's boat and the firing of a gun signalled the start. Miscellaneous craft, from canoes and sailing dinghies to a Manly ferry, listing ominously with her load, cluttered the Harbour. On shore, people peered from every available window. At Watsons Bay, Parsley Bay, South Head, Rose Bay, and from jutting piers, Sydneysiders saw the stately yachts pass along, as in procession. Rows of cars from the heights near Rose Bay testified to the enthusiasm which the event had evoked.

Within 48 hours of departing Sydney Harbour, a race milestone was achieved; one of the crews managed to communicate with the media back on shore in a fashion that was as unique as it was clever.

In the first two Hobart races no crew had been able to establish radio contact with shore bases so they could advise media outlets of their progress, the weather conditions being experienced, and what was happening around them. For the media, being the recipient of such an exclusive communication with a competing yacht was something any journalist wanted to secure – a scoop over rival reporters. Unfortunately though, the strength of the signal from the radio units the majority of yachts could carry was not strong enough to reach the shore, except over short distances.

However, such a circumstance did not deter the Sydney *Sun*'s yachting writer, Lou d'Alpuget, and budding young journalist, Frank McNulty, who was doing his first Hobart race as a crew member aboard *Moonbi*. The pair got together before the race and hatched a plan that would bypass the need for radio communications.

Unbeknown to all but the *Moonbi* crew, there were three additional 'guests' on board when the fleet set sail on Boxing Day, homing pigeons in a cage in the main saloon. On the second day, while *Moonbi* was still in relatively close proximity to the coast, McNulty fulfilled his end of the plan. He pencilled a brief report on the yacht's progress, its latitude and longitude, and the sailing conditions onto cigarette papers.

> When they were ready to go I took the pigeons onto the deck and released them, but they refused to leave. I think they must have been seasick!
>
> Each time I held them up so they could fly away they just fluttered back to the deck. Eventually I took a bird in my cupped hands and began swinging it towards the sky. After a few swings I let the bird go, and sure enough it flapped off towards the coast.

The bird found its way home to its coop. McNulty's message was delivered, and with that d'Alpuget had his scoop.

Interestingly, this pigeon post form of communication was seen to be so successful that, two years later, the organisers of the inaugural Brisbane to Gladstone race provided homing pigeons to the five competing yachts that were not equipped with two-way radios in case there was trouble.

*

Even in those embryonic years of the Hobart race there were sailors who became so enamoured with the event that they would go on to become legends of ocean racing, or more specifically, the Hobart race. One such identity in the 1947 race was young Tasmanian, John Bennetto – aka 'The Fish', after the bonito fish – who at age 21 was aboard *Kintail* as a first-timer. In the ensuing years 'JB' would go on to race from

Sydney to his home city another forty-three times before he passed away in 2005 aged 79. For the majority of those races he was at the helm of his much-loved 47-footer, *Mirrabooka* (an Aboriginal name for the Southern Cross).

During his ocean racing career Bennetto completed an unprecedented seventeen Hobarts with *Mirrabooka* without retiring (including the storm-ravaged 1998 race). More impressive though was the fact that he gave a countless number of young Tasmanian sailors the opportunity to access ocean racing by having them crew with him in the race. He instilled in every one of them that seamanship was forever the primary tenet in the sport. His own adage was that he would not ask any crewmember to do something during a race that he would not do himself.

In 1995 Bennetto revealed his most vivid memories of his race debut in 1947:

> *Kintail* was a stout yacht, but was not very well equipped. It was not what we had, but what we didn't have on board that I remember most. There was only one life jacket for the entire crew, there was no engine, she had storm sails that would have blown out in the first puff, and the skipper – who had the heart of a lion – was crippled from a war injury he suffered at Gallipoli. One thing *Kintail* did have was a stove – a petrol stove that threatened to explode every time we lit it!

It seemed nature had decided this wouldn't be a Hobart race without a southerly gale. Three storms bowled out of the south-west in rapid succession across Bass Strait and off Tasmania's east coast. The fronts were spread over a three-day period, and the last of them was so powerful that it ripped the roofs off houses along the coast.

Within a very short time three of the smallest yachts had retired – *Sea Tang* had a broken boom, while chronic seasickness among the majority of the crew aboard both *Mannara* and *Nautilus* caused those yachts to turn for home. At the same time there was concern for *Wanderer*, which had not been sighted or heard from for more than four days. On 4 January, reports reached Hobart that the yacht had just sailed into the Tamar River, in the north of the state, and all was okay.

Some waves were estimated to be in excess of 7.5 metres when the storms were at their worst. At one stage *Moonbi* – which was heading offshore – was pooped by a massive set of waves that loomed up from astern, burst across the deck and filled the cockpit to the brim with water. Fearing this would happen again and threaten the safety of the yacht, some of the crew bailed frantically using buckets and saucepans while others set large loops of rope off the stern to slow the yacht to a speed that was more manageable and therefore safer.

The force of wind and wave also brought tough times for the crew of the Livingston brothers' *Kurrewa III*. The wheel steering system failed, so the only way the crew could keep the heavy, 17.6-metre ketch on course was by using the bulky timber emergency tiller – no mean feat in such horribly rough conditions. In fact, when the wind was at its worst, crew members had to trim the sails – constantly easing them off and hauling them in for more than 5 hours to help keep the yacht under control.

Being on deck during this storm was a miserable existence. Sodden clothing was more a hindrance than an asset in conditions where the rain and spray struck like pellets and the chill factor from the howling wind made the temperature feel as if it was zero. In this era the best dressed man in heavy weather gear would be wearing a three-quarter length oilskin coat and probably a sou'wester. For added protection it was not unusual for sailors to soak a large size flannel shirt in linseed oil and turps, then when it was dry, wear it over a woollen singlet and under a woollen jumper. Waterproof trousers were unknown, as were seaboots and yachting gloves.

An excerpt from the logbook of the yacht *Horizon* gave a brief insight into life on board when the weather was at its worst:

Then we had another wild night; the wind howled like a banshee, the implacable sea into which the bowsprit churned at each second came sluicing green over the foredeck, the deckhouse, the cockpit; electricity from the over-charged atmosphere crackled in the rigging – whilst these naked men struggled with the sails like tormented gnomes in a Walt Disney fantasia.

The ferocity of this storm was such that 5 years later, the owner of *Morna*, by then, Sir Claude Plowman – who had already secured line honours in the Hobart race on three occasions – was still declaring the 1947 storm as the worst he had ever endured.

A story by J.S. McCauley in the Sydney *Sun* newspaper delivered some of Plowman's memories regarding that race:

Sir Claude describes the 1947 ocean race as the most gruelling he had sailed. In addition to gale force winds and rain, one of his crew members had a severe attack of blood poisoning and was rushed to hospital on arrival at Hobart.

Morna struck winds up to 80 miles an hour off the east coast of Tasmania, and the yacht covered 31 miles in 2 hours, 5 minutes.

'I will never forget the 1947 race; it was full of incidents from the start,' said Sir Claude today. *Morna* became mixed up with other yachts at the start, from then on we encountered many troubles and it was a relief to be over the finishing line.

'*Morna* struck a gale in Bass Strait, and at one stage we were logging 10 knots. The coastal passenger ship *Ormiston* was crossing the strait, and it was a great thrill to keep in sight of her for many miles.

'When *Morna* was bashing into the gale off the Tasmanian coast, conditions were so tough on deck that watches had to be changed every hour.'

In another incident, *Morna* was becalmed, with most members of the crew relaxing in their bunks. Sir Claude walked up on deck and had a premonition that a storm was brewing. He ordered all hands on deck to take down the majority of sails and double-reef the mainsail. Within 10 seconds of the job being completed, a gale hit the yacht and most of the crew was forced to take shelter below deck to stay out of danger.

Morna afterwards badly tore its mainsail, and it was a battered yacht that drifted first over the line in the Derwent River.

It was 5 days and 3 hours after departing Sydney, that *Morna* claimed a second successive line honours, however the interest of the locals centred on the arrival of George Gibson's locally designed and built, 12.5-metre-long sloop, *Westward*. It would be a 10-hour wait, but it was worth it.

Westward cruised across the line off Castray Esplanade in second place behind *Morna*. That alone was an impressive effort, but what made this more exciting for the people of Hobart, and Tasmania in general, was that the yacht's corrected time could not be beaten; as well as being declared the outright victor in the race, *Westward* gave Tasmania its first winner of what was by then an internationally recognised ocean racing classic. Young local sailor, John Bennetto, who would go on to become a Hobart race legend, was a member of the *Westward crew*.

The skipper of *Christina*, Bob Bull, did as he vowed he would immediately after the start in Sydney. Once in Hobart he lodged a protest against *Morna* relating to the incident on the start line. Part of his claim was that *Christina* lost 12 hours during the race while damage to rigging and the mast was repaired. The end result was not what Bull had expected; after a lengthy hearing by the Cruising Yacht Club's Protest Committee, *Morna* was cleared of any wrongdoing. However, in a shock move, the committee then announced that both *Christina* and *Defiance* had been disqualified; *Defiance* because the skipper did not report the incident immediately on reaching the finish in Hobart, and *Christina* for a breach of the sailing rules.

Bill 'Aubrey' Ratcliff

SAILING BIO

I have competed in and finished every heavy-weather Hobart since 1963. Rough weather doesn't put me off! I sailed my S&S 34, *Marara*, in eleven Hobarts with the best result being in 1993 when we won the *Storm Bay Cup* and came third overall against *Cuckoo's Nest* and *Ninety Seven*. Of all my Hobart races there has been only one where we could not finish – aboard *Takana* which suffered a broken rudder.

WHAT WAS YOUR BEST DAY SAILING IN THE SYDNEY HOBART?

In 1984 arriving in Hobart aboard my little S&S 34 *Marara* and seeing an empty dock. That confirmed we had survived what was considered to be the toughest Hobart race to date.

WHAT DAY OR EXPERIENCE WAS THE TOUGHEST OR MOST CHALLENGING?

The night in the horrific 1998 race when I was washed overboard from the helm of *Mercedes IV*. I was able to get back with the help of the one crewmember who had been on deck with me. My son Lucas then came on deck and took the helm and hove-to (no sails set) for the rest of the night.

WHAT KEEPS YOU GOING BACK TO THE HOBART RACE?

The friends I have met and made over many years at the CYCA and the Royal Yacht Club of Tasmania.

WHAT ARE SOME OF THE BIG CHANGES THAT YOU'VE WITNESSED IN YOUR YEARS ASSOCIATED WITH THE RACE?

There have been many design changes to make the boats faster, the rigs taller, the keels deeper and the rudders more prone to damage without consideration for crew safety.

CHAPTER 5

Facts, Fantasy and Growing Pains

In 1948, Boxing Day fell on a Sunday, and with religious attitudes holding considerable influence within Australian society at that time, sporting events were not staged on Sundays. This was a principle that the CYCA respected, and so the start of the fourth Sydney Hobart Yacht Race was rescheduled to Monday 27 December.

In the week prior to the start, the popularity of the race within the community was confirmed yet again when word went out around the waterfront and via the media that the yacht *Alice* would not be accepted as a starter unless the owner, Mr J.A. Callahan, could borrow two dinghies. These were required so that the yacht could comply with the rule stipulating that sufficient dinghies to accommodate the entire crew must be carried on deck by each competing yacht.

Within 24 hours more than 170 dinghies had been offered to him!

The 1948 race heralded the start of a transition for ocean racing in Australia. While the fleet of eighteen was ten down on the previous year's number of starters, there was a new design trend emerging – away from the bulky and heavy cruising style of yacht and towards more easily handled, performance-oriented designs. The yachts *Moonbi, Peer Gynt* and *Lass O'Luss* led the trend.

Even so, there was still much to be learned when it came to achieving maximum performance when racing offshore, no matter the conditions or the time of day. As a result, equipment and technology that related to boat speed and boat handling – like sail fabrics, sail shapes, rigging and deck gear – were improving dramatically. It wasn't realised at the time, but these developments would lead to Australia being recognised as a world leader in ocean yacht racing. This came two decades later when an Australian team of three yachts went to England and beat the world's best ocean racers, and in doing so, claimed the prestigious *Admiral's Cup*.

Also, a more intensely competitive attitude among crews was becoming apparent – the casual, she'll be right approach was very much on the wane. This trend was inspired in part by the close result on corrected time in the previous race: after taking 4 days and 24 minutes to complete the 628 nm course to Hobart, through weather fair and foul, the margin between first and second placed on handicap, was just 46 minutes. Minutes, not hours, mattered. The human element was also an increasingly important part of the equation.

The somewhat shambolic start the previous year, where three yachts came into contact and one also collided with the start boat, was an early indicator that there was a new attitude

137

emerging among crews – they were going all out to try to gain the upper hand and save seconds from the outset.

However, the CYCA's Sydney Hobart race organising committee obviously had not liked what they had seen at that start and introduced special precautions in 1948 in the hope such an incident would not be repeated. Club secretary, Earl Le Brun, announced that police launches would patrol the starting area to keep it clear of spectator boats and give competing yachts more room to manoeuvre. Also, each race yacht would fly a blue and yellow pennant in the rigging so they could be easily distinguished from spectator boats. In the International Code of Signals this pennant means 'Keep clear of me'.

There was another significant first that year: a description of the start was made via radio-telephone from three competing yachts and broadcast over Sydney radio stations.

The highly anticipated race for line honours between *Morna* and *Mistral V* held the greatest interest in this race. *Morna* was the more fancied of the two big boats, but the *Mistral V* crew was hoping a new nylon spinnaker which had cost an exorbitant amount of money – £100 – would be their winning weapon. When it came to handicap honours, an impressive new yacht, the 12.5-metre-long sloop, *Lass O'Luss*, was the favourite ahead of the previous year's winner, *Westward*. But there was also a theory among experienced sailors that *'The Lass'* might be vulnerable as it hadn't been tested in rough weather.

Westward's skipper, George Gibson, declared to the media that the race would be harder to win this year because the majority of the yachts competing appeared to be more highly developed. 'However, we have good gear, and a good crew, and if there are no hitches we should win again,' he said.

The sentimental favourite with the public was the 14-metre Tasmanian schooner, *Wanderer*, owned and skippered by seventy-five-year-old Eric Massey, who had been an active sailor all his life. He and his 'young' brother, sixty-year-old George, declared that, apart from wanting to win, they were hoping to teach the five youngsters in the crew – aged between twenty and twenty-two – how to best race a yacht offshore.

The eighteen entries and the colourful characters racing them fed the media's obsession with figures when it came to reporting on the race. The thousands of readers of the newspapers were informed that the combined fleet would carry a total of 14 tons of food costing £500; that the total value of the competing yachts was approximately £100,000. Also, many of the entries were not covered by insurance because their owners considered the extra charge levied by Lloyd's of London, based on the value of a yacht, to be excessive.

There was one detail the media could not agree on, however, and that was the length of the course. The most popular figure in newspaper reports for the early decades was 680 miles, but there is no indication anywhere as to how that distance came about. It is possible that it related in some way to the approximate distance the yachts would cover sailing upwind, downwind and across the wind to reach Hobart.

It was not until modern-day technology was utilised in 2002–03 that the CYCA was able to use Vincenty's formulae – a form of calculation where algorithms are applied in geodesy to measure the distance between two points on the surface of a sphere – to most accurately calculate the exact length of the course. The precise answer was that the rhumb line (shortest possible) distance for the Sydney Hobart race was 628.23 nautical miles.

*

On a perfect summer day where the waters of Sydney Harbour were shimmering, the azure sky was cloudless and a gentle breeze was fanning in from the nor'east, some 100,000 spectators were drawn to the scene to absorb the spectacle of the start of the fourth Hobart race. Never in Australia's history had such a huge crowd gathered to see a maritime event like this. Spectator boats, large and small, were bobbing about the starting line off Clark Island while others were scattered down the harbour all the way to the Heads. At the same time, many of those watching from the shore made it a family picnic day, while others could be seen lining the balconies of blocks of flats or standing atop them.

Jimmy Sim, from Melbourne, who was a crewmember aboard the 43-foot Victorian sloop *Merlan*, provided friends back home with this version of the start:

Ahead of the procession moved a fussy phalanx of 120 small yachts, 47 launches, and speedboats, a crowded ferry steamer, and sundry canoes marshalled by police launches trying, with only partial success, to keep the fairway clear. *Morna* was through the heads 7 minutes before the two recently-built Tasmanian cutters, *Mistral V* and *Sandra*. By noon the wind had reached a velocity of 30 miles an hour.

After some difficulty with her mainsail, *Mistral V* lifted her brand new £100 nylon spinnaker, and tore ahead after *Morna*. Then, suddenly, a strange thing happened. The seven following yachts ran into an unnatural calm just outside the Heads, and all the remaining competitors blundered into it. For 10 minutes sails flapped about helplessly, while thousands of sightseers lining the tall cliffs saw *Morna* and *Mistral V*, which escaped the calm, forge rapidly ahead of the field and vanish in the haze down the coast. Hundreds of motorists, who had been watching the progress of the yachts down the harbour from the heights of South Head, Rose Bay, and Vaucluse, set off in pursuit down the coastal roads, but the pace set by the leading yachts was so hot that they had to abandon the chase.

For the sailors, the first three days were memorable for all the right reasons. The yachts made good speed under spinnaker or a poled-out headsail and surged down perfectly proportioned waves amid a swathe of white water. But yet again this going would prove to be too good to last. The almost inevitable change came the following day. Just as the leading yachts were carving a course onto the waters of Bass Strait they were hammered by howling headwinds, a southerly gale that lasted four days and generated enormous seas.

The crew of Max Creese's yacht, *Sandra*, was so exhausted after battling the storm for more than a day they decided to seek shelter on the coast of Tasmania until the weather improved and they could resume racing. Aboard Guy Rex's *Mistral V* the men were manning the pumps and bailing frantically with buckets in a bid to stay ahead of the water streaming in through a hull leak that was below the waterline. It was a losing battle, so *Mistral V* became the race's first casualty with Rex opting to retire and head for a safe haven on the coast. Around the same time the crew of *Aloha* also surrendered to sheer exhaustion, while there was an emergency aboard *Lass O'Luss*. The heavily-heeled yacht had crashed off the top of a mountainous wave, and the force of impact as it landed had sent a pot of boiling tea hurtling across the cabin and onto a crewman who was sleeping in a bunk on the leeward side, scalding him badly. The yacht retired from the race immediately and set a course towards St Helens on Tasmania's north-east coast. It was met there by some locals who had come offshore in a rowing boat. The injured crewman was transferred to the small boat and taken ashore for treatment.

Poor radio communications with the fleet made it difficult to establish accurate position reports, however rough calculations indicated that *Morna*'s bid for a third consecutive line honours was on track. This proved to be the case when, 4 days, 5 hours, 1 minute and 21 seconds after departing Sydney, the big boat surged across the finish line in race record time. An understandably elated owner, Claude Plowman, had cause for a double celebration when *Morna* reached the dock in Hobart: once there, he was informed that he had been knighted by King George VI in Australia's New Year Honours list. Arise Sir Claude!

With the line honours winner confirmed, the focus in the race turned towards the corrected time result, and it appeared – after race officials had deciphered information that came from position reports by radio and through aerial observations – that it was going to be a close tussle between the previous year's winner and local favourite, *Westward*, and *Merlan* out of Melbourne. Unfortunately for the *Merlan* crew though, their chance for victory was unravelling around them, and they didn't know it! Crewman Jimmy Sim later wrote about some of his experiences in the race and what went wrong during a dramatic, and near tragic, last night at sea:

> Once outside [Sydney Harbour] we set a course in accordance with our planned strategy which took us well out to sea, over the Continental shelf, and about 150 miles off the coast. At about 4am the following morning, the breeze came in a bit fresher and we set our biggest spinnaker. We carried that huge kite for three full days, on the port gybe all the time.
>
> During this period we averaged about 190 miles a day, it was an absolute 'dream' sail and *Merlan* revelled in it. This took us a long way down towards Tasmania, where Lance [the yacht's owner] had predicted we would pick up a southerly. And sure enough, just at the right time, in it came. So, down came the spinnaker, up went the big genoa and a course was set for Maria Island. We were just five days out of Sydney which was very good going for those days. Off Maria Island we were greeted by planes with the press on board who took photographs of ourselves and the crack eight metre yacht, *Sandra*. *Sandra* was only about four miles ahead of us so, presuming that *Morna*, the 60ft scratch boat, was ahead of her, this put us in third placing for line honours. We calculated that at

that time our handicap allowance would be about
26 hours. So, therefore, we must have been in a strong
position to take out first placing on handicap as we were
only about 10 hours sailing time from the line and
anticipated that we should be finishing about midnight.

But things did not work out that way. We passed Cape
Pillar on the south-east corner of Tasman Island, but,
instead of turning north-west into Storm Bay, carried on
too far in the pitch black conditions, towards Bruny
Island. I was on watch about midnight as we ran on under
spinnaker at about 10 knots. I felt most uneasy; things did
not seem to be quite right. Too much time had passed for
us not to be sighting the Iron Pot light which marks the
entrance to the Derwent River. I went below, woke Lance
and told him of my misgivings. Lance shared my feelings
and we quickly dropped the spinnaker, put the boat up
into the wind, dropped the sails and put an anchor out
while we waited for daylight. Imagine our horror when
daylight came about 4am to reveal a line of huge rocks
rising from the ocean no more than 160 yards [150 metres]
off our bow! In other words, we had been no more than a
couple of minutes from sailing into disaster… a disaster,
the proportions of which did not bear contemplation. We
had been sailing straight towards the rugged coast of
Bruny Island! Weighing anchor, we set sail once more.
But now it was daylight and our course was clear. Late in
the afternoon, that same day, we sailed up the Derwent to
the finish. Our miscalculation had cost us about 16
precious hours and also, with little doubt, the race.

Sadly, there was worse to come for *Merlan*. On the return voyage to its home port of Melbourne, the yacht encountered a wicked storm when approaching the entrance to Port Phillip. There was no turning back and *Merlan* was overwhelmed by a huge breaking wave and driven onto a reef. The four crewmembers immediately launched the yacht's dinghy, which had been stowed on the deck, but as soon as they clambered aboard it was swamped by another breaking wave. Those onshore thought the sailors were destined to perish, but thanks to a remarkably heroic rescue effort by four local fishermen who were aboard a small open skiff, the sailors were saved.

Back in Hobart, there were jubilant scenes around the docks and across the city when race officials declared that, for the second consecutive year, the local yacht *Westward*, owned by George Gibson, had won the race. The result also stood as a fitting tribute to Jock Muir, a local who designed and built *Westward*, and who was a highly valued member of the crew. Some years later, when he looked back on the victory, he recalled: 'I remember it was savage weather for the last four days. It didn't worry me or the boat – the rougher it got the more the boat loved it, and so did I.' He then added a confession: *Westward* was not designed to win ocean races like the Sydney Hobart. The design parameters for the yacht – which he built in a paddock on the banks of the Derwent – were for it to be 'solely a fishing cruiser'.

When Muir passed away in 1995 at the age of 81, he was recognised as a legend in the world of boatbuilding and offshore sailing in Australia. During his lifetime he designed and/or built some 100 vessels, including many of Australia's best known ocean racing yachts of the era, like *Lass O'Luss*, *Waltzing Matilda*, *Wild Wave*, *Lahara*, *Van Diemen*, *Maris*, *Salacia*, *Balandra* and *Trevassa*. His passion was ocean racing or, more particularly, the Sydney Hobart race. He competed in the classic on nineteen occasions between 1946 and 1971, winning twice on corrected time and twice claiming line honours.

Westward was sold to a yachting enthusiast from Melbourne soon after winning the 1948 race. The deal obviously created great excitement within the city's yachting fraternity, so much so that a radio station seized on what it saw as a great opportunity to entertain local sporting enthusiasts. News of this came in a brief note published in the Melbourne *Age* newspaper:

> Highlights from the log of the cruising yacht *Westward*, dual winner of the Sydney to Hobart yacht race in 1948– 49, will be read by owner, Mr Lorls Solomon, and Tony Charlton in Sports Newsreel, broadcast from AW on Friday, June 30, at 6.30pm.

This was a yesteryear equivalent of the audiobook, an event that would convince even the most cynical of sporting enthusiasts that the Hobart race held high stature as an Australian sporting event.

*

One of the entries in the 1948 race would go on to be the corrected time winner 2 years later. It was the 13.7-metre classic, *Nerida*, then owned by Colin Haselgrove, the technical director of the highly successful South Australian winemakers, Thomas Hardy & Sons. The design for the yacht had been commissioned by Tom Hardy, father of the now famous *America's Cup*, Olympic and world champion sailor, Sir James 'Jim' Hardy. It was launched in 1933.

Nerida proved to be remarkably fast on home waters but a family tragedy intervened. In 1938, Jim's father was killed when the DC2 aircraft *Kyeema* crashed into the Dandenong Ranges east of Melbourne. There were no survivors. Jim was aged five at the time.

Tough times followed for the Hardy family as cash flow problems, and having to hand over their home to the military during the war, took a toll. At one stage, Jim's mother, Eileen, considered moving the family aboard *Nerida* just to save money. Fortunately though, that move was averted when Colin Haselgrove bought the yacht.

He subsequently decided to compete in the Sydney Hobart race with *Nerida,* and changed many features to make it more suitable for ocean racing. This included modifications to the rig, and replacing the tiller steering with a wheel. *Nerida* sailed to a creditable fifth in the 1948 race, and then took top honours in 1950.

Sir James, better known to his extensive circle of friends simply as 'Jim', always had a soft spot for *Nerida*, so he was overjoyed when the Hardy wine company purchased the yacht and brought it back into the fold. Some years later, when Jim moved to Sydney, he was able to take his beloved *Nerida* with him. Once there he decided to restore the yacht as close as possible back to the original design, including reverting to tiller steering. On hearing of this particular part of the restoration project, Haselgrove wrote to Jim, commenting: 'Hardy, if you put her back to tiller steering you are clearly much stronger in the arms than in the head!'

Nerida, with Sir James at the helm, was one of 371 starters in the 50th anniversary Hobart race in 1994, and one of the 62 retirements. He took personal ownership of the yacht that same year. Today Sir James, aka 'Gentleman Jim', still has great pleasure sailing *Nerida* on Sydney Harbour – with tiller steering.

Sir James actually made his Hobart race debut in 1955 as a twenty-three-year-old aboard the well-known South Australian yacht *Southern Myth*, which was owned by Norm Howard. It was an interesting experience, a real learning curve for him, he explained.

> Unfortunately Norm got himself hooked up into the handicap game. He believed that by reducing the area of the mainsail, *Southern Myth* would be more competitive because its handicap would be lower. Lower yes, but it was also a lot slower!

Southern Myth no longer had the horsepower needed to be competitive in light winds, and light winds prevailed for much of the course that year. However, there was one interesting first associated with this campaign; *Southern Myth* carried the first-ever mainsail in Australia to be made from terylene fabric. It was lighter and considerably stronger than the canvas sails the yacht previously carried.

Looking back on the twelve Hobart races he has completed, Jim's most memorable moment had nothing to do with storm-tossed seas or the result of the race. He explained:

It was a ridiculously funny moment in the 1976 race which we still laugh about to this day. I was sailing with Syd Fischer on his famous yacht *Ragamuffin*. The incident came when we were knocked down by a particularly nasty squall just as we were rounding Tasman Island. It was savage and quite dramatic as *Ragamuffin* was knocked onto its side, shuddering and shaking and with the sails flogging.

The panicked call that came from the guys on deck was 'Reef, reef, reef,' meaning we had to immediately, or sooner, reduce sail by lowering the mainsail. Crewman John Munson, aka 'Munno', who was off-watch and asleep in his bunk, had the job to operate the winch attached to the mast below deck which was used for raising and lowering the mainsail. He must've been half asleep when he leapt out of his bunk and battled his way to the winch while the yacht continued to lie on its side, almost capsized. Forever eager to please and quick to respond, Munno reacted to the call for reefing action with the question: 'Which way – up or down?' We couldn't stop laughing about it, and took the mickey out of him all the way into Hobart and all the time we were there.

Jim also recalled that the party scene at Constitution Dock in Hobart was always entertaining! Back then 'Moreton Bay

Porridge' – rum and milk – was the drink of the day literally around the clock. The crews seemed to have an endless supply of rum for the concoction but never enough milk. Fortunately, the local milko was quick to latch on to the new market that had suddenly appeared for him. So, no matter the hour, there was the milkman at the dock with his truck while crew from the race yachts were seen constantly running to him to replenish supplies.

The emerging Halvorsen brothers, Trygve and Magnus, were no doubt disappointed when their new yacht *Peer Gynt* finished seventh on corrected time in this race, but they were able to add a bright side to the effort. Knowing there was a severe beer shortage in Sydney, they loaded 600 bottles of the local brew aboard their matronly curved yacht, and took it back to Sydney for the benefit of the workers at their boatyard.

*

For many interested observers in 1949/50, there were concerns that the fleet size for the Hobart race was showing signs of stalling in the mid-teens, fifteen starters in 1949 and sixteen in 1950, even though media and public interest was being maintained.

One other impressive entry in the 1950 race was a 15.2-metre-long sloop built by Bjarne Halvorsen for prominent Sydney yachtsman and clothing retailer, F.J. Palmer. But five weeks before the race, when the £5000 yacht was almost ready for launching, a massive fire swept through the boatyard, located in Berrys Bay, near North Sydney. In total, twenty vessels valued at more than £75,000 were destroyed, including Palmer's yacht.

*

One of Australia's best-known and most successful offshore racing yachtsmen in the latter part of the 1900s and into the next century, Gordon Ingate, made his Hobart race debut in 1950.

It was apparent when he was in his mid-twenties that he was a rising star in the sport, so much so that English Colonel A.E. Saalfield, who was then living in Sydney, invited the young sailor to race the little, 8.8-metre-long sloop *Jasnar* to Hobart that year. However, there was one particular proviso attached to the offer – that the colonel's young daughter, Sally, must be part of the crew. Ingate accepted the offer and agreed to the proviso, which meant that Sally was among the first women to compete in the classic.

The race proved to be a tough test for Sally from the outset as the fleet had to contend with a punishing, 35-knot southerly gale for the first four days. Sally held vivid memories of that experience which she would later describe as being 'enjoyable'.

> I really don't know why, because I was buffeted beyond belief and slept on the floor with water dripping on my head… I lost a stone [6.35kg] from being thrown against the boat all day long – but I was not frightened by the rough conditions.

As *Jasnar* entered Constitution Dock some 6 days and 16 hours after leaving Sydney, a friend of the pair, 'Boy' Messenger, spotted Gordon and Sally standing in the cockpit waving to the crowd. Messenger shouted to Ingate, 'Why don't you marry the girl?' and on hearing that Ingate is said to have proposed right then, because, soon after the yacht was docked, Ingate hastily sent a telegram to the colonel in Sydney which read in part: 'Arrived safely... May I marry your daughter?' The colonel is said to have replied: 'Which one?'

Sally Saalfield and Gordon Ingate subsequently married, and over the ensuing decades he enjoyed considerable success across many facets of the sport including the Olympics, *America's Cup* and world championships. He is best remembered as the owner of *Caprice of Huon*, which was a member of the Australian *Admiral's Cup* team in 1965 and 1967.

The memories of *Jasnar* and that 1950 Hobart race obviously remained with Ingate over the decades because in 2016, when it came to his attention that the yacht was for sale, he bought it. In 2019 he was still actively racing the yacht – at age 93!

*

The disappointing number of entries was cause for the CYCA's committee to meet and discuss all aspects of the race and its future. Many theories and suggestions were put forward, the most controversial being that the race be held every second year, and that the start should alternate between Sydney and Hobart. Both proposals were soundly rejected, so it was a case of carry on regardless and do the best we can.

There was a similar sentiment in Hobart. A news item published in *The Mercury* reported that consideration was being given to starting the race each alternate year in Hobart, and that it might be staged every 2 years. This was not well received in that part of the world, the local theory being that, because of the cost and effort needed to get yachts to Hobart for the start, the fleet number would only decrease, not increase.

The consensus was that the Hobart race numbers were remaining static chiefly because Australian society was still struggling to recover from the war. In essence, as life improved for the populace so too would the fleet size for the race. However, if there was one person who reflected the ultimate determination to be part of the Sydney Hobart at that time, it was Merv Davey.

He was one of the sailors who, when cruising Sydney Harbour, was recruited by Peter Luke to become a member of the CYCA in the very early days. He was member number 25.

Merv Davey's love for offshore sailing, in particular the Hobart race, and his desire to help guide the club during its embryonic years, saw him elected to the position of Rear Commodore between 1947 and 1949, then Commodore from 1949 to 1951.

A decade earlier, before the CYCA or the Hobart race existed, Merv had decided to design and build a 13.3-metre-long steel cruising yacht. He certainly held the necessary credentials for the task: he was Sydney University's youngest ever graduate in both science and engineering.

When he set about designing the yacht, he paid no heed to any form of handicap rule; instead he drew up the plan for his desired accommodation then sketched the hull lines around that. With that done, he had a local steel fabricator construct the bare hull then trucked it to a vacant paddock next to his home on the shores of Sydney Harbour where he set about completing the project. Budget constraints and the limited availability of equipment, including the engine, saw Merv apply a practical approach to every part of the project. The yacht, which would be named *Trade Winds*, had a wooden deck covered in canvas so it was as watertight as possible. The timber mast was not stepped through the deck, but on it, Davey's theory being that if it ever broke and went over the side, it wouldn't take a large part of the deck with it. The yacht's small petrol engine, which originally powered a tiny baker's van and could only be started using a crank handle, had a propensity to leak petrol and oil into the bilge, creating a perpetual fire risk.

Regardless of this seemingly basic approach, it soon became apparent that Davey knew what he was doing. Once he entered the racing fold of the CYCA, his desire to cruise became secondary. *Trade Winds* placed sixth on handicap in both the 1946 and 1947 Hobart races.

Encouraged by these results, Davey designed and fitted a larger rig to *Trade Winds* and subsequently won the 1949 Hobart race.

*

The CYCA remained homeless until 1 August 1951 when the membership received the news they had wanted to hear ever since the club was founded 6 years earlier. It finally had a home!

Kelshaw's Boatshed, a somewhat rundown structure tucked away in the south-east corner of Rushcutters Bay, on Sydney Harbour, was purchased for £10,000 and has been headquarters ever since. While this was exciting news for the membership, the acquisition proved to be as much a burden as a milestone. The cash flow derived from the on-going boatshed business was not as strong as anticipated, and worse still, the condition of the building attracted the attention of the local authorities, including the licensing police.

The dilapidated structure dated back to the late 1800s, so, not surprisingly, its facilities were far from modern. In fact one visitor, who later became a club member, recalled how shocked he was when he first visited the club that ran the Sydney Hobart Yacht Race. The actual structure had suffered the ravages of salt air and had a serious problem with white ants, but unfortunately the club's cash flow difficulties meant there were insufficient funds to effectively rectify these problems. The management committee was persuaded to take the advice of the local licensing sergeant and leave it to the court to decide what improvements needed to be undertaken. This had the potential to be a major mistake.

Alan Campbell, who was then the Club Secretary, recalled that 'the court had a field day' when the club's case was heard. It seemed that the long list of problems with the clubhouse that was presented to the judge gave him the opportunity to demonstrate to the community that the court was doing its job. The licensing sergeant got up and read to the 'beak' his findings regarding the building; it was a fire trap, it had no fire escape, the doors of the ladies and gents toilets were too close to one another … the list went on. The situation became even worse for the club the following morning when the *Daily Telegraph* published a double column story under the headline: 'Club Declared Fire Trap'. The future for the CYCA was looking bleak, but the Board decided to attend to what modifications they could with the little cash that was available.

With those modifications complete, Campbell returned to court with a well-known Sydney solicitor, Ken Smithers, so the judge could consider what improvements had been made to the premises. Campbell's heart sank when he realised he was to go before the same judge, until good fortune intervened. The judge recognised the club's new counsel, and this led to him saying: 'Oh, Mr Smithers, I see you are representing this applicant'. Then, while Smithers outlined the club's plans and detailed what work had been carried out to date, the judge seemingly ignored him and busily initialled the pages he had in front of him. That task complete, he put his pen down, interrupted Smithers and said, 'Licence granted. Next case please.'

It was still a long and hard road over many years for the club from there, but today the CYCA's headquarters is a very modern and impressive clubhouse standing on that same site.

*

The 1951 Hobart was a milestone event and a record breaker. Media interest continued to grow as did public interest nationally. Newspapers across the country tapped into syndicated stories such as the following, which appeared in *The Advocate* in Burnie, on Tasmania's north coast on 24 December:

Fourteen Yachts to Battle Out Sydney Hobart Race

Preparations in Sydney are almost complete for the start of Australia's greatest ocean yacht race, the Sydney Hobart. The 680-mile event has become such a good box office attraction that a commercial radio station has arranged special radio-telephone coverage of the yachts' progress four times daily for the duration of the race. Sixteen yachts were entered for this year's event, but only 14 will jockey for position round the naval starting launch at Clark Island at 11 a.m. on Boxing Day. The biggest contestant, *Nirvana*, a 63-foot cutter from Newcastle, was scratched last week as she could not be got ready in time. The only New Zealand entry, *Rangi*, was wrecked and burnt on rocks at Norfolk Island while en route to Sydney. A fine day is forecast for the start and Sydney Harbour is expected to be crowded with small craft. The Cruising Yacht Club of Australia, which sponsors the event, has chartered a palatial tourist ferry, the showboat *Kalang*, to take spectators to the start. Leading in favouritism is the crack ocean-racing yawl *Margaret Rintoul*, which won the Montague Island race earlier this year. The yawl has been sailing remarkably well and with Frank Barlow as skipper is generally expected to be first across the finishing line. Although unplaced in the last race, a strong contender this year will be the Halvorsen brothers' sloop, *Solveig*, which is generally expected to improve on her last performance, as a result of the valuable experience her skipper and crew gained in the Los Angeles-Honolulu race. The newest yacht in the fleet is the Hobart-built *Lahara*, owned and skippered by New Guinea patrol officer, DN Ashton. Yachtsmen who have seen her sailing claim she is as fast as her name denotes – 'north-west monsoon'. Another boat to watch is *Nocturne*, which this year will rate a trifle better than last, having had her mast shortened and equipped with new standing and running rigging and a dog-house. The low-rater, *Nimbus*, a 34-foot cutter owned and skippered by Sydney yachtsman Tony Cohen, is also strongly tipped to be among the leaders, as are Tom Williamson's 35-foot sloop, *Struen Marie*. All variations of fore and aft rig are represented in the fleet. There will be four sloops, four cutters, three schooners, two yawls and a ketch. The first boat should cross the finishing line in the Derwent River on New Year's Eve.

Unfortunately for the crew of handicap favourite *Nimbus*, good fortune didn't go their way. A handwritten note discovered in recent times explained what happened:

Lost mast in Bass Strait. Jury rigged to finish 10th. Went between Tasman Isle and mainland – dangerous but necessary as we would not have made [cleared] Tasman Isle. The result was the Committee made Tasman Island a mark of the course the next year.

Nimbus was the last yacht to reach Hobart in the fleet of fourteen, taking 5 days, 3 hours and 25 minutes to complete the course – an average speed of 5 knots.

Tom Williamson, owner of corrected time winner *Struen Marie*, told the media after his yacht reached Hobart that good luck more than good management had led to it winning the race. He explained that *Struen Marie* was running downwind under spinnaker when it was suddenly hit by a squall so powerful that the crew was unable to lower the spinnaker – it was too dangerous a manoeuvre to execute. They could only hang on and hope that everything would hold together as they rode out the squall for some considerable time. He said that this moment, as dangerous as it was, turned out to be quite fortuitous in that the yacht was driven offshore at high speed. Williamson added that *Struen Marie* '... travelled through, and sometimes over, the water faster than her makers ever expected her to move.' *Margaret Rintoul*'s elapsed time was 4 days 2 hours 29 minutes, an impressive 3 hours 32 minutes inside the record.

When that time was being posted there was another record of sorts being established out on the course. It involved the tiny ketch *Katwinchar* which, when *Margaret Rintoul* crossed the finish line, was little more than halfway to Hobart. This same yacht had arrived in Sydney just three weeks before the race started, having been sailed by a three-man crew all the way from England, a distance of 15,000 nm. The primary purpose of their journey to Australia was to migrate to Tasmania. However, while planning their passage, they realised they could include the Hobart race as part of their adventurous voyage.

But the story did not end there. In the decades to come, *Katwinchar* would create a sentimental link spanning the intervening 68 years between the 1951 race and the 75th in

2019. However, the remarkable details surrounding this yacht's resurrection would not emerge until a few months prior to that start of the anniversary race.

*

The 1951 race was seen to be historic in that for the first time a 'radio mother ship' – the well-travelled 17.3-metre ketch *Kurrewa III* – escorted the fleet to Hobart. It was introduced as a safety precaution, but ironically the only real drama during that race involved *Kurrewa III*. Co-owner, Frank Livingston, contracted a serious bout of blood poisoning when the yacht was mid-Bass Strait. An emergency radio call went out and, soon after, an attempt was made to drop drugs to the yacht from a flying boat, but it was unsuccessful. *Kurrewa III* then set a course for St Helens, on the north-east coast of Tasmania. Once there, Livingston was transferred to shore and soon after, flown to Melbourne for treatment.

Despite this, from that year onwards, there has always been a radio relay vessel accompanying the fleet. For the 75th anniversary Hobart race in 2019, the 70-foot motor yacht *JBW* will be accompanying the fleet to Hobart or the fifteenth time. The impressive vessel is loaned to the CYCA each year by owner John Winning, and has been manned on every occasion by former CYCA Commodore, David Kellett, and skipper Andrew 'Steak' Copley.

*

Just after the finish of the race there was unexpected news published in The *Hobart Mercury*. It confirmed the race had achieved an international following:

> According to advice received from the Agent-General (Mr von Bibra) Tasmania has received a splendid advertisement in London from the Sydney Hobart yacht race.
>
> Each day the progress of the yachts was plotted on a map of Australia and Tasmania in the window of the office of the Agent-General.
>
> Mr von Bibra has advised the Chief Secretary (Mr White) that great interest was shown in the race and that each day Londoners gathered at the window to see how the boats were faring.
>
> Mr White said that, through the courtesy of the Managing Editor of *The Mercury* (Mr CE Davies), some splendid photographs of yachts which competed in the 1950 race had been displayed along with the map of the race route.

*

Hobart race organisers at the CYCA were desperately hoping that the 1952 race would see a fleet larger than 1951's fourteen starters. That happened, even if the final number was only three more. Much to everyone's satisfaction, the media's fascination with the race remained strong. For the majority of sailors, the irony of this was how so many journalists who knew absolutely nothing about ocean racing took to reporting on it.

Many of these colour writers applied their own theories and 'facts' to their stories in a bid to provide maximum interest for the readership.

In 1952, Ipswich, located 40 kilometres inland from Brisbane, was a town of less than 40,000 residents. Its local newspaper is *The Queensland Times*, and Ward McNally was one of the paper's feature writers. Less than two weeks before the start of the race that year, the paper published McNally's overview of the event. He actually misinterpreted a few facts, but it certainly made for an interesting article for his country readership. The feature appeared under the headline:

Sydney Hobart Yacht Race Now Famous

With the announcement by a big shipping company that it will run a special cruise to cover the opening of the Sydney Hobart Yacht Race, the race has really entered the ranks of the world's great ocean yachting contests.

The shipping company was the Lloyd Triestino Line which announced last week that the post-war luxury liner, *Australia*, would leave Sydney Harbour on Boxing Day morning in the wake of the yachts taking part in the race.

The liner will carry up to 500 passengers paying £6 a head. It will follow the race until dusk and then return to Sydney.

But the people who go on the *Australia* will be only a fraction of the crowds who see the frail cockle shells off on their battle through the empty, storm-swept wastes of the Pacific.

On Boxing Day morning, up to 50,000 Sydneysiders will converge on wharves, jetties, and harbour beaches to watch the start of the now-famous ocean yacht race.

Several thousand more will ride out to the starting line aboard gaily decorated ferries to watch the racing craft break out sail, and overseas liners in port will blast a salute as the little ships head for the open sea.

And Hobart will get ready to turn on a real Tasmanian welcome.

Sydney and Hobart have been doing this sort of thing for seven years now.

It all started when an RN bloke called Illingworth — Captain John Illingworth, 'kingpin' of England's Royal Ocean Racing Club — was in Sydney at the tail end of the war. Illingworth was amazed to find that a country so rich in cruising waters didn't have an ocean race worth talking about.

So he did something about it.

Seven years ago he sales-talked the Royal Cruising Yacht Club of Australia into sponsoring what has in seven years become widely recognised as the third most important ocean race in the world.

There were plenty of Aussie yachtsmen back in 1945 who reckoned that Illingworth was 'mad'; that a yacht race 680 miles down the coast was too risky to be worth the candle.

But 'Captain Johnnie' guffawed those arguments right out of the picture, pointing out that in England men had been racing yachts across oceans for upwards of 70 years.

163

'And what was yachting for if not to get out into a decent sea and pit your skill against the winds and rain?' asked Capt Illingworth.

So, on the morning of Boxing Day, 1945, a fleet of 20 small ships set course for Hobart.

Smallest yacht in the race was *Ranji* [*Rani*], skippered by 'Captain Johnnie' himself.

Following the 'ocean' racing pattern of the day, 19 of the fleet sailed from land point to land point, never shifting far from sight of the coast.

ON OPEN SEA

But the 20th yacht, *Ranji*, made straight for the open sea and was quickly lost to sight.

Five days later, she was seen again – luffing up the Derwent River, just a day and a half ahead of her nearest rival!

That Illingworth man certainly showed us a thing or two about ocean racing …

These days, the Sydney Hobart always attracts a classy fleet.

It gets Australia-wide interest, and it's challenging the Bermuda ocean race in yachting importance.

Take a look at the record book and find out why.

Last year the race was highlighted by a dramatic sea rescue. Skipper Frank Livingston, of the radio-mother ship, *Kuwerra* [*Kurrewa*] III, was smacked on the left knee by a swinging boom, developed blood poisoning, and an SOS was sent out.

Livingston was 'air-lifted' to Melbourne, where he underwent an emergency operation.

Then, just to liven things up a bit, the Sydney yacht *Nocturne* ran smack into a southerly buster, took a beating for 17 hours, and finally struggled out with her main-mast snapped off at deck level like a rotten carrot.

She limped the remaining couple of hundred miles to Hobart.

But most dramatic of all incidents happened three or four years ago.

Lass O'Luss was racing before a storm down the Northern Tasmanian coast when a member of the crew was heaved against the ship's oil stove.

Lass O'Luss streaked for St Helens and tried for two hours to get through the bar, but was kept out by swirling seas.

Finally a local fisherman got his boat alongside the yacht, took the injured man off, and rushed him to hospital, where he was treated for first degree burns to the face and chest.

Interestingly, the CYCA had not been granted the Royal Warrant some members had long hoped for but McNally gave the club one anyway.

*

Just one week before the 1952 race, and two days after McNally's story appeared, Sydney yachtswoman and journalist Sheila Patrick wrote a lengthy feature which was designed to benefit the women whose menfolk were participating in the Hobart race that year.

It appeared in Sydney's *Daily Telegraph*:

Wives and 'sweet-hearts' of local yachtsmen complain that the Sydney Hobart yacht race has become a disease with their menfolk.

Many skippers and crews have to compromise and go to Hobart only every second year, spending alternate Christmas holidays with their family and friends.

Most wives send up a silent cheer when their husbands decide to give the classic race the go-by for a year.

For every yacht which crosses the starting line on Boxing Day means spoiled Christmas celebrations for at least six families. Not only do most skippers and crews spend every weekend of November and December ocean sailing to train for the tough 680 miles to Hobart, but they also have to refrain from too much festivity on Christmas Day because rich food and alcohol can cause severe seasickness days later.

Worse, annual holidays are often taken up entirely with sailing to Hobart and back, away from their families.

However, despite feminine protests, 25 boats from four States, New Zealand and Holland had entered for this year's race up to yesterday. Entries are accepted up to next Wednesday, three days before the race starts.

One well-known Sydney skipper of a big cutter is notorious for denying that he is going to Hobart, and assuring his wife and children that nothing would be more pleasant than spending his Christmas holidays camping at Pittwater with his family.

However, in the last few days, the fascination of the race proves too much for this otherwise well-meaning husband and father. In a great panic he rushes to lodge his entry, organises a crew, and makes desperate last-minute arrangements. He invariably crosses the starting line on Boxing Day, and usually does very well.

He is again a non-entry this year, but as usual is reported to be showing serious signs of weakening.

One extremely keen Hobart race skipper makes his crew go to bed at 9.30pm for a month before the race:

'Crews can't stand long hours, wet and cold, in bad weather unless they are physically in top condition,' he says. 'I've known men to get very seasick in a small boat, only because they are not in good physical condition.'

And to his wife he says: 'No Christmas parties for me. You can go, but count me out.' The wife does go to some parties, and has to explain to puzzled hostesses that her husband is 'in training', 'resting up' or 'indisposed'.

Wives also come in for plenty of odd jobs: 'Pick up that chronometer at the instrument-makers, please dear,' said one husband as his wife staggered off to do her Christmas shopping.

'Oh, yes, there is £6/15/- to pay.'

When the wife blanched, and murmured '£6/15/-, just for repairs!' the husband-skipper said with irritation,

'Everything must be in good order; you want us to win, don't you?'

Another skipper gets his wife to push the stroller all the way to Lane Cove [the local shopping village] to pick up a new winch for the boat. 'Pick a cool afternoon,' he says. 'Can't go to sea with faulty deck winches, dear.'

Other wives have to take the sails to the sailmaker during the week with long explanations about the repairs to be done.

A job for wives and families is preparing food for eating during the race.

'Most of my good screw-top jars are taken to Hobart,' says one wife. 'I don't get them back; that would be too much to expect.'

She spends many nights before the race making savoury stews, thick soups, and puddings to go in the jars, and cooking corned beef and roast lamb to eat cold.

One skipper is an orange-juice fan, and buys several cases of cheap oranges, which he press gangs his small children into squeezing for a flat rate of 3d a dozen.

One member of a Hobart race crew who was engaged to be married tried to put the wedding off until after the race. But his fiancée insisted that they marry before the start of the race, and carried him off to Bowral [in the Southern Highlands] for the honeymoon so that he couldn't even see the others sail away without him.

The race, which starts at 11am on Saturday, December 26, is the ninth in the series. Preparation is one of the secrets of success in this tough ocean battle of wits and seamanship. Skippers today also spend many months in planning for the five day battle down the eastern coast and across the turbulent waters of Bass Strait.

First, the boat must be thoroughly overhauled for any weaknesses. Inside and out she is tested to withstand the worst the sea can produce. The boat must drive on through almost any kind of weather in an ocean race, and this type of treatment soon finds the weak spots in a hull.

Three months before the race, the proposed crew is called together and the race discussed from every angle, from lifesaving gear to food and courses.

A master list is made of every possible job which needs to be done before the race, and each crew member is given a small list of his special jobs.

One crewman will be in charge of victualling, and will have to order, pick up, and stow all foodstuffs. Another will see to the hiring of the radio, and learning to service it. A third will go over all the standing and running rigging of the yacht thoroughly to see whether it is fit for the tough test ahead.

Arrangements must be made for last-minute slipping, and perhaps a quick rub with car polish or some other preparation concocted by the skipper. Smooth bottoms win races, too.

Food is a problem. It must be nutritious, easy to prepare, and easy to eat. The crew mustn't wear themselves out cooking messy meals in bad weather. One hot, nourishing meal a day, supplemented by eggs, tomatoes, biscuits, and plenty of fruit, dried or fresh, is the answer.

Lemons keep well at sea, and many lads develop a great longing for celery, which is 'nourishing and easy to eat'.

The only hot food some yachts have is beverages. Everything else is eaten cold, and has been prepared beforehand and stowed in big jars.

Food is usually served in deep dishes to prevent it spilling. Cake tins also make excellent plates for ocean racing.

Every man must have adequate oilskins, sou'westers and 'eatin' irons' [knife and fork] and a marlin spike, as well as warm sweaters and spare shorts to change into when wet.

One pair of long, thick, warm slacks is useful, too, as it gets very cold sailing on the ocean at night, especially down south.

Of course, the women do their bit to get the men and their craft ship-shape for the tough five or six days' race, for the truth is that most wives and girlfriends are secretly very proud of their men who go deep-sea racing.

Fraser Johnston

SAILING BIO

I started my sailing on VJs on Middle Harbour in Sydney in 1957, and two years later became the NSW Junior State Champion. Sixteen- and eighteen-foot skiffs followed, then I went into offshore keelboat racing aboard Horrie Godden's Tasman Seabird 36, *Kaleena*. I had a break for a couple of years then returned to ocean racing in 1969. Since those days, I have been ocean racing or doing coastal deliveries virtually non-stop. My racing career has taken me to the *Admiral's Cup* and regattas in Japan, Key West, Miami, Porto Cervo, the UK, Monaco, San Tropez, Hawaii, Spain and Hamilton Island Race Week.

WHAT WAS YOUR BEST DAY UNDER SAIL IN THE SYDNEY HOBART?

The first night and second day of the 1983 race. I was aboard *Challenge II* and we waited until dark on the first night before we set a spinnaker – just so our opposition out to windward of us didn't see what we were doing. It was a tactical move which, over the next 24 hours, put us in a position where we would be very difficult to beat on corrected time. Everything went our way with the weather down to Tasman Island and across Storm Bay, so much so that we won by a handsome margin on corrected time.

WHAT DAY OR EXPERIENCE WAS THE TOUGHEST OR MOST CHALLENGING?

Two events spring to mind. The first came in the '93 race when we lost John Quinn overboard from *MEM* when we were approaching Bass Strait. It was a very traumatic experience for all of us as we did our best to recover him. The fact that he was saved was nothing short of a miracle. The second harrowing time occurred when I was crew aboard Lou Abraham's *Challenge Again* and we lost Gary Schipper overboard. It was a terrible time for everyone on board, but through a great team effort, we recovered him safely.

WHAT KEEPS YOU GOING BACK TO THE HOBART RACE?

Racing on well-prepared, well-crewed, well-found yachts where you meet the challenge of wind and waves and nature's often unpredictable moods!

WHAT ARE SOME OF THE BIG CHANGES THAT YOU'VE WITNESSED IN YOUR YEARS ASSOCIATED WITH THE RACE?

I recall sails made from cotton, and *Kaleena* having the first aluminium mast on a racing yacht in Australia! Now the sport is as much a space race as a yacht race – and it's still good fun.

But iron men on wooden ships will always challenge themselves, alone or with their mates, and the sea can break any man-made object: wood, steel or carbon!

CHAPTER 6

The Future is Assured

In the first half of the 1950s the number of starters in the Hobart race remained in the low to mid-teens, and while this figure was less than hoped for, some local individuals who would become legendary in the world of ocean racing and yacht design were emerging within the event. In particular Alan Payne, Trygve and Magnus Halvorsen, Vic Meyer, and soon after, the American design group, Sparkman and Stephens, all made their mark on the race.

A decade later some other equally famous names were added to this exclusive list: notably Australia's legendary Ben Lexcen; and the Kiwi, Bruce Farr, who, like Lexcen, cut his teeth on designing and racing high-performance 18-foot skiffs. In later years both transferred much of that design philosophy into ocean racing yachts and, to some degree, the *America's Cup*.

It is near impossible to nominate a name to stand atop this select group, all of whom made their Hobart race debut over a 25-year period. However if one looks back to the early days, it was Alan Payne who initially showed the way, with the Halvorsens not far behind. Payne was a free-thinking young man who had a remarkable feel for efficient hull shapes as well as overall design concepts – designs that would prove to be fast, seaworthy and safe. Also, like Lexcen, Payne went on and made a name for himself within the prestigious *America's Cup* circle of sailing, designing Australia's first challenger, *Gretel*, which impressed the world in 1962, then *Gretel II* 8 years later.

Payne migrated from England to Australia with his parents and brother in the late 1920s. The family lineage was deeply rooted in seafaring and sailing, and he would stay on that same course by becoming a naval architect, or more particularly, a yacht designer.

There is no doubt however that thirty-one-year-old Payne's experience aboard the yacht *Horizon* in the inaugural Hobart race, when it was feared that the rampant storm had claimed the yacht and its crew, remained deeply etched in his mind. From that he learned the design parameters needed for an ocean-racing sailboat to survive in such threatening conditions. He would sail in another four Hobart races before the pressure of his business caused him to spend more time at his desk than under sail. However, the *Horizon* experience and those that came later with other yachts, convinced him that the best concept for an offshore racer at that time was an easily driven, heavy-displacement design with a hull shape that provided the same handling characteristics no matter the angle of heel.

When he ventured into the Hobart race arena in 1952 with his 35-foot design, *Nocturne*, he took everyone by surprise as it was a significant departure from the existing trend. Yachts of that period were generally deep-hulled, heavy-displacement, strongly built and featured a long keel with the rudder attached to the trailing edge. Instead, *Nocturne*'s hull was more the shape of a dinghy – shallow with a short keel and separate spade rudder mounted near the stern. The design could be likened more to the Scandinavian 30 Square Metre class of the era – light-displacement, light construction and remarkably fast in light winds. When compared with the existing heavy-displacement offshore racers of the time, *Nocturne's* sail area was quite small because the fine lines of the hull made it easily driven.

Launched in 1949, *Nocturne* was built for Bob Bull, who previously owned the 1946 Hobart race winner, *Christina*. Its Hobart race debut came 2 years later, and the result was impressive; *Nocturne* crossed the finishing line just 3 hours behind line honours winner *Margaret Rintoul*, but was placed ninth on handicap in a fleet of just fifteen. Much to Payne's delight the yacht had lived up to his expectations. It was exceptionally fast when sailing downwind and reaching across the wind. These design traits helped the yacht to finish first across the line in 1952, and fourth on handicap.

The 1952 race also saw the debut in Australia of the design group Sparkman & Stephens (S&S), a New York based company that became a world leader in almost every field of yacht design, including the *America's Cup*. S&S was formed in 1929 by twenty-year-old Olin Stephens and friend Drake Sparkman, two highly talented men who within 2 years became the go-to pair in the United States for ocean racing yacht designs.

Olin's father certainly helped launch the business as he placed an order for the design of a 16-metre-long yawl suitable for ocean racing and cruising. When the design was complete Olin's younger brother, Rod, supervised the construction of the yacht, which was launched in 1931. It was to be named *Dorado*, after a species of dolphin, but somewhere along the line prior to launching it was misspelled; it became *Dorade*.

Its narrow beam and sleek lines saw the design declared revolutionary, and that it proved to be. With Olin at the helm and his father and brother in the crew, *Dorade* set out in the 3000 nautical mile 1931 Trans-Atlantic race from Newport, Rhode Island, to Plymouth in England. The yacht was declared the winner on handicap by almost four days – a stunning achievement that immediately cemented Sparkman & Stephens at the top of its field.

The same yacht – which has been superbly restored and maintained in recent years – was in Australia in 2017 to compete at Hamilton Island Race Week and the Rolex Sydney Hobart Race. Despite being 86 years old, *Dorade* placed second in its division at both events.

In the first 5 years of operation, the S&S business grew impressively on design commissions from within the United States, but the business partners were always hoping that a commission would soon come from Europe and consequently present a valuable chance to expand. Instead, the first international design commission came a decade before the inaugural Hobart race from Hobart, Tasmania! It's distinctly possible Sparkman & Stephens didn't even know where Hobart was, but regardless, it was seen as another satisfying business opportunity.

Thus, when Hobart-based yacht builder Percy Coverdale launched the 13.4-metre-long *Landfall*, from his shed on the banks of the Derwent in 1935, it was the first S&S design to be built outside the USA. It was originally rigged as a yawl, then some years later converted to a more efficient sloop rig. In 1952, 17 years after being launched, the yacht became the first S&S design to contest the Hobart race. *Landfall* started in another four Hobarts over the next six decades, before then owner Michael Strong returned to the race in 2014 to celebrate *Landfall*'s 80th birthday.

Landfall turned in an impressive performance in its Hobart race debut. It was an intense battle for line honours over the entire course and when Hobart was reached, no more than an hour separated the first three yachts. *Nocturne* was first across the line, 36 minutes ahead of *Landfall* with the impressive 16.5-metre yawl, *Ruthean*, third home. The South Australian entry, *Ingrid*, owned and skippered by James Taylor, claimed the *Tattersall Cup*.

*

'The Hobart race is here to stay,' *The Sydney Morning Herald* trumpeted in a Boxing Day preview of the 1953 race. The story revealed that the fleet was the second-largest since the inception of the race, and up by more than 60 per cent on the previous year – from fourteen to twenty-three.

This obviously exciting news saw an estimated 100,000-strong crowd view the start from land and sea. When it came to the cannon being fired at 11am, the initial scene was more about colour and collisions than the sight of the race yachts churning their way towards Sydney Heads amid a huge spectator fleet.

The drama came when *Wild Wave*, skippered by the Tasmanian legend Jock Muir for owners Geoff and Lindsay Keats, tried to wedge its way back through the race fleet after having broken the start (crossing the starting line prior to the start signal). It meant *Wild Wave* needed to get back behind the line and restart if it was to be a legitimate competitor in the classic, but none of Muir's rival skippers seemed to care. It was a logjam and as a result there was a series of unavoidable collisions which were accompanied by the sound of splintering timber and tirades of abuse.

'The scene began to take the shape of a battle royal, reminiscent of the good old days of grappling, galleons and boarding parties,' Hobart race legend, Norman Hudson, who was aboard *Kurura*, said on looking back at the incident. 'However no yacht was dismasted, and after an impressive exchange of salty language between the crews involved, everyone got going for Hobart.'

As well as announcing that the future of the Hobart race was assured, *The Sydney Morning Herald*'s story included an interesting assessment of some of the fleet from the CYCA's secretary, David Allworth:

It's the most open field ever this year. The class of boat is much better than last year and the field is very strong. *Ripple* and *Solveig* are both old war-horses ... *Ruthean* is most likely for line honours this year ... *Gipsy Queen* is a good boat, but there's nothing particular about her ... *Nimbus* could easily win on handicap. Tony Cohen, the skipper, knows his way up and down the coast ...

178

Nocturne is quite capable of taking line honours; she's sailed by Bob Bull and a crew of four. They start racing when the gun goes and they don't stop until the judge's pistol goes at the other end. They're a very tough crew. If a sail has to be changed 50 times it'll be changed to keep that boat going ... *Wraith of Odin* is owned and skippered by BR O'Brien, a lecturer at the University of Sydney. He and his family live aboard. He could win if he had a hard crew; but I think he bears in mind that the *Wraith* is his house and there's not much point in bashing it. *Kurrewa III* has sailed more miles than any of them ... *Isis* is one of the best kept yachts I have ever seen. She's a big boat for 32ft, and she's magnificently kept, thanks to the owner's charming wife, Margaret May. There's definitely a feminine touch about *Isis* ... *Flamingo*, the newest entry, is the only RNSA [Royal Navy Sailing Association] we've seen in Sydney. *Flamingo* was designed by Laurent Giles, one of the crackerjack English designers, in collaboration with Captain John Illingworth, who conceived the idea of the Sydney Hobart race and won the race in *Rani* ... *Onrust* is a Dutch-built ketch with wooden spars, owned by a Dutch Naval officer who sailed it to New Zealand single-handed. He met his fiancée there and the two of them are taking a crew of five and black kittens with them to Hobart.

Melbourne's *Age* newspaper also set the Hobart race scene for Victorian readers:

The race is one of the toughest events of its kind in the world. To the landsman this may seem a crazy way of spending a well-earned Christmas holiday, with an inch of wooden planking separating one from some of the roughest waters around the Australian coast. Before them there may be hours of thrashing into head winds with the heartbreak of sails torn to shreds, flooded cabins, smashed spars. Bad leaks may develop as the wooden hulls pound into the big ocean rollers. Or as in last year's race the boats may find themselves slipping silently through drifts of thick fog in the middle of Bass Strait ... Indeed, the quick change from the festive atmosphere of Christmas to a storm-tossed ocean swell has often meant that only the abstemious have avoided feeding the fishes. But to the devotees of 'ocean-walloping' few sports offer the enduring satisfaction and adventure that come from bringing a small yacht safe to port ahead of all its rivals.

One reason for the increase in fleet size was, no doubt, that the CYCA decided to split the fleet into two divisions and provide more trophies – the major prizes would be awarded to the upper echelon of yacht while the more cruising oriented entries would race for their own trophies. Also, there would be prizes for the first three yachts across the finish line, regardless of what division they were in. Each entry would be assigned to one division or the other after its rating was calculated using a series of measurements, including overall length, beam, draught and sail area.

The first 24 hours was a dream run for the yachts as they sailed down the New South Wales south coast under spinnaker and on the face of a summer nor'easter, but as is almost always the case in the Hobart race, it was too good to last. Little more than 24 hours after the start, the sign of an approaching southerly buster was there for all to see – an ugly, grey-black, cigar-shaped cloud formation stretching from one horizon to the other rolling their way from the south. No doubt there was the same call given on every yacht: 'Get the storm sails on deck!'

Norm Hudson later described the squalls as 'real bottlers'.

The fleet had been warned of the storm hours earlier by Jack Amos, a Qantas flight crew radio operator who was aboard the race's radio relay vessel, *Lauriana*. The following day he made a radio call to the CYCA telling of the storm experience:

> The comparative calm of today is in sharp contrast with last night when we were tossed around like corks. The storm lasted all night and the wind at times reached 55 knots. The gale abated early this morning and at daybreak we were running into a stiff southerly breeze. *Kurrewa* had reported via radio that a huge shark inspected the yacht during the day. It was the biggest ever seen by anyone on board.

John Livingston, the new owner of *Kurrewa IV* with his brother Frank, reported by radio of a great fight the crew had put up to save the mainsail after it had fouled aloft during the gale. The 130-square-metre sail had arrived from England only a week before the race. Livingston said all hands 'had worked furiously on deck'. One of them, Doug Robertson, had climbed the

20-metre mast in the dangerous conditions to free the sail. Robinson had '... battled perilously among the crosstrees for more than half an hour before untangling the sail, while the yacht sliced through the water at a dangerous angle'.

By the morning of Monday 28 December, the gale had been replaced by a flat calm as the leaders entered Bass Strait. Overnight, Jock Muir again exhibited his talent as a yacht designer and ocean racing skipper as *Wild Wave* more than recovered from its poor start to become race leader. Muir wrote in his biography, *Maritime Reflections*, that before the start the decision was made to minimise drag, so the yacht's propeller was removed and the aperture filled in – an action that was then legal under the race rules. He said:

> It was a race of complete weather contrasts; setting off in strong, fair winds down the coast of New South Wales, and 40-knot storms across Bass Strait (where we had a 206 mile spinnaker run in one day); to north-easterlies down the east coast of Tasmania and then a relative calm in the final days.

That same year, the Sydney Hobart went close to seeing its first tragedy. The schooner *Brilliant* was mid-Bass Strait when rigging broke and catapulted crewman Alan Campbell over the side. Incredibly, he was able to hang on to a piece of wire and stay in contact with the yacht: then suddenly, a large wave came along and washed him back onto the deck.

Thousands of locals flocked to the finish line at Battery Point and to the docks when it became obvious that local yachtsman Jock Muir was destined to take line honours with *Wild Wave*, and almost certainly win on corrected time. The apparently victorious *Wild Wave* was welcomed to Hobart with rapturous applause and cheering but sweet soon turned to sour. Numerous protests were lodged against *Wild Wave* following the fracas at the start, and they were upheld by the Protest Committee. The Halvorsen brothers' yacht *Solveig* was then recognised as the winner of line honours while another Sydney sloop, *Ripple*, owned by CYCA member Ron Hobson, was awarded the *Tattersall Cup* as the winner on corrected time. Muir later commented:

> ... it was a hearty welcome we received from Tasmanians
> on our arrival in the Derwent and as we crossed the line,
> but this soon turned to disbelief as the race and fourth
> place on handicap were taken away from us within the
> walls of the Royal Yacht Club of Tasmania.

That aside, the Race Committee was forced to rewrite the rules after the 1953 race. This was due to some yachts in 1951 and again in 1953 cutting the corner at Tasman Island, which is at the eastern entrance to Storm Bay. While it was generally accepted that the 300-metre-high island was to be kept to starboard by race yachts when entering the bay, a number of crews read the fine print and realised that the rules did not stipulate that. So, with the sea and wind conditions being favourable, they sailed through the narrow gap.

*

For the Halvorsen brothers, Trygve and Magnus, being awarded the line honours trophy following the disqualification of *Wild Wave* must have felt like they were receiving an award by default. The family name had been associated with the race since 1946; they built the corrected time winner, *Christina,* and sailed their own yacht, *Saga*, into second place that year, but all subsequent efforts to win had failed. They returned for their eighth try in 1954 – the fifth attempt with their sweetly proportioned, 11-metre-long, double-ended sloop, *Solveig*, which Trygve had designed and the family company built. Fittingly, it was the 1000th vessel – sail, power, military, commercial and pleasure – built by the Halvorsen boat-building business in Sydney. The usual armada of spectator boats was on the water while tens of thousands of avid race followers crammed onto every vantage point on the shore – all to farewell the fleet of seventeen yachts representing five states. There was an additional vantage point that year. A helicopter was hovering over the yachts, filming all the action and colourful scenes for British television. Meanwhile, few people, if any, realised there were two notable absentees from *Solveig*'s crew: Magnus and Trygve had both been laid low the previous day with a gastric illness so severe they were incapable of taking their places on the yacht. All they could do was hand over the helm to their highly respected and talented navigator, Stan Darling, and wish him and the rest of the team good luck. The pair was no doubt disappointed about not being aboard *Solveig*, and it was a bitter-sweet moment when the yacht reached Hobart where *Solveig*, competing in its fifth Hobart race, was declared the winner on corrected time! The victory was attributed to the unrelenting effort by the crew when it came to driving the yacht to its limits in strong winds and big seas, upwind and downwind. The entire fleet had contended with strong southerly headwinds and bold breaking seas as soon as they cleared Sydney Heads. Two days later the wind turned to the north-east, but it was still blowing a gale. Undeterred, the *Solveig* crew pushed the yacht as hard as possible across Bass Strait under spinnaker to the degree where they were forever on the verge of broaching – a rapid, uncontrolled and often violent 90 degree change of course across the wind to where the yacht is usually knocked flat. To keep everyone at 100 per cent concentration when it was their turn to steer, a novel rotation system for the helmsmen was established. Each time the yacht broached, the helmsman at the time was 'sacked', until all five crewmates had had their turn – then they set a smaller spinnaker! As it turned out, the procedure had dire consequences. Crewman Norm Hudson went overboard! He later explained that he was on the foredeck during a spinnaker change when the incident occurred:

> Suddenly a rope beneath me sprang to life. It was attached to the spinnaker going aloft. As the sail filled, it lifted me up into the heavens and over the side. Instantaneously Trevor Gowland darted to the rail as *Solveig* gave a timely lurch to leeward, and he grabbed me by the scruff of the back while I was still in a horizontal position in mid-air, bringing me back to the foredeck.

Solveig led the fleet into Storm Bay only to be snared by a glassy calm. The crew had to then watch in sheer frustration as three yachts sailed around them and led them home. As disappointing as that was, some quick calculations confirmed that *Solveig*'s elapsed time for the course was good enough for it to be declared the outright winner on corrected time. Line honours in that race went to *Kurrewa IV* – formerly *Morna* – which the Livingston brothers had purchased only months earlier from Sir Claude Plowman and renamed.

*

The following year, 1955, the eleventh Hobart race was more a cruise than a race as light weather prevailed for almost the entire distance. Even the final 11 nm from the river entrance to the finish, was a drifter for many of the seventeen competing yachts. One point of interest that year was the return to racing of F.J. Palmer, who had lost his near-completed yacht, to be named *Even*, in the boatyard fire in Sydney just prior to the 1950 race. The new yacht of the same name was almost identical to the one that was destroyed. Palmer's endeavour was well rewarded as *Even,* which had Hobart race legend Jock Muir as sailing master, claimed line honours in what was a lacklustre event. For Hal Evans, the owner of *Moonbi*, persistence finally delivered a dividend. After scoring two second places and a third on corrected time, this was the year where he finally got to stand atop the podium and accept the *Tattersall Cup*.

While this race lacked the dramatic moments and excitement of previous years, the dockside crowd was agog on hearing remarkable news of a shark attack! It came from the crew of *Even* when the yacht reached Hobart. At one stage during the race their speed measuring equipment – a shiny, bullet-shaped spinning device towed behind the yacht on a long line – was attacked and swallowed by a large shark. When the crew pulled in the line the shark was still attached, until it reached the stern of the yacht and disgorged its inedible prey. The enraged shark then fell back into the water and locked its jaws onto the yacht's rudder, shaking it violently. Doubters on the dock were quickly convinced the story was true because the teeth marks in the rudder were there for all to see.

Michael Hesse

SAILING BIO

I started sailing in VJs when I was twelve. I've participated in three *Admirals Cups*, two *Sardinia Cups*, one *Clipper Cup*, five Fastnets and five *Southern Cross Cups* including twenty-seven Hobarts (two wins, numerous top ten finishes and one line honours).

WHAT WAS YOUR BEST DAY SAILING IN THE SYDNEY HOBART?

The 1973 Hobart on *Queequeg*. We ran all the way south under spinnaker in clear sunny weather. We only had to tack once to clear the Heads, and then needed to tack only two more times in the Derwent to reach the finish line.

WHAT DAY OR EXPERIENCE WAS THE TOUGHEST OR MOST CHALLENGING?

The 1975 Hobart on *Mercedes IV*, running all the way south under spinnaker in murky weather to find, on the last morning as the weather cleared, that we had sailed thirty miles past Tasman Island, and had to beat back while watching smaller yachts slip around the Island and reach across to Cape Raoul.

WHAT KEEPS YOU GOING BACK TO THE HOBART RACE?

Nothing – I have no intention of doing another Hobart!

WHAT ARE SOME OF THE BIG CHANGES THAT YOU'VE WITNESSED IN YOUR YEARS ASSOCIATED WITH THE RACE?

Apart from lighter (and much faster) boats relying on crew weight for stability, exact weather forecasting on board each boat, and professional crews who fly out from Hobart before most boats have finished; clearly the biggest change is the ability of the 100-footers to complete the course in a little over a day, often leaving the smaller boats to sail a quite different race with completely different weather patterns.

CHAPTER 7

Sailing Solo

The debut of the new 17.4-metre sloop *Solo* in the 1955 race almost went unnoticed and the yacht's profile was not much higher after the race, as it finished eleventh on corrected time and was no threat for line honours.

But that would change the following year ...

The foundation for the *Solo* story started immediately after the First World War. In 1919, fourteen-year-old Vic Meyer and his older brother were in bunkers in the bowels of a cargo ship shovelling the coal used for its steam engine. It was a work-for-passage arrangement that was taking the brothers from their native Switzerland to South America – the start of a 'see the world' adventure. But, despite their best intentions, this escapade proved to be a brief one. Soon after they reached Buenos Aires, Vic's brother received word from home that he was to inherit their father's successful iron foundry located in Solothurn, in north-western Switzerland. So the brothers returned home.

Six years later, that same spirit of adventure was still flowing through Vic's veins. In August 1925, aged 19, he boarded the migrant passenger ship *Ballarat*, which was bound for Sydney. Once there, he took up accommodation in a boarding house close to the city and found employment in a local foundry. Through hard work and determination it took young Vic just a few years for him to have sufficient funds to establish his own foundry in the inner Sydney suburb of Marrickville. He quickly made a name for himself in the industry and consequently the business became increasingly successful, so much so that in 1946 he rewarded himself by purchasing the 13.8-metre Halvorsen-designed and built motor yacht, *Siesta*. Many maritime adventures followed and Vic's love for the sea grew proportionately. Unfortunately, in mid-1950 *Siesta* was so badly damaged in a fire it was deemed to be not worth salvaging. Undeterred, Meyer immediately started to look for a new boat and just four months later, in October that year, he bought one of the most impressive vessels on Sydney Harbour, the 21-metre double-ended cruising ketch, *Lauriana*. He became a member of the CYCA and, soon after, stepped up to assist the club's efforts to purchase the waterfront premises in Rushcutters Bay by joining with Merv Davey and Colonel Albert Saalfeld to guarantee the loan from the Bank of New South Wales that was needed to secure what would become the club's headquarters.

Meyer's relationship with the club continued to strengthen to the degree where, in 1952, he provided *Lauriana* for the role of radio relay vessel for that year's Hobart race. The round trip to Hobart and back was a life-changing experience for him. During the return voyage from Hobart to Sydney he got to experience, for the first time, passage-making under full sail. As the ketch cruised through the afternoon and into the evening, Meyer realised he had found a new love and convinced himself that extended cruising under sail was far more pleasurable than being under power. Some years later, in his biography, *Man of Iron, Ship of Steel*, Meyer is quoted as saying: 'We were sailing up the coast without the engine, which had stopped for some reason, and I realised how wonderful it was. So quiet; and we were going just as fast.'

Meyer's thoughts became locked into cruising under sail, and that led to him sitting down with Alan Payne and discussing his concept for a new yacht. Payne wasn't sure about a steel hull, but Meyer was emphatic for two reasons: strength; and the fact that the yacht would not leak. Initially the plan was for a sloop measuring 14.3 metres overall, but Meyer's demand for a powerful 100 horsepower diesel engine, and a comfortable cruising interior, saw it stretched to 17.4 metres.

Construction of the yacht started in early 1954 and on 2 January 1955 it was launched and christened *Solo* – the name being an abridged tribute to Solothurn, the region in Switzerland where Meyer spent his childhood.

On seeing the yacht for the first time many of the local experts were sceptical about the concept, even though it floated perfectly on the designer's lines. The principal concerns aired by these naysayers were that it was too heavy, would rust and would not live up to performance expectations.

Time would tell...

*

While the design parameters for *Solo* were based around cruising, the yacht's speed under sail on Sydney Harbour and short passages off the coast had many experienced sailors convinced that it could be competitive as an ocean racer. So, not surprisingly, Meyer was soon lured by friends at the CYCA into doing some short coastal races, and the results were not disappointing.

Meyer obviously enjoyed those offshore experiences because, only a matter of months later, *Solo* was entered in the 1955 Hobart race and from the day the race started Vic Meyer became an ocean racing aficionado.

Despite *Solo*'s disappointing result in that year – fourth across the line and eleventh on handicap – there was no holding back Meyer's desire to be a starter in the 1956 race. His preparations led to him improving the rigging by purchasing a number of new sails, and assembling a highly experienced crew.

The fleet of twenty-eight was equal in size to the record number of starters in 1947. The breakdown of the entries saw sixteen yachts from New South Wales, six from Victoria, four from Tasmania and two from South Australia. As expected, much of the public focus was on the classic *Kurrewa IV,* which was chasing a fifth line honours, while the Halvorsen brothers' new sloop, *Anitra V,* was the favourite among experienced offshore sailors who were looking for the likely winner on corrected time. There was only cursory interest for one-year-old *Solo.*

The composition of the fleet confirmed that the race was going through a significant transition period. The old-style, heavy-displacement cruising yachts no longer made up the bulk of the entries. Instead, they were being replaced by modern designs that targeted performance. Heavy cotton and canvas sails were being superseded by sails made from synthetic fabric, in particular terylene and nylon. Additionally, race organisers had placed a greater emphasis on safety. They drafted new regulations relating to all facets of the sport, and went to considerable lengths to ensure every yacht met the required standards.

The popular topic among the competing sailors who were enjoying a few beers in the CYCA's bar on the eve of the race was the weather forecast. A strong southerly change was predicted for the first night at sea, and indications were that it would be heavy going almost all the way to Hobart. That was an understatement! What eventuated was the roughest, toughest and most challenging Hobart race in its eleven-year history.

*

Media reports relating to the start confirmed that the race had not lost its popularity. On the water, some 2000 spectators were aboard boats of all shapes and sizes milling around the start line. It was one of those boats that provided the most drama during the countdown. The magnificent 20-metre-long cutter *Kurrewa IV*, was manoeuvring for the start when a small spectator boat, which had two young ladies sitting atop the cabin, crossed the yacht's bow. The inevitable collision resulted in the ladies being hurled into the water. That led to another spectator boat weaving its way through the race yachts and rushing to their aid, but in its haste it struck the two women. Both were subsequently rescued and taken to hospital suffering arm, chest and back injuries.

When the New South Wales Governor, Sir John Northcott, fired the starting cannon, *Kurrewa IV* did as expected by leading the fleet through Sydney Heads and onto the open sea, and continued to lead going into the evening.

A sample of the conditions that lay ahead came on the first night when a solid change roared in unannounced from the south-west and caught the majority of crews unaware, none more so than the crew of *Wraith of Odin*. In a matter of seconds the yacht was at an alarming angle of heel, shuddering and shaking until there was the sickening sound of the timber mainmast splintering and crashing over the side. Worse still, as it fell, some loose rigging caught on the mizzen mast and levelled that as well. About the same time, *Southern Myth*'s forestay snapped like a dry twig, causing the mast to bend like an archer's bow. Only quick action by the crew and helmsman kept the rig in place. *Southern Myth* was then Sydney-bound.

Kurrewa IV revelled in the tough going overnight and opened up a 40 nm lead over *Solo* and *Anitra V* at Green Cape, which is recognised as the entrance to Bass Strait. But there was no welcome mat waiting for the fleet; a second and equally savage front rolled in from the south-west, bringing with it howling winds and large breaking seas. These conditions were tailor-made for *Solo* which closed the gap on *Kurrewa IV.*

Meanwhile, some distance astern, the 11-metre schooner *Ranston* speared off the top of a mighty wave and crashed into the trough that followed with such force that hull planks split open and water began gushing in. A mayday call went out by radio while the crew manned the pumps and buckets in a desperate bid to keep the yacht afloat. At that stage the north-east coast of Tasmania was closer than mainland Australia, so the crippled yacht was held on a course to the south.

Phil Davies, who was one of the eight crew aboard that yacht, explained what happened:

> It was impossible to stop the leak, and as time went on, and there being no sign of help, we began to get really worried. On the second day the leak got worse. We were working in bailing shifts to fight the water – three men on buckets and one on the pump. By Monday we were bailing desperately in shifts of 30 minutes and then collapsing in an attempt to get some sleep. At that time we had given up hope of sailing the yacht to land. We were getting ready to abandon ship when a southerly buster hit us 80 miles east of Eddystone Lighthouse and our rubber dinghy and lifebelts went overboard. By then, land seemed to be a million miles away. We were forced to use bottles to bail because our hands were red raw and our arms felt like lead weights. We were at the end of our tether when we heard a shout outside. It was a fisherman aboard a trawler hailing us. We had never seen anything so wonderful. He got us undertow and headed for Oyster Bay, 30 miles away, while we still bailed to keep the yacht afloat.

Ranston sank while being beached in Oyster Bay.

While the *Ranston* drama was unfolding, another of the smaller entries, *Vailima*, owned by Jim McLaren, was also in danger of sinking.

McLaren was an enthusiastic member of the CYCA who found himself in this predicament in a circuitous way. He competed in his first Hobart race in 1953 as a member of the crew of *Gipsy Queen*, which finished tenth across the line and tenth on handicap. The experience was enough to convince him that he should build his own ocean racing yacht, so having made that decision he set about dealing with the most difficult task first – finding the lead ballast needed for the keel.

With it being only a few years since the war, lead was still in very short supply, so no doubt McLaren thought he had struck gold when he saw an advertisement in a newspaper offering a suitable amount of the precious product for sale. He high-tailed it to the address in the advertisement, located in Sydney's south, met the seller and asked if he could see the lead. The owner then casually pointed to a small yacht moored in the bay behind the house and said, 'It's out there under that!' After going out to the yacht and having a good look at it, McLaren did some quick calculations and a deal was struck: he bought the lead and the yacht attached to it!

Over the next few years that yacht became the focus of family fun for Jim, his wife Joy and their four daughters, all of whom loved sailing. One of those daughters – Kay – became so passionate about being under sail that some years later she went on to be recognised across Australia and internationally for a remarkable achievement: in 1988, Kay Cottee became the first woman to sail single-handed, non-stop and unassisted around the world.

While enjoying happy family times aboard the yacht, Jim did not lose sight of his ultimate goal to race his own yacht to

Hobart. That led to him selling the family yacht and entering the 1956 Hobart race with his new acquisition, *Vailima*, a 9.1-metre-long double-ended sloop.

The yacht was prepared for the race, but with 48 hours to go to the start, McLaren had a major problem – no navigator! His only hope was to pin a note on the CYCA noticeboard under the 'crew wanted' category. Soon after, a chap remembered only as John answered the call. McLaren quickly decided John had the necessary qualifications to get the yacht to Hobart safely, so welcomed him aboard *Vailima* as navigator.

Soon after the start, 'John the navigator' proposed that the initial course should take the yacht well offshore, to the 100 fathom line, where it should pick up a favourable south-flowing current. He then became violently seasick, so disappeared below deck and was not seen for three days. He later wrote:

When I came to, the boat was becalmed: ate some baked beans, had a glass of rum and felt OK. There was no sun so I was unable to demonstrate my navigator skills with my sextant. The boat had done some 200 miles through some quite rough seas but we were out of sight of land and nobody had a clue where we were. My decision to go out to the 100 fathom line, 20 miles out to sea, had taken care of that; there was no point in apologising to anyone concerning this or to explain how a veteran seaman became seasick. Fortunately for my ego, half the crew were sick as well.

At the time, Jim McLaren described the race as being one where not much happened, but his recollection over four decades later confirmed that plenty did in fact happen:

> We had a southerly when we cleared Sydney Heads, another southerly change off the New South Wales south coast, then a third, a beauty, as we entered Bass Strait. Three bloody fronts before we got to halfway. The last one was from the south-west. The wind got to 86 knots – bloody hard. I don't think the seas were as big as those experienced in the 1998 race, but the same wind and rain were certainly there. You couldn't sail in it. We had to go down to bare poles. We did manage to set the sea anchor but it took only one big wave to break the rope attached to it. The same wave took out the forward hatch. After that we could only run with it. We felt like we were heading for New Zealand. I was getting a bit worried because we could only hang on and hope. We were like that for 24 hours.

Vailima was nearly inverted when it was rolled by the huge wave that took the sea anchor with it and ripped off the forward hatch. When the yacht came upright, it was half-full of water, the batteries and engine were under water, and the two-way radio had taken a bath. Also, it was soon realised that the yacht's inflatable dinghy and lifebuoy had gone overboard.

Everyone was bailing frantically but, with the forward hatch missing, it was a losing battle. One of the crew then realised that the timber chart table lid was about the same size as the forward hatch, so it was removed from its mountings and handed to John, along with a hammer and nails. He had volunteered to go on deck and crawl forward in the hope he could cover the hatch hole with the lid. He did so – a remarkably brave move considering he was not wearing a safety harness and that *Vailima* did not have any lifelines.

Through a valiant effort by the crew, *Vailima* remained afloat, but John was still unable to confirm its position. He explained:

> The boat continued towards New Zealand at a frightening rate but eventually we were able to turn round and head back to where we thought Tasmania should be. On 4 January the sky briefly cleared and I was able to get our latitude by sextant. That gave us a reasonable idea of where Hobart should be, but we didn't know how far away it was.

With both *Vailima* and *Ranston* being unable to transmit position reports, there was growing concern back on shore regarding their wellbeing. Newspaper headlines were already suggesting that both yachts may have sunk. *Ranston's* fate became known when it reached Oyster Bay, but it was some days before *Vailima's* lot was established when the crew of a light plane spotted it near Storm Bay.

*

There was only a faint breeze blowing when *Solo* led *Kurrewa IV* into Storm Bay, 40 nm from the finish, but *Kurrewa IV* proved its superiority in those conditions and took the lead. However, it wasn't long before a 70-knot south-westerly gale roared in. From that moment, it became a hammer and tongs battle for the honour of being first into Hobart. Both crews knew that to reduce sail would mean capitulation. Then suddenly the *Solo* crew had the decision whether or not to reef the mainsail made for them when the sail could no longer cope with the pressure of the wind and blew apart.

Solo's crew could then only watch as *Kurrewa IV* sailed away to take line honours by the narrowest margin in the race's twelve-year history – 32 minutes 16 seconds. But the greatest prize was *Solo*'s, whose corrected time for the course could not be beaten in the race for the *Tattersall Cup*. *Solo* was the race winner.

Vic Meyer had arrived!

David Kellett

SAILING BIO

I have ocean raced out of the CYCA since 1968 and have participated in forty-five Hobart races: participating in twenty-six and subsequently, for the past nineteen years, being responsible for the safety net aboard the radio relay vessel. I've also competed in two *America's Cups*, as well as the Bermuda and Fastnet races.

WHAT WAS YOUR BEST DAY SAILING IN THE SYDNEY HOBART?

Taking line honours and the handicap, as skipper aboard *Sovereign* in the 1987 race, thus becoming the first Australian yacht to take the double. Bernard Lewis, the owner, had given me a marvellous opportunity to assist with the design and supervision of the construction and then sailing the 83-foot maxi yacht.

WHAT DAY OR EXPERIENCE WAS THE TOUGHEST OR MOST CHALLENGING?

During the 1970 race, aboard the Cole 43 *Bacardi*, we experienced 60–70 knot winds for more than 18 hours with big seas. (I was aboard Charles Curran's *Sydney* in the 1998 race, and we were forced to turn back with rudder problems before the weather bomb hit.)

WHAT KEEPS YOU GOING BACK TO THE HOBART RACE?

Initially it was the challenge, but now it's the camaraderie and, by conducting the radio skeds with the fleet, giving something back to the sport I have been so passionate about since I was a young boy.

WHAT ARE SOME OF THE BIG CHANGES THAT YOU'VE WITNESSED IN YOUR YEARS ASSOCIATED WITH THE RACE?

The increased awareness and training of safety among all crews and the thorough checking of the suitability of the yachts in construction and stability. Also, the speed and efficiency of the yachts.

CHAPTER 8

A Word from the Master

In the weeks preceding the 1957 Hobart Race, Captain John Illingworth, whose few fateful words 12 years earlier led to the creation of the classic, penned a personal note in London and forwarded it to the CYCA Commodore, Merv Davey:

Many races have been sailed since we crossed the line in 1945 for the first Sydney Hobart. At the time, it was in the minds of some of us that we might be laying the foundations of the third of the world's classic ocean races, and it is good to know that our hopes were not unfounded.

By happy chance, the length of the course matched that of the other two – the Fastnet and the Bermuda Races. By happy chance, also, the course provided one of the most sporting and interesting passages imaginable. At least one complete change in wind and weather can be relied on; and more often several of these. Strong winds are usual, but most races include a patch or two of light wind racing, calling for other crewing and skippering techniques.

I had planned to bring the *Mouse of Malham* to race again in 1955/56. We had won the Championship here at home in our class in 1954 and we were longing to race again with you, particularly the Olympic Year. Unfortunately, my mother's illness prevented this, but it is my firm intention someday, Dieu Voulant [God willing], to have another go.

By the same token, I hope very much that one of the modern Australian yachts will come over and make a strong bid for the Fastnet someday soon, or, if this should prove impracticable, we would always welcome an Australian crew and arrange for them to take over one of our better boats.

I sometimes wonder whether it is realised in Australia how much interest is aroused here in Britain, year by year, by the Sydney Hobart. But it is a fact that the renown of the event is world-wide.

And, so the great game goes on, and the race gains stature year by year. Good sailing to all of you who are going this year. I wish I could be with you.

The CYCA membership reacted accordingly: Captain John Illingworth RN, the 'Father of the Sydney Hobart Yacht Race', was elected a Life Member of the club.

*

Over the 75 years of the Sydney Hobart Yacht Race the CYCA has been recognised as a world leader when it comes to issues relating to safety in ocean racing. That was certainly the case in 1957 when the club announced that two-way radios would be a requirement for all competing yachts, and that regular and compulsory radio 'skeds' (schedules) during the race were to be established. Apart from the safety aspects associated with this directive, the radio 'skeds' would be of great value to the media reporting on the race and also provide a comfort zone for the families and friends of competitors.

Even so, the new regulation did not sit comfortably with all yacht owners. For example, Tasmanian yachtsman Dudley Burridge, who contested the 1955 race with his yacht *Fantasy*, wrote to the CYCA:

> Once again the small boat is being forced to carry more weight, the smaller crew will have more work to do and in general will suffer more than the larger craft. Surely we must be the only country in the world where such a requirement is made for ocean racing. I am sure that no owner of a boat of less than 35ft in Tasmania at present will be willing to buy one. In the event of an urgent emergency I would say no radio would be of any assistance and in an ordinary emergency the navigational problems seem to suggest little hope for assistance without a lot of luck. No seaman should rely on such doubtful assistance in considering his safety at sea.

The new rule remained in place.

From the early hours of Boxing Day 1957, the crews of the twenty yachts contesting the race were all smiles. A brisk westerly wind was whipping up white caps across Sydney Harbour, confirmation of the weather prognosis suggesting it could be a record-breaking race. A few hours later, when the fleet was lining up for the 11am start, the surface of the harbour looked something like a snowfield as wind gusts in excess of 40 knots ripped in from the west and turned the water white. It could only make for a spectacular start.

The Livingston brothers' cutter, *Kurrewa IV*, which was the largest yacht in the fleet by some three metres over *Solo*, did as expected and led the charge towards the Heads while clocking an impressive 10 knots. But before long *Solo* began to throw out a challenge until the helmsman was forced to make a dramatic change of course to avoid a collision with the classic, 50-metre-long Sydney Harbour pilot ship, *Captain Cook III*, which for some inexplicable reason held its course and demanded right-of-way over the fleet.

Once the yachts cleared the Heads the crews experienced Five Star conditions – sails were eased and a downwind course was set directly towards Bass Strait.

Unfortunately for Bill – later Sir William – Northam, his Hobart race debut was to be short-lived. His stylish sloop, *Caprice of Huon* looked very impressive until a savage westerly squall brought about a rigging failure, and with that the timber mast went crashing over the side in countless pieces.

As evening approached there was another drama, this time aboard *Kurrewa IV*. A powerful gust of wind caused the yacht to heel dramatically, and the resulting wave of water that surged along the leeward deck washed two crewmen, 'Jumbo' Gothard and Scotty Macbeth, over the side. Incredibly, both were able to grab rigging as they went and hang on until crew could rush to their aid and drag them back aboard. They were uninjured.

The following two days and nights at sea saw the crews of the leading yachts *Kurrewa IV, Solo, Anitra V* and Mac Brown's *Catriona* experiencing exhilarating rides down the New South Wales south coast, across Bass Strait and on towards the next major turning point, Tasman Island.

The *Catriona* crew told of an amazing and unprecedented spinnaker run across the Strait. A 40 plus knot northerly wind drove the yacht so hard down the face of the big waves that it was like a surfboat in full flight. At times a massive and roaring white bow wave burst skywards, two metres above the deck on both sides.

Meanwhile, race leader *Kurrewa IV* was setting a cracking pace, covering more than 200 nm in a day. It was an achievement that would be recognised at the time as one of the best runs ever in international yacht racing history.

Unfortunately for the smaller and slower entries, the wind faded to a bare breath off Tasmania's east coast, but worse still, an oily calm was awaiting them when they rounded Tasman Island and entered Storm Bay. Regardless, Tom Flower and his crew aboard *Eos* decided to make good of the time: they cast out the lines and caught 15 large fish.

Kurrewa IV did as the pundits predicted by taking line honours and setting a new course record time: 3 days 18 hours 30 minutes and 39 seconds – 7 hours 58 minutes and 25 seconds inside the record set by *Margaret Rintoul* in 1951. Making this result even more meritorious was the fact that this was the big yacht's sixth line honours; an achievement that was admired in offshore sailing circles the world over.

However, the biggest celebration in Hobart awaited Trygve and Magnus Halvorsen aboard *Anitra V.* Finally, after years of trying, the ocean racing brothers had the unforgettable experience of sailing their yacht to a win on corrected time, and consequently got to hold the *Tattersall Cup* aloft for all to see.

*

In the latter half of the 1950s the CYCA had an active fleet of yachts that contested short ocean races out of Sydney on a regular basis. Many of the competing yachts participated in those races as part of their preparation for that year's Hobart race.

Sadly, one such race, staged on the weekend of 14–15 June 1958, over a course from Sydney Harbour to Bird Island, 45 nm to the north, then back to Pittwater, was struck by a tragedy.

It involved the famed Hobart race line honours yacht *Kurrewa IV.*

At the time the yacht was returning from Pittwater to Sydney Harbour on the morning of Sunday 15 June. It was off North Head and only a short distance from entering Sydney Harbour when a 70–80 knot south-westerly squall descended unannounced from the clifftops and hammered the yacht. The staysail blew to shreds almost immediately and the yacht began to heel alarmingly. The crew rushed to lower the remaining sails; a near impossible task in the conditions.

The vertical cliffs of North Head, where a mighty surf was breaking, were rapidly becoming a serious threat to the yacht, so *Kurrewa IV*'s internationally acclaimed helmsman, Ron Robertson, was doing everything possible to regain control and get steerage. Without warning, *Kurrewa IV* speared its bow through a large wave which swept along the deck and into the cockpit.

'The wave knocked me into the scuppers,' crewmen Fred Thomas later recalled.

> Ron was gone! I saw him in the water. Someone immediately threw a life ring and he got into it. The yacht was stalled so we didn't have steerage. We saw Ron in the water for maybe 10 minutes or so, but we couldn't get momentum to pull the yacht away and get back to him. The motor wouldn't start and lots of water was coming in.
>
> Ron disappeared! But, just prior to that, I could still see him and he waved to us. It was not a wave as in 'Oh shit, I am in trouble!' It was as if to say, 'Just stay calm, I'm gone! Save the boat.'

The crew caught one last glimpse of Robertson just after they managed to get the yacht under control. He was close to the rocks in a position where it would have been impossible for them to reach him in any safe manner.

*

There had been a sprinkling of international entries in the thirteen Hobart races prior to 1958, but they were all cruising-oriented designs whose owners were participating more for the pleasure than the prizes. But in 1958 an entry was received that confirmed the high standing the race then held on the international scene. Prominent and successful English ocean racing yachtsman Geoffrey Pattinson shipped his successful 11.6-metre offshore racing sloop, *Uomie,* from London to Sydney in the hope he could repeat Illingworth's effort in 1945 and take top honours. There was also a historic element associated with his entry – *Uomie* would become the first yacht in the world to compete in the three majors: the Fastnet, the Newport to Bermuda and the Hobart.

Once more *Kurrewa IV* and *Solo* were expected to fight for line honours, but there was also an unknown element to the battle. The Livingston brothers had decided to fit a more modern rig in their yacht, and had made a wardrobe of new, more efficient sails, all in a bid to stave off the inevitable challenge from the ever-improving *Solo.* In its eight Hobart race starts, *Kurrewa IV* (previously *Morna*) had been first to finish on six occasions and set the record time mark for the course. Unfortunately though, while *Kurrewa IV* was crashing and bashing its way across Bass Strait in a 40-knot southerly headwind, the power of the new rig proved to be too much for the ageing hull; caulking between the hull planks began to fall out, and with that, water started pouring in. The only option was to turn and run for Eden while crew manned the pumps and bailed with buckets.

It was a similar scenario for Don Mickleborough's ageing sloop *Southerly.* The power of the wind coupled with the thunderous pounding from the head-seas caused the seams between the hull planks near the bow to open up and consequently a significant amount of caulking fell out. When the level of the water reached bunk height it became obvious that the amount of water coming in exceeded what they could bail out with buckets and pumps, so Mickleborough sent out an SOS by radio. However, soon after, the crew traced the source of the leak and quickly stemmed the flow by jamming strips torn from tea towels into the cracks.

No doubt Mickleborough – who over the next decades became one of the more colourful characters associated with the race – was pleased two-way radios had been made compulsory. Even so, while the daily radio reports from the fleet back to the radio relay vessel were being received, there was growing concern for one yacht that had not been heard from since the start, Sydneysider Graham Newland's 11.6-metre-long sloop, *Siandra*.

With *Kurrewa IV* retired, the race for line honours became a great battle between *Solo* and Sir Arthur Warner's 15.8-metre ketch, *Winston Churchill*. It took the two yachts six days to reach the Derwent after their progress was slowed dramatically by a large area of calm off Tasmania's east coast. At the mouth of the Derwent *Solo* held a narrow lead over '*Churchill*', which, despite having set a huge spinnaker, was unable to close the gap. Vic Meyer kept the momentum going with *Solo* and sailed on to his first ever Hobart Race line honours prize by just 14 minutes!

At that stage it was anyone's guess as to which yacht would win the *Tattersall Cup*, and with *Siandra*'s position still unknown because its radio remained on the blink, there was added intrigue until later that day when the crew of a spotter plane sighted the yacht in Storm Bay. After a quick calculation it became apparent that if the wind held for *Siandra* it would almost certainly be the winner. *Siandra* did excel in the conditions as the navigator's log revealed: '0700 hours – going like a rocket. 1600 hours – Sailing like a bat out of Hell.'

That year the *Tattersall Cup* belonged to Graham Newland and *Siandra*.

Englishman Geoffrey Pattinson sailed *Uomie* into fourth place on line honours and fifth on corrected time. Once moored in Constitution Dock he declared to the waiting media: 'Your ocean racing technique is like the Americans' and somewhat better than ours.'

*

In 1959 – 3 years after television was introduced to Australia – the Sydney Hobart race laid claim to a world first: the start of the race was televised live to audiences across Australia. Neither the Fastnet Race nor the Newport to Bermuda Race had ever been featured in this way.

The thirty starters that year made for a record fleet, two more than in 1947 and in 1956. The regular combatants, *Kurrewa IV* and *Solo*, were tipped to duel again for line honours while it was anyone's guess as to which yacht would win on corrected time.

In what was seemingly becoming a tradition, the fleet copped a hammering out of the south during the first night. Norm Howard, the skipper of *Southern Myth* and the veteran of six Hobart races, put things into perspective: 'It was the most ugly storm squall I have ever seen. It came at about 70 mph and lasted about an hour. The most horrifying thing was when it whipped up a waterspout near us.'

Within 24 hours, though, the Hobart had become a downwind race, conditions that saw *Kurrewa IV* open up a 20 mile lead over *Solo*. But the advantage was to be short-lived: another southerly gale was tailor-made for *Solo*. Meyer and his crew elected to take an offshore course and were consequently rewarded with line honours by 40 minutes over *Kurrewa IV*. This would also prove to be a historic and notable race for yacht designer, Alan Payne. Apart from having designed *Solo*, the corrected time winner *Cherana* was one of his exciting new 11-metre Tasman Seabird class yachts, a design he created with the Hobart race specifically in mind.

In 1960 the Sydney Hobart race's reputation for being one of the roughest toughest ocean racing tests in the world was shattered. It was as if, through divine intervention, the Tasman Sea and Bass Strait had finally been tamed. In fact, for many skippers the most challenging part of the 628 nm course was the first 3 miles from the start line to Sydney Heads. Thousands of small craft, the majority crammed tight with spectators, had descended on the harbour and created a virtual obstacle course through which the yachts had to weave their way to reach the open sea. However, there was one crew among the thirty-two contesting the race that came well prepared: they had a crewman perched on the bow armed with a loudhailer, his sole task being to 'politely' warn those aboard spectator boats how to keep out of the yacht's way.

There was renewed interest in the race for line honours with Peter Warner arriving on the scene with his elegant 22.2-metre schooner *Astor*, the largest yacht ever to contest the race. *Kurrewa IV* had a massive spread of sails set, and the power that generated drove it into the lead soon after the start.

Kurrewa IV, Astor and *Solo* vied for the lead across Bass Strait and down Tasmania's east coast until Hobart legend, Jock Muir, played his local knowledge card and took *Kurrewa IV* close to the coast in search of better breeze. It was found and consequently the big boat got across the line in Hobart with an advantage of more than 2 hours over *Solo* and 4 hours over *Astor*.

The race for handicap honours was even more intense with *Siandra* and the similar-sized *Kaleena, Malohi, Rival, Norla, Joanne Brodie* and *Janzoon* all in with a chance.

Here again it was a tactical move off the coast that decided the result. Graham Newland took the gamble and sailed *Siandra* through the narrow and reef-strewn waters around the Hippolyte Rocks (just 6 nm north of Tasman Island) at night. There were anxious moments. Newland later recalled:

> We knew we might run aground, but our odds of
> succeeding were improved by the fact that the seas were
> calm and the wind light. I had some of the crew lie on
> their bellies at the bow, shining torches onto the bottom
> so we could pick our way through the rocks.

In a remarkably close finish *Siandra* claimed the *Tattersall Cup* for the second time, this time by just 16 minutes over *Kaleena* with another 33 minutes to *Malohi*.

*

The 1960s proved to be a spectacular period in the evolution of the Sydney Hobart race. It came in the form of exciting new yachts; strong international interest in the race; and breakthroughs in yacht design, construction and equipment; plus some party antics that are now entrenched in yachting folklore.

The 1961 race broke new ground when popular Sydney yachtsman Russell Slade entered Australia's first ocean racing yacht built from fibreglass, the 12.2-metre sloop, *Janzoon II*.

Slade's passage through life to this point had been an interesting one. He attributed much of his commercial success in life to sailing; school held little appeal for him, both academically and in sport. However, the moment he set sail in a small dinghy that all changed: he knew he had found his vocation in life. In no time sailing became his passion and within a few years he became the youngest person ever to win a New South Wales State Championship in the 16 foot skiff class.

Commercial success followed. At a young age, intuition and research convinced Slade and his brother, Hermon, there was a future in plastics so they established Polymer Corporation. The company provided a considerable amount of product to the war effort, then continued post-war as a successful chemical business in Australia. Slade later explained it was a perfect commercial match: 'My brother was a chemical genius but couldn't sell a thing, but I could.'

Some years later, when he had grown to enjoy offshore racing, Slade became chairman of the large Australian clothing manufacturer Bonds Industries. In the mid-1950s he purchased the ten-year-old, 12.8-metre sloop, *Janzoon*, and raced it to Hobart in 1955, '56 and '57, his best place being third on handicap in 1955.

During this period Slade and his highly experienced crew began to consider the next yacht; the consensus being that they should look to the future and start with a clean slate. There was no doubt Alan Payne was the man for the design, and that it was worthwhile considering fibreglass as the construction material. Slade and his crew would have known that just a few years earlier five enthusiastic sailors in Oregon, USA, decided to build the Chinook 32, the first yacht to be constructed from the then revolutionary material, fibreglass. They then put the Chinook 34 into production and it proved to be a huge commercial success; they built 600 boats in the first 3 years of business.

Slade's knowledge of plastics complemented Payne's penchant for being a pioneer in his field and the decision was made: *Janzoon II* would be the first all-fibreglass ocean racing yacht in Australia, possibly the world. For Payne, this project was also a stimulating diversion away from his other major project – the design of Australia's first America's Cup challenger, *Gretel*.

The design task for *Janzoon II* was a two-year program. Payne worked hard to grow his knowledge of fibreglass structures while at the same time looking to extract every possible advantage there was to be had under the RORC (Royal Ocean Racing Club) design rules – the handicap rule at the time. Consequently, *Janzoon II*'s hull shape was unlike anything seen before: pinched in at both the bow and the stern to gain measurement advantages and a long, flat underwater section back aft. In profile it was not dissimilar to Payne's already proven Tasman Seabird design.

The new, pale-blue hulled *Janzoon II* was part of the record fleet of thirty-five for the 1961 race and destined to start as one of the favourites for a handicap win. It was also a record when it came to the number of spectators at the start on Boxing Day with the media quoting a figure of 500,000.

This Hobart would prove to be a superb event – an excellent challenge for the entire fleet in widely varying conditions – rough seas and gale force winds for the first 48 hours then light conditions off the Tasmanian coast. It caused Trygve Halvorsen to comment in Hobart: 'It was the finest all-round test of a vessel and crew I've yet experienced in a Sydney Hobart race.'

There was an additional drama on the first night at sea – a man-made one: the crew of *Sylvena* spotted a rusting World War II mine wallowing in the waves off Jervis Bay. Race organisers and all competing yachts were advised by radio of the danger and a search was initiated by the navy, but it was not sighted again.

The battle for the honour of being first to Hobart turned into a rollercoaster ride: at one stage *Solo* led the schooner *Astor* by some 50 nm, but at dawn on the fourth day at sea the *Solo* crew could not believe their eyes. *Astor* was on the horizon, six miles ahead! Astor went on to claim line honours by 48 minutes, a result that prompted *Solo*'s skipper, Vic Meyer, to declare: 'It's what the Lord gives that we take advantage of in ocean racing. I was beaten by a good boat and an excellent crew.'

Making *Astor*'s win even more meritorious was the realisation that the yacht had been 'wounded' for almost all the distance from Sydney. The pounding it took from a 60-knot blow during the first 24 hours caused some planks to open up and water to rush in at a rapid rate. The crew was forced to man the pumps for 20 minutes in every hour for the rest of the passage to Hobart.

Alby Burgin and Nelson Rundle's 10.7-metre-long sloop, *Rival*, from Lake Macquarie, was the winner on corrected time over the fibreglass *Janzoon II* by little more than 30 minutes.

Peter Shipway

SAILING BIO

I've chalked up thirty-one Sydney Hobart races for two overall victories and five line honours wins. Additionally, I've sailed in eight *Admiral's Cup* series for Australia (for first, second and third – one as Australian team captain), two *Southern Cross Cup* victories, eight Fastnet races and one *America's Cup* in Newport, Rhode Island.

WHAT WAS YOUR BEST DAY SAILING IN THE SYDNEY HOBART?

Sailing up the Derwent River in a fresh and squally southerly to capture overall victory in the 1974 race aboard *Love & War*.

WHAT DAY OR EXPERIENCE WAS THE TOUGHEST OR MOST CHALLENGING?

Losing the 1985 race on protest after being declared the provisional overall winner aboard *Drake's Prayer*.

WHAT KEEPS YOU GOING BACK TO THE HOBART RACE?

Boxing Day is special – a unique experience – along with the friendships and camaraderie among the crew throughout the race. Also, the rugged beauty of Tasman Island and Cape Raoul. Finally, the finish up the river and in Hobart is unequalled anywhere in the world.

WHAT ARE SOME OF THE BIG CHANGES THAT YOU'VE WITNESSED IN YOUR YEARS ASSOCIATED WITH THE RACE?

My first Hobart race took 6 days 1 hour and 42 minutes (1968 aboard *Cavalier*). Forty years later we took 1 day 20 hours and 34 minutes (aboard *Wild Oats XI*). Apart from the shrinking duration, I've witnessed breathtaking progress in design, equipment and the skill of the crews.

CHAPTER 9

The 'Yankee Yawl', Delphine and a Submarine!

It was inevitable that the Sydney Hobart race and New York shipping magnate, Huey Long, would come together one year and 1962 was that year.

In the eyes of many, Long could be described as a 'Pot Hunter' – he loved ocean racing and lived to win trophies, especially at major international events like the Fastnet Race and the Newport to Bermuda.

Now, with the Sydney Hobart having been contested on fifteen occasions, Long and his magnificent new 17.4-metre aluminium yawl, *Ondine*, were lured into the southern hemisphere and on to Sydney for the 1962 race.

By Australian standards the no-expense-spared *Ondine* was a showstopper. It was the world's first all-aluminium ocean racer so, quite understandably, everything about it appeared to be superior to anything seen locally – hull, fittings, fit-out, mast and sails. Unprecedented crowds flocked to the CYCA just to ogle at this two-masted beauty with its heavily varnished timber work that shimmered in the sun.

Despite it having been raced hard since its launch, and having sailed all the way from the US to Australia just to contest the Hobart race, a number of local 'experts' had qualms about the 'Yankee Yawl': principally the structural integrity of its aluminium hull, and its stability should it be a rough race, mainly because *Ondine* was fitted with a retractable centreboard instead of the conventional fixed keel.

They need not have wasted their time worrying, even though *Ondine* didn't get it all its own way from start to finish.

Watching the start of the Hobart race had, by this time, become very much a Boxing Day tradition in Sydney. So, as usual, tens of thousands of spectators made the pilgrimage to vantage points around the harbour, or onto spectator boats of all shapes and sizes. It was an overcast day where the two-masted *Ondine*, with its snow-white sails and a large Stars and Stripes ensign flying proudly from the stern, was a stand-out.

With *Ondine*'s reputation preceding it, no one was surprised when it bolted away from the record fleet of forty-two starters and led them all to the Heads. But seasoned sailing souls were quick to remind the uninitiated that this was a Hobart race and only 3 of the 628 nm had been covered. Minutes later their words rang true. As the leading yachts rounded South Head, and sails were trimmed to suit a course to the south, Peter Warner's mighty *Astor* picked up pace then powered past *Ondine* and into the lead.

A day later *Ondine*'s predicament was a lot worse: it was trailing *Astor, Solo, Winston Churchill, Ruthean* and *Ilina*, the latter yacht owned by prominent young Australian media man Rupert Murdoch, who was making his Hobart race debut.

The pressure was on, and consequently, before the day was done, *Ondine*'s highly respected Australian navigator, Bill Fesq, (the only Australian on board) opted to risk his trump card and sail an offshore course down the Tasmanian coast. Less than 24 hours later, when Tasman Island was reached, the *Ondine* crew was elated. They could see *Astor* on the horizon ahead – becalmed!

When *Astor* finally broke free of its windless predicament, line honours and a race record time still looked a certainty – if the wind held. But soon after rounding The Iron Pot and entering the Derwent, the situation went from bad to worse for the race leader. An ebb tide was running against *Astor* and the wind went from light to lighter. A period of pain followed as the *Astor* crew watched *Ondine* gaining on them from behind, turning it into a bow-to-bow race. One nautical mile from the finish and it was still anyone's prize. In a matter of moments though it became apparent that *Astor* was winged; the crew was unable to gybe the spinnaker as the spinnaker pole was broken. The *Ondine* crew were able to complete their gybe successfully and sailed on to claim line honours by just 100 metres – the closest finish ever. Rubbing salt into the wounds of the *Astor* crew was the knowledge that *Ondine* had lowered *Kurrewa IV*'s 1957 race record time by almost a day.

Once *Ondine* was docked and the media scrum descended on Huey Long, he and the rest of his American invaders must have wondered where the Hobart race's reputation for being a rough, tough and often gear-busting experience had come from. It had been an armchair ride, primarily downwind – the easiest race ever. At that time Long must have been hoping that the wind would again die on the Derwent as the only yacht that could steal away the double of line and handicap honours from his yacht was Vic Meyer's *Solo*. But the wind held so, much to Long's chagrin, *Solo* charged to the finish under spinnaker and claimed the prestigious *Tattersall Cup* – the corrected time winner by less than an hour.

There was one other result in this race worth noting. A tough-as-teak Sydneysider named Syd Fischer – a newcomer to the sport after being a surfboat sweep for many years – made his Hobart race debut with the 36-foot Lion class sloop, *Malohi*. He finished a highly creditable fifth on corrected time, beaten only by such luminaries as Meyer, Long and Australia's first *America's Cup* challenge skipper, Jock Sturrock. Despite having started life in a broken family at the tough end of 'Struggle Street' in an inner Sydney suburb, Fischer went on to become one of the all-time greats of the sport in Australia with his yachts named *Ragamuffin*. In 1971 he made international headlines by winning the storm-lashed Fastnet Race, becoming the first Australian to take the coveted prize, while in the *America's Cup* Fischer shares the record with Sir Thomas Lipton of five personally funded challenges.

*

Unfortunately, Huey Long's disappointment at not taking both line and handicap honours in the race ran deep, to the point where the dockside celebrations in Hobart soured. At some point someone brought to his attention that a photograph of

Solo published in a Launceston newspaper clearly showed that *Solo*'s life raft was not on deck, as required under race rules (Vic Meyer was adamant that the life raft was stowed on the cockpit floor, which was legal). In next to no time Long was on his way to Launceston, desperate to see the photograph which would – hopefully – enable him to lodge a protest against *Solo,* should he be convinced the life raft was not on deck.

Long's desperation to be awarded the *Tattersall Cup* prompted considerable contempt towards him among his Australian rivals. This became a hot topic some hours later at a dockside party taking place aboard Peter Warner's *Astor.* Those present included Rupert Murdoch, one of his senior managers, Curley Brydon, and some of the Hobart race legends from the CYCA, in particular the celebrated trio, 'Thunder' (Harry Kerslake), 'Raw Meat' (George Pearce) and 'Earrings' (John Love) – three affable rogues who, having departed the ranks of the spectacular 18-foot skiffs, had taken up ocean racing, primarily aboard F.J. Palmer's *Even* and Murdoch's *Ilina.* In the early hours of the morning, when the party was still going strong, the conversation turned to the fact that Long had not shown any hospitality towards his Australian sailing rivals in either Sydney or Hobart. Consequently, it was suggested that those aboard *Astor* move that party to *Ondine* there and then. But Mickleborough came up with a better idea: they should organise a proper 'no-host' party on board *Ondine* the following day and invite everyone possible to attend. By early morning, the plans were in full swing. Murdoch pulled his publishing strings in the town and had 1000 invitations printed.

Mr Huey Long

requests the pleasure of your company

at a

small Informal Party aboard

'Ondine'

Drinks

8.00 pm Wednesday

January 2, 1963

The invitations were duly distributed to all and sundry: the State Governor; Hobart's Lord Mayor; the Marine Board; waterside workers and their wives; local firemen; a highland pipe band; and nurses from the local hospital.

At this stage Long was still in Launceston pursuing evidence against *Solo*, so Mickleborough called his brother who happened to live there and asked him to send a telegram to *Ondine*'s boat captain, Sven Joffs. It read: 'Prepare *Ondine* for a party tonight – Huey.'

The upshot of all this was the most amazing party in the annals of Sydney Hobart history.

Through quick thinking and smart planning, twenty 18-gallon kegs of beer arrived at the dock and were set up in front of *Ondine* by bar staff who had been hired from various local pubs.

At the designated hour of 8pm it was estimated that more than 1000 people had already gathered for the event, every one of them in a party mood.

Realising what was happening, Joffs hastily eased off all of the yacht's dock lines so no one could go aboard *Ondine* – not even the Lord Mayor, who had arrived in his chauffeur-driven Bentley, much to the delight of a cheering crowd. At this stage Don Mickleborough was standing alongside *Ondine*, and his presence and manner was enough for the Lord Mayor to go up to him with his hand extended and say: 'Mr Long, you've done a good job.'

The party went on well into the night.

When Huey Long returned to Hobart from Launceston without any evidence against *Solo,* and saw plenty of evidence of the party, he was far from happy.

*

Mickleborough (whose nickname was 'Don Two' because there already had been a 'Don Juan') along with Thunder, Raw Meat and Earrings, were among the most colourful characters of the Hobart race in the 1960s. Their antics over the years brought great mirth and entertainment to fellow competitors and race followers alike. Thunder, who spent much of his working life with the railways and as a blacksmith's striker, gained his nickname because his huge and powerful physique reminded many of a stallion named Thunderhead which featured in a popular movie at the time. Raw Meat received his moniker after a remarkably slow Hobart race – about a week. All the yacht's provisions having been consumed days earlier, as soon as the yacht had docked, George leapt ashore and headed for the local shops where he bought a pack of steaks. By the time he returned to the yacht he was so hungry that he tore the pack open and started devouring them raw, much to the amazement and amusement of all around him.

Another Raw Meat story etched deeply into Sydney Hobart folklore had its beginnings in a particularly wet, wild and generally miserable race in the early 1960s. He had either no wet weather gear, or what he had leaked very badly, so much so, he was soaked through. For some reason he refused to put on dry clothing for each of his watches; instead he would put on dry clothing over the already wet clothing. Before long he was taking on the proportions of a Sumo wrestler. But that wasn't a problem for his crewmates – it was the smell, which got worse as the race progressed. Days later, when the yacht finally reached Hobart and docked, no one wanted to be anywhere near Raw Meat. However after a few celebratory drinks were consumed the rest of the crew decided it was time to get square. They carried him to the ablutions block nearby and threw him under the shower, clothes and all. But the story goes: 'Raw Meat was defiant to the end – he ate the soap!'

John Love, aka 'Earrings', got his nickname through being forgetful. He had been dancing with a young lady somewhere in Sydney whose clip-on earrings continually slipped off and fell to the floor. Eventually, he picked them up and put them in his pocket, then later forgot to return them to his dancing partner. As a result, when he arrived home he had a terrible time trying to explain the origin of the earrings to his wife.

*

The 1963 race was historic in that the fleet of forty-four yachts saw all Australian states represented for the first time. The race would also have been recognised as one of the easiest on record ... had it been from Sydney to Tasman Island! It was idyllic downwind sailing all the way from Sydney to the island, then all hell broke loose.

Navigators became concerned as they watched the barometer drop like a brick – a sure sign that a mighty storm was brewing. Anxious crews kept a lookout towards the southern horizon, day and night, always ready to reef sails or set storm sails. The front, which had developed in the Southern Ocean, came across Storm Bay with the power of a locomotive. In no time the yachts were battling 80-knot winds and wicked waves, the faces of which were near-vertical and capped with a foaming white mass. It was so rough that, at one stage, the Halvorsen brothers' new double-ended sloop, *Freya*, which had a reputation for being an exceptional sea boat, was completely buried by a massive wall of breaking water.

Bill Ratcliff, who was aboard Don Mickleborough's sloop, *Southerly*, later gave a graphic account of his experience that year in Storm Bay:

It was blowing so hard, and the seas were so big, it took us three tries before we actually got around Tasman Island. Once in Storm Bay the seas were just as bad – don't ask me how bad because we were too scared to look up at them. The fact that a big ship was hove-to near Cape Raoul, unable to make headway, gives fair indication of the conditions. Three of us, Bruce Jackson, Phil 'Yogi

Bear' Musgrave and I, had to go to the bow to secure the jib on deck. We were on our hands and knees hanging on for dear life. Next thing *Southerly* stuck her bow through a huge wave and we were submerged. The wave washed us along the deck until we finished up in a heap against the safety rail at the back of the yacht. All we got out of Don was: 'You blokes better get back into the cockpit before you keep going over the side'.

Well to the north, at a position some 40 nm north-east of St Helens in Bass Strait, the storm was still raging. The wind was howling in from the south-west at more than 50 km/h while the sea state could best be described as 20 times 10 – 20 metres apart and 10 metres high. It was like a boiling cauldron, and unfortunately for the 10-metre sloop *Lolita*, which was in the middle of the maelstrom, there was nowhere to go but onwards. The yacht was well proven over four previous Hobarts, but this was the first under the new owner, John Farren-Price.

Suddenly, their situation went from hellish to horrendous. A breaking wave about 15 metres high loomed onto the scene and completely overwhelmed the little yacht, rolling it over 360 degrees not once but probably three times. During the final roll it remained with its keel pointing skywards for an agonisingly long time. Noted navigator Bob Young, who was the only person on deck at the time, was trapped beneath the upturned hull desperately trying to hold his breath. He decided not to detach himself from the yacht by unclipping his safety harness, reasoning that it was better to drown attached to the yacht than to get washed away, 'and no one know what had happened to me'. Then

Lolita suddenly righted itself and Bob took what he would later describe as 'the best breath of air I've ever had'. Still, yacht and crew were far from safe; the mast had gone over the side and taken the radio aerial with it, and the water level in the cabin was above bunk height. One more wave like the one just experienced would cause the yacht to founder, taking the crew with it.

When the water was pumped and bailed out to a safe level, the crew set about drying out the electrics and setting up a jury rig. The electrics were dried out by tipping rum over the bits that mattered and setting fire to them with a match. It worked! A jury rig of sorts was also put in place, and while that was happening Bob Young managed to get a good sun sight with his sextant and plotted their position on the chart. Considering that the coast of Tasmania was directly upwind in still heinous conditions, it was decided there was only one way to go – directly downwind to New Zealand, 1000 nm away to the east.

While this was still being contemplated, a miracle came into play. Bob Young was a noted radio operator with Qantas Airways and he somehow managed to turn the metal and wire lifelines around the deck of the yacht into a crude radio aerial. He then tapped out a brief SOS message in Morse code, giving the yacht's approximate position. Incredibly, moments later, the message was picked up by a fisherman on a trawler who could understand Morse code, and he in turn notified Hobart Radio of the distress signal. A return Morse message was sent soon after, advising *Lolita*'s crew that a rescue effort was under way, and the estimated time of arrival for that vessel.

By that time, the storm had abated and the sea was a millpond, but the crew could see no sign of a rescue vessel anywhere on the horizon, which caused Bob Young to start thinking that he may have calculated their position incorrectly.

While this was being discussed by the crew who were gathered in the cockpit, there came a sound and sight almost beyond belief; little more than 20 metres away the British submarine HMS *Trump*, surfaced, right alongside the yacht!

The crew of the submarine managed to get a long tow line to *Lolita*, and sent across a 44-gallon drum containing desperately needed food, cigarettes, rum, cake, biscuits, cups, plates and cutlery, the latter three items having been inadvertently thrown overboard days earlier in the rush to save the sinking yacht.

Before the near three-day tow to St Helens started, the submarine's captain advised that a crewman on the yacht must be positioned at the bow at all times, armed with a suitably large and sharp cutting implement. He then explained why: should strong crosswinds be encountered at any stage during the tow, the towline would have to be cut because in those conditions the submarine could be in danger of turning turtle – capsizing! The captain added that the *Lolita* crew would have fair warning – he would sound the submarine's horn prior to submerging!

Bob Young, the hero of this near tragedy, was part of a total of seventeen Hobart races – eleven by yacht and six as a radio operator aboard the race's radio relay vessel.

*

The 1963 race is recognised as the one where the Halvorsen brothers, Magnus and Trygve, made their first big impression on the classic via the success of their new yacht, *Freya*. The

11.8-metre double-ended sloop proved to be superbly competitive in all conditions, but especially when the going was rough and tough. That year *Freya* claimed top honours on corrected time over another double-ender, the slightly smaller, *Cavalier* (Dr L. McDonnell), by more than 2 hours.

That was only the start: this remarkable yacht would go on to make it a 'three-peat' over the following 2 years – three consecutive wins on corrected time, a world first for an annual and major ocean race anywhere, and an achievement that might never be seen again.

The Halvorsens' domination came as the by-product of a unique approach to the sport that combined the best features of their five previous yachts with the experiences they shared over fifteen Hobart races.

Making this achievement even more meritorious was the fact that the pair designed, built and raced their yachts. In an interview with the CYCA's Peter Shipway in 2012, Trygve, then aged 92, gave an interesting insight into the secrets of their success over so many years:

> We had a crew that was very interested in every one of our projects. They helped build the boats and contributed to our ideas. *Peer Gynt*'s hull was designed by Magnus and I did all the profile, layouts, sail plan and all the engineering. She was made strong because of the Bass Strait gale we experienced with *Saga*.

Trygve went on to explain that *Anitra V*'s record of three second placings and an overall victory should have been two wins and two second placings: 'The official measurer made a mistake in the sums,' he explained.

Then along came *Freya*.

Here, Trygve told how, apart from the design, many other factors had contributed to their success with the yacht:

> The watch patterns were really important. We had three helmsmen – 1 hour on and 2 hours off. If they were needed for a sail change, it came out of their 2 hours below. We found that 2 hours off watch was enough. If they spent any more time in the bunk they would get too dozy. It took them too long to wake up and be alert.

When asked to reveal the heritage of the *Freya* design, Trygve explained:

> All our yachts were cruising boats as well as racing yachts. They had carpets on the floor, big bunks and all that sort of thing. *Freya* also had a long keel – Magnus' idea because a long keel meant a yacht could sit on the bottom more safely if required when the tide went out [and the yacht was alongside a dock]. But, it was *Freya*'s hull form that was the real secret to her success. We worked hard to minimise the pitching motion. She was a very sea-kindly boat, and that helped in rough weather because we could push the boat much harder, simply because of the hull shape. Also, *Freya* had quite a short rig because Magnus wanted to go cruising, yet it was still fast.

Trygve then disclosed the Halvorsen philosophy when it came to ocean yacht racing, saying:

> You have to cross that finishing line in order to win. So the reliability of the boat is tops. We would often give up training sessions just to make sure the boat was ready for a race. That was our first priority. Also, we never had a pre-race plan – we took the weather as it came.

*

The start of the 20th Hobart race in 1964 confirmed that ocean yacht racing in Australia was developing rapidly; fifteen of the thirty-eight starters that year were new. Jim Polson's small all-aluminium sloop, *Yampl*, had to be rushed by road from South Australia to Sydney to be in time for the start. Legend has it that it was so new that crewmen were seen painting the yacht's deck as it passed through the New South Wales country town of Gundagai.

The Halvorsens didn't need to prove a thing when it came to ocean racing, but that year they wanted to win on corrected time with *Freya* so there was no doubt that the yacht's inclusion in the first Australian team to challenge for the world championship teams trophy, the *Admiral's Cup*, in England that year, was justified. Another Australian team yacht, Ron Swanson's *Camille*, was also in this race. The third team member was *Caprice of Huon*.

The usual crush of spectator craft dogged the yachts as they departed Sydney Harbour. Surprisingly, the glamour boats,

Peter Warner's *Astor* and Rupert Murdoch's *Ilina*, were not prominent. The impressive new Alan Payne designed 15.2-metre-long steel sloop *Bacchus D*, owned by Phil Deaton, led the fleet south from Sydney, carrying its spinnaker well into the night – until a southerly change arrived. The shout for the off-watch sleeping below was 'Everyone up!' so the spinnaker could be lowered as quickly as possible and an upwind headsail set. Within a matter of minutes what had been a pleasant sail through the night had become a wet and bumpy ride. Even so, there was no doubt the happiest of all crews was aboard *Freya* – the yacht was in its element. By the time the bulk of the fleet was in Bass Strait, it was downwind sailing once again and here the new *Bacchus D* began to impress. As the day progressed so too did the larger *Astor* and *Ilina* which were carrying every sail possible. It worked, because by nightfall they were first and second in fleet.

Once again Storm Bay lived up to its reputation and bowled a howling south-westerly blow at the front runners – *Astor* was then leading *Ilina* and *Bacchus D*. Approaching the Derwent, *Bacchus D* was suddenly hit by a brutal, 40-knot squall, so powerful that its towering aluminium mast – the largest ever produced in Australia – buckled and crashed over the side.

Astor sailed on to claim line honours for the third consecutive time in its Hobart race career, beating *Ilina* home by 2 hours. However, an element of disappointment accompanied this result as both Warner and Murdoch announced they would be retiring their yachts from racing.

There was great jubilation from yachties and spectators alike, who were on the docks and aboard boats on the river

The ultimate prize: The superbly ornate Tattersall Cup is the ultimate prize for the Sydney Hobart classic. Struck by silversmiths in Sydney in 1913, the hand-wrought sterling silver cup and plinth was considered at the time to be *'the finest piece of workmanship to have been done in Australia'*. The trophy displays the name of every yacht and owner that has won the race on corrected time.
Getty Images/Saeed Khan

2013 Hobart race start: On a typical Sydney summer day, hundreds of spectator craft escort the ninety-four yachts out of Sydney Harbour and onto the open sea, while tens of thousands of spectators watch from the shoreline. This was the most competitive fleet ever. It included twenty-two international entries; five supermaxis; three Volvo 70s and seven former race winners.
Fairfax/Brendan Esposito

Rani *memento 1945:* This wooden bowl was presented to Captain John Illingworth, skipper of the yacht *Rani*, by the Royal Hobart Regatta Association in recognition of his yacht winning the inaugural Sydney Hobart Yacht Race in 1945. The bowl is made from a variety of Tasmanian timbers. It was a presentation piece to Illingworth, not the winner's trophy. *ANMM Collection*

Inaugural race start – 1945: The tiny sloop *Rani* establishes and early lead over *Saltair* and *Mistral II* soon after the nine competing yachts exited Sydney Harbour and headed south for Hobart. *Fairfax*

1945 Kathleen *crosses the finish line:* Jack Earl's sturdy ketch, *Kathleen*, crosses the finish line in third place in the inaugural Hobart race. The yacht's elapsed time was 8 days 6 hours 20 minutes. A welcoming crowd was on hand for the finish of each yacht, no matter the hour. *Fairfax/Harry Martin*

1945 – *The crew of* Rani *in Hobart:* The legendary English offshore yachtsman, John Illingworth (right) and his crew gather aboard *Rani* in Hobart after being declared the winners of the inaugural Sydney Hobart race. *Rolex Collection*

*1946 – **Ready to race:*** Claude Plowman's 18.8-metre gaff cutter, *Morna*, is towed away from its dock in Sydney and readied for the start of the 1946 Hobart race. A fleet of nineteen yachts valued at £80,000 contested in the classic that year. *Morna* claimed line honours. *ANMM Collection Gift from Louis D'Alpuget*

*1947 – **Mistral II:*** Robert Evan's 19.2-metre schooner, *Mistral II*, appears to be a clutter of sails and rigging as the crew prepare it for the start of the 1947 race. *ANMM Collection Gift from Louis D'Alpuget*

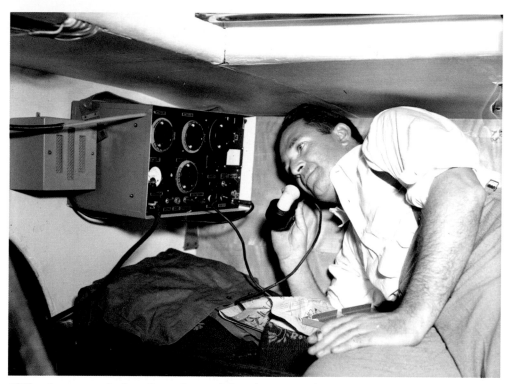

1948 – *A crewman checks radio equipment before the start:* Radio communications were notoriously unreliable in the early days of the Hobart race – in fact so unreliable that the crew of one yacht reverted to using homing pigeons to get a race progress report to a Sydney newspaper. *Fairfax/ Frederick Halmarick*

1949 – *A new knight:* *Morna*'s owner, the recently knighted Sir Claude Plowman, explains the course he took in the 1949 race for an eager audience tuned in to Sydney radio station 2SM. *Fairfax*

1961 – One of nature's grandstands: Sydney's South Head was one of many vantage points around the harbour where tens of thousands of spectators could watch the fleet set sail and head for the open sea. *Fairfax/ Barry Gilmour*

1962 – Dash to the finish: American Huey Long's highly fancied entry, *Ondine* (left), trailed local favourite *Astor* all the way from the start to Storm Bay. Then a calm slowed the leader to the degree where the American yacht closed the gap by a considerable margin. *Astor* was able to maintain its lead until about 1 mile from the finish when a spinnaker pole fitting failed and impacted the yacht's speed. *Ondine* then sailed by and claimed line honours by a mere 100 metres – the closest finish ever. *Libraries Tasmania AA193/1/26*

1962 – The sweet taste of victory: The crew of Vic Meyer's mighty steel sloop, *Solo*, gathered aboard the yacht in Hobart's Constitution Dock to celebrate after the yacht was declared the winner of the Tattersall Cup. *Newspix*

1965 – A historic year: There was a swarm of spectator craft on Sydney Harbour in 1965 to farewell a record fleet of fifty-three starters (many of which came from overseas) lined up for the 21st staging of the classic. Yachting history was made when the Halvorsen brothers' yacht, *Freya*, won the race for the third consecutive time. *Keystone Press/Alamy*

1968 – A broken mast didn't stop them: After being dismasted in the Indian Ocean while sailing to Sydney for the 1968 race, and a herculean effort to re-rig the yacht and get it to the start line, the American ketch *Ondine II* delivered the goods for owner Huey Long and his crew by claiming line honours. *National Archives of Australia*

1970 – Mercedes III, Southerly *and* Matika *show the way: *Mercedes III* (left) was the first ocean racing yacht design influenced by famed America's Cup winning designer, Ben Lexcen. It was a joint effort where Lexcen drafted the hull lines while the sail plan was drawn by the owner Ted Kaufman. *Rolex Collection*

1971 start – You parked the car where? Over the decades, spectators have gone to extraordinary lengths to view the always spectacular start of the Hobart race – but probably none as extraordinary as this! *Atomic/Alamy*

1972 **American Eagle – *'The Mouth from the South':*** Highly popular American media man, Ted Turner (affectionately known as 'The Mouth from the South') returned in 1972 for his second consecutive assault on the Hobart race with his America's Cup class yacht, *American Eagle*. His effort was well rewarded – *American Eagle* won both line and handicap honours. *National Archives of Australia*

1979 Syd Fischer – An ocean racing legend: Syd Fischer is considered by many to be Australia's greatest ever ocean racing sailor, primarily with his series of successful yachts named *Ragamuffin*. He is also recognised for giving many promising young sailors the opportunity to enter the sport. At age eight-eight Fischer became the oldest skipper to compete in a Hobart race. *Jonathan Eastland/Ajax News & Feature Service/Alamy*

1976 Ballyhoo – Dodgems on departing: Jack Rooklyn's Ben Lexcen designed aluminium maxi, *Ballyhoo*, had to play dodgems with small craft at the start of the 1976 race. Once clear of the hazards, the yacht went on to be first to Hobart. *Newspix*

1982* Styx – *A blast then no mast: Joe Abrahams' impressive sloop, *Styx*, was blasting past Tasman Island on the face of a north-east squall in the 1982 race when this image was taken. Minutes later the yacht was dismasted. *Richard Bennett*

***1986* Windward Passage – *There is a little* Windward Passage *in every sailor's heart:* In 1986 the maxi yacht scene in Australia received a mighty boost when yachting enthusiast and media man, Rod Muir, purchased the world's most famous big boat, the American maxi, *Windward Passage.* The ageing beauty was second to Hobart that year. *Rolex Collection*

1997 Karakoram – *Lachlan Murdoch at the helm:* In 1997 Rupert Murdoch's son, Lachlan (right) followed his father's course into the Sydney Hobart yacht race with his own yacht, *Karakoram. Torsten Blackwood/AFP/Getty Images*

1998 start – Smooth start, hell over the horizon: It was a sparkling summer day for the start of the 1998 Hobart race, but 48 hours later tragedy struck. *Jean-Paul Ferrero/Auscape/Alamy*

*1998 tragedy – **Stand Aside:*** Marauding seas and a howling an 80 knot wind created life-threatening conditions. *Newspix*

*1998 tragedy – **Stand Aside:*** Fear and fatigue are etched on the faces of the crew of *Stand Aside* as they survey damage to the cabin top. The yacht had been rolled over by a huge wave. *AAP Image/ Sport The Library/Rod Hunter*

2004 Veterans – reminiscing: Race veterans John Gordon (left) and John Walker remember the good times and the tough times. Gordon competed in the inaugural Hobart while Walker raced his yacht, *Impeccable*, to Hobart twenty-five times, the last time when aged eighty-five. He migrated to Australia from his homeland, Czechoslovakia, with his wife in 1949. After arriving in Sydney Walker changed his name to that of his favourite tipple, Johnnie Walker, as no-one could pronounce his Czech name. *Fairfax/Dallas Kilponen*

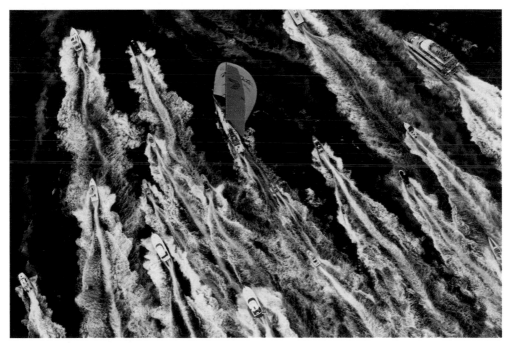

2011 Wild Oats XI – a starting escort: Creating wakes like vapour trails, a small armada of support boats escort the Oatley family's supermaxi, *Wild Oats XI*, out through Sydney Heads. Going into the 75th anniversary race, *Wild Oats XI* stood as the most successful yacht in the history of the classic, having claimed line honours on nine occasions and won the Tattersall Cup twice. *Fairfax/Ben Rushton*

2019 – Before and after: One of the most remarkable stories associated with the 75th anniversary Hobart race emerged before the classic started. The 115-year-old, 9.75-metre long English designed and built ketch, *Katwinchar* – which contested the 1951 race after sailing 15,000 nm from England to Sydney – was in a derelict condition when located in Newcastle (top) through a fortuitous set of circumstances in 2017. Once retrieved, it was superbly restored then relaunched in time for the start of the 75th anniversary race in 2019. *Murray Waite*

when the Halvorsen brothers guided *Freya* home to a remarkable third across the line. Most importantly, though, when its corrected time was calculated, *Freya* was declared the outright race winner. And, much to the delight of those associated with the *Admiral's Cup* team, the result, coupled with *Camille* being placed second on corrected time, was a very positive sign for the Australian challenge.

*

By this era in the 1960s, the dockside post-race parties in Hobart contributed much to the appeal of the race, even though the majority of these events occurred on a whim and without planning. And it was due to such spontaneity after the finish of the 1963 race that 'Delphine' became part of the history of the Hobart.

The story goes that Curley Brydon and Don Mickleborough, who had crewed aboard *Ilina* for the race, had been enjoying a few cold beers, along with countless other sailors, at a dock-front pub one afternoon. Later, while heading back to the yacht, they passed Delphine's Frock Shop, and there in the window was a somewhat glamorously attired dressmaker's mannequin. Mickleborough stopped immediately and said: 'Curley, let's go and buy her and give her to Raw Meat. He's having no luck trying to win a girl here in Hobart.'

Great idea!

The pair went into the shop and asked the owner if they could buy the mannequin, frock and all, but the woman politely refused. However, she told them she had another mannequin out the back of the shop. It had slightly damaged eyes and they could have it for £40. It was a deal! Curley then ducked into the chemist shop next door and bought a pair of cheap sunglasses for the appropriately named 'Delphine' to wear so the damaged eyes were not obvious. They also chose a colourful frock and a wig for her to wear. Much to their delight, Curley and Don's new-found friend, Delphine, soon looked very stylish and remarkably lifelike.

Raw Meat's new girlfriend soon joined the post-Hobart race social whirl and quickly became the talk of the town. She even attended the State Governor's Hobart race welcome party with him (where Raw Meat signed himself in as 'Sir Loin') and was seen to be 'dancing' with a number of the sailors. However, her most famous appearance in Hobart that year came at the official presentation of the race trophies at the Town Hall.

Legendary navigator 'Sighty' Hammond suggested that, instead of Delphine merely making an appearance at the function, there should be an element of fun attached to her presence; in short a prank. He suggested that Curley Brydon's girlfriend, Dotty Sawyer, be dressed as Delphine – frock, wig, sunglasses et al. – pose as Delphine the mannequin at the function, then suddenly come to life at the height of the celebrations. Dotty was confident she could carry it off, so she then went aboard *Ilina* and dressed in Delphine's attire. That done, Curley and Raw Meat carried the rigid-as-a-post Dotty through Hobart and to the entrance of the Town Hall. By that time they were brimming with confidence, so they carried the still rigid 'Delphine' straight past the doorman, into the main hall and up onto the stage where the race trophies were set out.

Once there, they lifted Delphine into place – lying her on top of the grand piano – amid rapturous cheering, applause and laughter from those present.

CYCA Secretary, Merv Davey, who sometimes struggled to find his sense of humour, was far from impressed. He went straight up to Curley and Raw Meat on the stage, poked Delphine in the ribs and said, 'Get that thing out of here!'. In a flash Dotty sat bolt upright and said in a most indignant tone: 'Don't you touch me!'. Poor Merv went close to having a heart attack on the spot while Delphine, having been assisted down from the top of the piano, left the stage to more cheers, applause and peals of laughter, then joined the rest of the crowd.

The Flag Officers of the Royal Yacht Club of Tasmania were not amused, so much so that a letter went from that club to the Commodore of the CYCA. It requested that the crew of *Ilina* be banned from participating in future Hobart races. The CYCA did not go to that extreme, instead opting to suspend Rupert Murdoch, Curley Brydon, Don Mickleborough and the rest of the *Ilina* crew from the club for three months. The entire crew was also ordered to write letters of apology to the State Governor, even though the majority were not part of the prank.

*

The Sydney Hobart came of age in 1965, establishing a milestone with a record fifty-three entries which, for the first time, saw every Australian state and the ACT represented. There were also entries from New Zealand, Britain, Italy, South Africa and Hong Kong. The calibre of this fleet was unquestionably the highest the race had seen, so much so that *Freya* would have to excel if it was to make it three in a row. There were two yachts of note from overseas: *Stormvogel* and *Fanfare*. South African registered *Stormvogel* was a radical, 22.5-metre light-displacement ketch, owned by Dutch plywood manufacturer, Cornelius Bruynzeel, and billed as the largest and fastest ocean racing yacht in the world. *Fanfare*, owned by Geoffrey Pattinson, was out of the UK. The Italian Navy was represented by *Corsaro II*.

One of the more interesting entries, a new 12.3-metre-long Alan Payne design for Russ Williams had been built in a deconsecrated church at Eagle Farm, in suburban Brisbane. The church was destined for demolition so the builder of the yacht put to good use what he could of the ageing structure. Floorboards were used for deck planking, much of the fit-out was made from the cedar window frames and the keel was cast in the church grounds. When launched, the yacht was given a most appropriate name: *Fare Thee Well*!

If the weather was expected to provide the drama this year then it certainly didn't come to the party. Winds were generally light over the entire 628 nm. But it wasn't a race without high drama. The two most serious incidents involved the Italian Navy entry, *Corsaro II*. The skipper and navigator had to be replaced on the eve of the race after they were injured in a car crash in Sydney, then, soon after the start of the classic, a spectator launch collided with the yacht as it sailed towards the Heads. No-one was injured though people were hurled into the water and the small powerboat was left half-submerged. Worse was still to come for the Italians in the race.

The Halvorsens staked their claim for handicap honours soon after reaching the open ocean by making a daring move. Instead of staying inshore and paralleling the coast, which was the norm, they opted for what was considered a long, losing leg out to sea. It was a good gamble: once out there they found the stronger winds they had anticipated. The dividend came that night when they tacked *Freya* back towards the coast. They were confident they were well ahead of their main rivals, but they didn't expect to be ahead of *Stormvogel*. Yet, at sun-up, the crew of *Stormvogel*, believing at that time they were leading the fleet, were shocked to see *Freya*, which was little more than half their size, 2 miles ahead!

The fleet had an easy passage across Bass Strait and down the Tasmanian coast – but there was a shock for all crews at 6.30am on 30 December when *Corsaro II* sent out a distress call, advising that the navigator, Lt Commander Franco Barbalonga, had been catapulted overboard by a flaying rope while the spinnaker was being set. All nearby yachts immediately changed course towards *Corsaro II* and joined the search. Thirty minutes later the yacht *Corroboree*, skippered by CYCA member Gordon Marshall, arrived on the scene and soon spotted Barbalonga. In a matter of minutes, the very shocked and extremely lucky sailor had been plucked from the water.

Tony Cable, who was aboard *Fare Thee Well,* took up the story: 'I was in the galley when the anxious Italian voice interrupted the radio sked with the news that they had a man overboard. *Corroboree* was behind it, on the same track, and picked up the Italian in no time. He was naked except for one sock, which he gratefully presented to Gordon Marshall as a souvenir. Gordon had it mounted and proudly placed the plaque on his wall at home.'

Stormvogel spread its wings during the day and regained the lead, and the crew thought that from there they could not lose. For them and the rest of the fleet, the remainder of the race was easy going. *Stormvogel* cruised into Hobart 4 days and 6 hours after departing Sydney and *Freya* was just under 10 hours behind. It was another superb effort from the Halvorsen brothers and crew, *Freya*'s corrected time ensuring it was declared winner by more than 2 hours.

The 'three-peat' was complete. History had been made. No other yacht in international ocean racing had won a major annual event three consecutive times. The *Freya* crew were the legends of Hobart.

Once docked, the crew of *Stormvogel* realised they had been extremely lucky over the entire course from Sydney. A crewman who was sent aloft to check the rig discovered significant cracks in the metal rigging attachments. After a thorough inspection, the conclusion was that had the yacht experienced strong winds at any time, it would probably have been dismasted.

Michael Green

SAILING BIO

I have sailed in forty Hobart races from 1970 to 2018.
I was sailing master aboard the line honours winner
Ninety Seven in 1993, sailing master on the handicap
winner *Quest* in 2002, the TP52 *Quest* in 2008 and the
TP52 *Balance* in 2015. I have also garnered five second-
placings on handicap, and two third-places on handicap.
Internationally, I have competed in four *Kenwood Cups* in
Hawaii and two *Admiral's Cup* regattas in England.

WHAT WAS YOUR BEST DAY SAILING IN THE SYDNEY HOBART?

The approach to the finish of the 1993 race and securing
the line honours trophy. Sailing into Hobart in that
circumstance is something you never forget.

WHAT DAY OR EXPERIENCE WAS THE TOUGHEST OR MOST CHALLENGING?

Crossing Bass Strait in the ill-fated 1998 race. I have never
seen seas so big, powerful and threatening.

WHAT KEEPS YOU GOING BACK TO THE HOBART RACE?

It's all about the excitement of the challenge – giving it
all as a team and knowing when we reach Hobart that we
could not have tried harder.

WHAT ARE SOME OF THE BIG CHANGES THAT YOU'VE WITNESSED IN YOUR YEARS ASSOCIATED WITH THE RACE?

The changes in navigation equipment has impressed me
most – we have gone from the sextant and sun sights to
GPS satellite navigation. Also, the steady improvement in
safety training and equipment has been important to the
sport.

CHAPTER 10

The Boy from the Bush

In March 1936 in the outback town of Boggabri – 300 kilometres inland from Coffs Harbour on the New South Wales north coast – Ethel Doreen and Edward William Miller welcomed into the world a baby boy, whom they named Robert. It was towards the end of the Great Depression, and the baby's parents, like so many others, were struggling to make ends meet. They spent a considerable time living in tents in bush camps where Edward sought work as a timber getter and Doreen, when possible, worked as a barmaid. With time it became a very dysfunctional family and young Robert's strongest memories were of physical fights between his parents. When he was 7 years old, his parents abandoned him to the care of Boys' Town, a home for disadvantaged children. After a brief stay there, his mother, who had by then separated from her husband, sent him to live with his grandfather in Newcastle.

One day young Bob took himself to the local ocean beach where he saw children of a similar age racing small model yachts in a large rock pool. The speed and manoeuvrability of these little sailboats intrigued him, so he went home and set about making his own model which, after some modifications, became the fastest on the pond.

This was a prescient start to life for a young lad who went to the school of hard knocks and fundamentally educated himself, because some three decades later, having changed his name by deed poll to Ben Lexcen, he achieved national and international fame for his design of *Australia II*, the yacht that ended the longest winning streak in international sport (132 years) by winning the *America's Cup* for Australia in 1983.

Over the decades preceding that historic day, Bob Miller/ Ben Lexcen revolutionised the 18 foot skiff class and became a world champion sailor. Subsequently, he made a name for himself as a sailmaker, designed successful ocean racing yachts and also represented Australia at the Olympics in Munich in 1972.

In 1965, his name became known on the international ocean racing scene after he joined forces with Star Class sailor, Ted Kaufman, who had approached him for the design of a 12.8-metre offshore racing yacht to be named *Mercedes III*. It was to be a joint effort where Lexcen drafted the lines of the hull, designed the keel and created the initial sail plan. It was built by master craftsman Cec Quilkey in southern Sydney, and when launched it was recognised as being the first offshore racer in the world to be built using the cold-moulded laminated timber method of construction.

Mercedes III became a world-beater. It won nine of the first fourteen races it contested then, in 1967, led the three-yacht Australian team (which included Sir Robert Crichton-Brown's *Balandra* and *Caprice of Huon*, sailed by Gordon Reynolds) to victory in what was considered to be the world championship of ocean racing, the *Admiral's Cup*, which was contested in Cowes, England.

But not every post was a winner for Lexcen in that era.

The man was beyond being a lateral thinker when it came to life in general and all things nautical. He seemed to pull concepts and theories from places where few people's minds dared venture, then develop them for a project. But not all of them worked. This became evident the same year as the *Mercedes III* project when Ben decided to take the theory of ferro-cement construction into a new realm – ocean racing yachts. It was a building method that had been known to the maritime world since 1848, but no one had dared take it to where Ben was thinking. Frenchman Joseph-Louis Lambot, who invented the technique (later to be known as reinforced concrete) introduced it to the world of boating by building *un petit bateau*. This same small boat – which to the astonishment of many actually floated – is still on display at the Brignoles Museum in southern France.

Ben decided he and some well-known sailing mates – Carl Ryves, Pod O'Donnell and Dick Sargent – should design and build a ferro-cement yacht for the specific purpose of racing to Hobart.

No one was surprised by the final design – it was a hybrid – a light-displacement yacht, the hull of which appeared to include the best features of an 18 foot skiff, an Olympic Flying Dutchman class dinghy, and a light-displacement offshore racer.

Some years later, Carl Ryves took up the story about the yacht:

Some way-out Professor convinced Ben that concrete, or more specifically ferro-cement, was the future in boatbuilding. He declared that a hull could be built lighter and stronger than anything else, even steel.

Benny came up with a concept for a light displacement 11.5 metre ferro-cement race boat which, by his calculations, would have a hull that was just 6.5 millimetres thick – but it would be twice as strong as steel.

Somehow we managed to scrape up enough money for the project so set about building the hull in a small factory in Balmain [close to the shores of Sydney Harbour].

We spent countless hours bending steel rod into the desired shape of the hull, wrapping it in mesh and tying it all together with wire as we went. Needless to say our hands were cut to pieces, but we pressed on.

After months of work the structure was ready for the cement to be applied using hand trowels. We thought we were going well until we realised when we had finished that the ferro-cement was more like 25mm thick, four times more than the desired 6.5mm. In short, it was a disaster as the hull would be grossly overweight. So, we grabbed a high-pressure hose and blasted all the still wet concrete off the mesh, from bow to stern as well as across the deck so we could start again. It has to be said though that it was only because of Ben's enthusiastic leadership that we kept convincing ourselves it would be ok.

The second concreting effort was far more successful, so once the ferro had cured, we set about fitting out the hull. One particular day I was fitting some of the wooden deck beams when I dropped a G cramp. It fell into the bilge and on impact there was the sound of a mini explosion: the G cramp had smashed a hole the size of a coconut straight through the ferro-cement hull, showering the guys below with concrete dust.

We all stood around for a few minutes inspecting the damage, then without any hesitation unanimously agreed: 'We are not going to Hobart in this thing'.

Instead, we gave the hull away to some guy who had dreams of cruising around the world, and never saw it again!

Despite this setback, Ben would go on to design some of the world's most successful offshore racing yachts, plus *America's Cup* challenge yachts and even a radical skateboard for kids.

*

On today's international ocean racing scene, Australians and New Zealanders are considered to be among the world's best crew. It is safe to say for both nationalities that the Hobart race is where the majority of these elite sailors have cut their teeth in the big league.

Yet, while the evolution of Australian sailors came from the very first race in 1945, it was not until the 1966 Hobart that the Kiwis made their mark.

It came in the form of Jim Davern's 18.5-metre sloop, *Fidelis*, a lean and low-slung sloop that was often referred to as 'the snake box' simply because it was so narrow.

When the yacht crossed the Tasman from Auckland and arrived in Sydney for the 1966 race no one really considered it when it came to picking a favourite for line honours. Instead, the bulky American entry, *Nam Sang* (nicknamed *Dim Sim*), was installed as favourite by the experts and public alike for both line and handicap honours, while Bob Crichton-Brown's highly impressive new yacht, *Balandra*, was second choice.

With *Freya* not among the forty-six starters, the corrected time winner was expected to come from the stable of Sydney yacht builder and designer Ron Swanson. His unusually proportioned yachts, based on a vintage design, had won every major ocean race out of Sydney except the Hobart.

The big American entry didn't disappoint its supporters when it led the fleet out of the harbour on Boxing Day, and in doing so created a new entry for the Hobart race history books. The yacht's sailing 'master' was noted American yachtswoman Peggy Slater. By being at the helm when the yacht reached the Heads she became the first woman to steer a yacht out of the harbour at the head of the fleet.

But once on the open sea *Fidelis* left no doubt it was a light-weather flyer. Incredibly, a day later, *Fidelis* had established a demoralising lead over the rest of the fleet – 80 nautical miles! It was unprecedented in the twenty-two-year history of the race.

Later, while *Fidelis* glided down the Tasmanian coast and extended its lead, twenty of the yachts immediately behind it lay almost motionless on a glass-topped ocean, all within sight of each other.

When the flying Kiwi machine went on to claim line honours 4 days and 8 hours after leaving Sydney, Davern and crew had plenty of time to celebrate as *Balandra* did not reach the finish in second place until 17 hours later. The result for the highly fancied *Nam Sang* was a bitter disappointment for its crew. The yacht crossed the line in seventh place, a full day behind *Fidelis*. Then, to make matters worse, when it entered Constitution Dock it was greeted by a sign in *Fidelis*'s rigging which read 'Where's you bin, *Dim Sim*?'

Inevitably, Davern was asked by the media in Hobart how his yacht performed offshore in rough weather, and he had a very positive reply. The procedure was simple: 'We close the hatches, sound the klaxon horn as we submerge and breathe through the mast!'

For a while it appeared *Fidelis* would take the double – line and corrected time honours – but a favourable breeze brought the smaller entries in the Derwent home at a rapid rate. Consequently, the 30 foot sloop, *Cadence*, owned by offshore veteran Jim Mason, became the smallest yacht ever to win the race, and in doing so, ended the drought for Ron Swanson who was its designer and builder. Swanson finished second with his similar yacht, *Salome*, and another of his designs, *Mister Christian* (Peter Kurts), was placed fourth behind *Tamboo* (R.J. Green).

*

Fidelis's success and the staging of the inaugural *Southern Cross Cup* – which had the Hobart race as the feature event – was enough to lure it and eight other yachts across the Tasman to be part of the 1967 Hobart.

The CYCA created the *Southern Cross Cup* series as a consequence of Australia's stunning victory in the *Admiral's Cup*. Based on that regatta's format, it was to comprise a series of races out of Sydney then have the Hobart race as the grand finale. The one difference was that instead of it being open only to international teams comprising three yachts, Australian states were also allowed to enter teams.

The star attraction for that year's Hobart was the unconventional aluminium French schooner, *Pen Duick III*, designed and sailed by the legendary Eric Tabarly. The clipper-bowed, black-hulled and bland looking yacht arrived in Sydney with a daunting reputation. During the previous European summer it had won every major offshore race that mattered, including the Fastnet, and consequently won the RORC [Royal Ocean Racing Club] 1967 Class 1 Championship with a perfect score of 100 per cent.

Noted English yacht designer, Julian Everitt, later wrote of *Pen Duick III*:

> One of the most successful and effective 'Rule' exploiting boats of all time. Designed by the great man himself, Eric Tabarly, the schooner rig gained an enormous amount of 'free' sail area under the RORC rule and this combined with the tiny fin keel, separate spade rudder and ballast bulb created a speed combination that resulted in an overall win in the Fastnet Race in 1967.

When the yacht arrived in Sydney, Tabarly made an immediate impression on local yachtsmen. He deftly steered the 18-metre yacht, which was under sail only, through the densely packed field of moored boats off the CYCA, then with perfectly calculated timing, called on the crew to lower the sails. *Pen Duick III* glided into its marina berth at the club with the perfect degree of momentum and came to a stop without touching the dock. A round of applause was heard coming from members in the CYCA bar.

Unfortunately, the start of the 1967 race was exciting for all the wrong reasons – in fact it was chaotic. The rounding mark positioned off South Head broke free from its mooring just as the race got under way, and drifted more than a kilometre north-west, towards the entrance to Middle Harbour.

Champion New Zealand yachtsman Chris Bouzaid devoted considerable space to this incident in his book *Go Rainbow Go*:

> The vanished mark caused even the most [good]
> humoured helmsmen to grind their teeth and call upon
> their Maker in baffled rage.
>
> A clump of about fifty yachts converged at that point
> where the buoy should have been. Failing to find the
> mark, they all proceeded downwind in search of it. Booms
> tangled with shrouds. Crews lined rails to fend off yachts
> which were fending off other yachts. The air was blue
> with regrettable language. The missing buoy was located
> only 300 yards from the cliffs and cries for sea room were
> heard above the general angry din.
>
> Meanwhile, a smaller percentage of skippers had
> decided that if a mark was not where the sailing directions
> said it would be, they were entitled to ignore it – and they

there-upon put to sea, gaining maybe half an hour on the bulk of the fleet.

On realising they had a calamity on their hands and would inevitably face a mass of protests in Hobart because of this unprecedented situation, the CYCA's Race Committee radioed all yachts and announced the race would not be restarted or cancelled, but should any yacht owner consider they were unfairly disadvantaged by the wayward buoy, they could state their case with race officials after arriving in Hobart.

Experienced sailors and the media alike declared the clashes between *Fidelis* and *Pen Duick III* for line honours, and between *Mercedes III* and *Pen Duick III* for first on corrected time, would be the highlights of the race. But it didn't quite pan out that way.

The race forecast was for generally light winds from the start to Storm Bay and that was what the majority of the sixty-seven-yacht fleet encountered – easy going. *Pen Duick III* and *Fidelis* lived up to predictions; 24 hours into the race the Kiwis led the Frenchman by just 1 nm. But 48 hours later the positions had reversed, and by a significant margin. The wall of sail that Tabarly was able to set from the yacht's two masts in such light weather gave *Pen Duick III* a demoralising turn of speed for those that followed, so much so that the Frenchman then led by 25 nm. From that point Tabarly continued to sail away from the rest of the fleet until he crossed Storm Bay and reached the entrance to the Derwent. By then *Pen Duick III* was leading by such a margin that it looked certain to take the double: first home and first on corrected time. But the old adage that a yacht race isn't over until it's over was heard once more. The dreaded demon of the Derwent struck. It was a 'glass-out' between the river entrance and the finish line; as if a giant vacuum had descended on the scene and sucked up all the wind. After hours of frustration a faint breeze arrived – enough for *Pen Duick III* to glide across the line in first place. But, as satisfying as that was, the yacht's crew were well aware that their only chance remained in the hands of the weather gods: should the wind evaporate once more, *Pen Duick III* would be declared the winner on handicap.

Instead, the weather went very much in favour of the smaller yachts. A howling north-westerly gale with gusts to 45-knots created rapid downwind sailing off the Tasmanian coast. It was everything that Bouzaid and his crew aboard the 11.5-metre One Ton Cup class yacht, *Rainbow II*, were hoping for. Their yacht was in its element.

The navigator's log from another race yacht, *Catriona*, said it all:

> *Rainbow II* came screaming past us carrying a huge masthead, blood-red spinnaker. It was broaching, rolling, shaking and shuddering, thrashing wildly about, being knocked down with a report like a cannon then staggering to her feet and rushing onwards.
>
> I've never seen a boat sailed like it in the eight times I've been to Hobart. *Rainbow* ran through us like the old packet of salts. Every time she broached, the spray would shoot up as her spinnaker hit the water, the kite [spinnaker] would spill and, as it filled again, there was a

report like a gunshot as the sails and rigging tightened …
and with this banging, roaring and spray going up, off she
flew out of sight.

If ever a boat deserved to win, *Rainbow* did.

That superhuman effort was well rewarded: *Rainbow II* became
the first Kiwi yacht ever to win the Hobart race on handicap –
but by only one hour over *Pen Duick III*.

The inaugural *Southern Cross Cup* series saw the trophy
awarded to the New South Wales team of *Calliope* (Chas
Middleton), *Mercedes III* (Ted Kaufman) and *Moonbird* (Norm
Brooker).

*

The 24th Hobart race in 1968 made premature headlines in
mid-December due to a near tragedy on the Tasman Sea, and a
Herculean effort to get the star of the race, American Huey
Long's latest *Ondine II*, to the start line.

It was early December when the 45-foot light-displacement
New Zealand sloop, *Matuku*, owned by Kem Cox, departed
Wellington. It was en route to Sydney for the Hobart race
when, in the middle of the Tasman Sea, it collided with a
whale. The yacht's hull was so badly smashed by the force of
the impact that it started sinking immediately. Fortunately for
the crew, they managed to inflate the life raft and clamber
aboard just prior to the yacht going under. It was five days
before they were rescued and their lives were spared by what
some might see as divine intervention as they had decided to

borrow the life raft before leaving New Zealand only because the Hobart race rules required competing yachts to carry one!

Long's new *Ondine II* a stunning, 73-foot aluminium ketch with a powder-blue hull – was dismasted in the Indian Ocean while sailing to Sydney for the race. Only a superhuman effort by Long and crew got the yacht to the start line. *Ondine II* arrived in Sydney just three days before the race, as did its new aluminium mast, which was air freighted to Sydney from Germany.

Boxing Day was a glamorous Sydney summer day, so no one was surprised to see more than 1000 spectator boats on the harbour to farewell the fleet. And, as usual, huge crowds packed the shoreline.

When the start gun boomed out its signal at 11am, it was not *Ondine II* but another American yacht, Homer Denius's 16-metre-long sloop, *Rage,* that burst forth from the pack and led the charge all the way to the Heads. Unfortunately for the already weary *Ondine II* crew, any hope they had for being first to the open sea was stymied when a large tear appeared in its massive headsail. It had to be lowered and a smaller replacement hoisted.

The crews aboard the sixty-seven yachts enjoyed a pleasant spinnaker run down the coast until later that first day when a fierce south-westerly change, harbouring gusts to 40 knots, made an unwelcome appearance. From that moment the upwind battle was on – a battle that suited quality yachts like Syd Fischer's superb new *Ragamuffin*, Dennis O'Neil's *Koomooloo* (a development of *Mercedes III* and undeniably the most beautiful yacht built in Australia at the time), plus Bob Crichton-Brown's *Balandra*. They revelled in the rough going, and their efficient designs and competent crews combined to see them make significant gains over their rivals. At the same time *Ondine II* could not find its stride – the crew was struggling to race the yacht while at the same time making sure the new rig stayed in one piece. That slow progress saw it back in 14th place in the fleet at that stage.

Rage continued to lead when approaching Bass Strait, but then came a disaster. The yacht speared into the air from the top of a large wave then crashed into the trough that followed. The force of the impact proved too much for its aluminium mast, which exploded into three pieces.

Ondine II picked up the pace down the Tasmanian coast when a favourable north-easterly wind arrived and it sailed back into the lead. But the yacht's slow progress over the first half of the course wrecked any chance of a record time.

There was an enormous welcome from the always enthusiastic Hobart crowd when *Ondine II* powered across the finish line and claimed line honours. The 'sailing Steinway' *Koomooloo* reached the finish line some 7 hours later and set a corrected time that would not be beaten. The *Tattersall Cup* was Denis O'Neil's. Second place was a surprise – the new, radical and somewhat unusual-looking Peter Joubert designed *Boomerang VII*, while *Ragamuffin* was third. All three had gained the benefit of a good weather pattern once in Storm Bay and from that point they were unbeatable.

*

The following year – 1969 – the British arrived in force for the 25th Hobart race celebrations, their primary objective being to spoil the party and win the *Southern Cross Cup*, which was being contested that year. However, if one of their yachts won the classic, they would happily take that. Leading the challenge was high profile newspaper publisher Sir Max Aitken, with his superbly proportioned 19-metre sloop, *Crusade*, plus the Rt Hon. Edward Heath (who became Sir Edward Heath in 1992) with his yacht *Morning Cloud*.

Heath, who had always enjoyed his sailing, bought the 10-metre-long production yacht off-the-shelf with a view to winning the 1969 Fastnet. But things didn't go to plan: *Morning Cloud* sailed home in 30th place. That very disappointing result caused him to put the Hobart race and the *Southern Cross Cup* on his agenda for later that year, but as his navigator, Anthony Churchill, recalled in an interview written for the London *Telegraph* in December 2009, before committing 100 per cent to the project, Heath called a crew meeting:

> He gathered us together and told us we were going to do the Sydney Hobart race later that year, but that if we didn't intend to win, we may as well not go. He was absolutely determined and quite confident we would win. We all were.

The British challengers for the *Southern Cross Cup* reminded themselves that it was the great Captain John Illingworth (RN) who had suggested back in 1945 that the proposed cruise to Hobart become a race and he had swept all before him. So, in that 25th anniversary year, they should work hard for a repeat performance.

Prior to the Hobart race, Syd Fischer's superbly prepared and well sailed sloop *Ragamuffin* had dominated the *Southern Cross Cup* and was installed as favourite to win the big one. Also, the British hopes for line honours with Sir Max Aitken's 62-foot *Crusade* were under threat from a radical new local yacht, *Apollo*, designed by Ben Lexcen and owned by a young and emerging Perth property developer, Alan Bond. It was Lexcen's first solo foray into offshore racing, and *Apollo* certainly looked fast.

Before leaving England, Illingworth met with the British team and passed on a piece of advice to the man who later became Prime Minister: 'Stay well offshore after departing Sydney.'

Heath did just that, as did a number of other competitors in the record fleet of seventy-nine yachts, and made considerable gains down the New South Wales coast and into Bass Strait. While they all romped along under spinnaker, the inshore yachts, living in hope of a south-westerly change, only found calms.

It didn't last, as Churchill remembered:

First we came across a load of killer whales, then halfway down the course we ran into a southerly buster ... an enormous storm halfway between a gale and a hurricane. We started taking on water and were close to sinking but we bailed out and carried on.

That storm hit most of the yachts when they were well down the Tasmanian coast. At that stage those offshore were perfectly placed to benefit most, so it was obvious the race winner would come from that group – a group that did not include *Ragamuffin*.

In the battle of the big boats, the *Crusade* crew were confident they held a considerable lead over *Apollo* and were in no danger of losing the line honours trophy. How wrong they were! The sleek and slick *Apollo* carved 20 miles out of *Crusade*'s lead on the slog towards Tasman Island and Storm Bay. The first thing the Brits knew about *Apollo*'s close proximity was when a rain squall lifted – there in full view and closing fast was *Apollo*. It was a battle royal from that point all the way to the finish line, where *Crusade* got the gun by less than 19 minutes.

Still out on the course, Edward Heath and his polished team of sailors were driving *Morning Cloud* hard, and the yacht was responding brilliantly. Smart tactics also made a significant contribution, and once the little sloop reached Storm Bay it was obvious only a disaster could rob them of victory.

Such was the interest in Britain in this David and Goliath battle that the BBC gave half-hourly updates on their progress in the closing stages of the race. But it was far from a foregone conclusion: 'The wind dropped when we were 10 minutes from the finish,' said Churchill at the dock, 'and I knew that we had to be across the line inside 15 minutes to win overall.'

Edward Heath and his crew became worthy winners of the 25th Sydney Hobart.

As Leader of the Opposition, Heath was met on the dock by the British consul in Hobart, who took him off to celebrate with a dinner at Government House. Heath went ashore in his salt-encrusted sailing gear, since his street clothes had not arrived from Sydney.

On corrected time, *Morning Cloud* beat another British team yacht, *Prospect of Whitby* (Arthur Slater) by almost an hour, with Sydney-based yacht *Salacia* (Arthur Byrne) third. *Ragamuffin* was a disappointing 17th.

*

His actual name is Terrot Angus Dalrymple-Smith, but in the world of ocean racing he is known simply as Butch. British by birth, this colourful character became an acclaimed sailor and yacht designer, working for many years in Ireland in Ron Holland's superyacht design office. For the past couple of decades he has lived in La Ciotat, on France's Mediterranean coast, primarily working on the design of classic style yachts and their restoration.

He was aboard the Swan 65, *Sayula*, when it won the inaugural Whitbread round-the-world race in 1973–74, but before that in 1969, aged 25, he arrived in Sydney from the UK as a member of the crew of Arthur Slater's *Prospect of Whitby*, one of the three yachts in the British team challenging for the *Southern Cross Cup*.

Sydney felt like a new-found home, so much so that he stayed for years. In that time he got to race 18-foot skiffs, won the One Ton Cup World Championship in New Zealand in 1971 when sailing with Syd Fischer aboard *Stormy Petrel,* built a midget speedboat for commuting on Sydney Harbour, and made what was possibly Australia's first ever waterbed. He holds fond memories of those years:

When I first got to Sydney in 1969 I could only sense that I was a long, long way from Europe. It felt very strange and foreign. The rest of the crews and I were met by a kind member of the CYCA who asked where we would like to be taken, so he took us around to our respective hotels, dropping each person off, until I was the last one in the car. What he didn't know was that I didn't have money to pay for a hotel room. Some weeks earlier, I had written to Peter Hemery, whom I met at the *Admiral's Cup* in Cowes in 1967, and asked him if he had a spare bed for the time I was in Sydney, but I had received no reply. I explained my dilemma to our host and suggested he take me to the CYCA which he did. When I got out of the car with my one small duffle bag outside the Club, I felt far from home and very lonely, so with some level of trepidation, I slowly climbed up the steps and into the Clubhouse. I looked around the bar then heard 'G'day Butch'. It was a couple of Australian *Admiral's Cup* team guys I had met in England two years earlier.

Suddenly, I felt I was home!

Soon after, Peter Hemery arrived and was profusely apologetic because his house was being renovated and in total turmoil. However, he told me his mother had a lovely apartment overlooking the yacht club and had a spare room.

We finished second in the Hobart race that year, but the British team did not win the *Southern Cross Cup*. Still, the fact that I had so much fun during my time in

Australia, made it easy for me to decide to stay in Sydney a while longer – but how much longer I didn't know.

I was fortunate enough to be invited to join the crew of John Court's *Ilina* for the 1970 Hobart. I was really looking forward to it as I had heard that the chef from the Chevron [at the time Sydney's most prestigious hotel] was joining us – but I got it all wrong – he was the doorman, not the chef!

It was an interesting race, especially when we rounded the Iron Pot and sailed into the Derwent. Suddenly, all the guys who had been below for the entire race, started popping their heads up – typical lee-rail Vikings, waving to the crowd as we approached the finish. Then, when we were ashore and celebrating in the bar, these guys were the ones telling all the girls the most lurid tales relating to the race and their heroic participation.

*

On Boxing Day morning 1969, while the docks at the CYCA were crammed with crews, family and friends, there was a soon-to-be-highly-prized invitation being handed out particularly to the foreign crews but also to many locals. The invitation was to what would later become known as the Quiet Little Drink post-race party in Hobart, the organisers being two experienced and well-known local yachties, Tony Cable and John Dawson.

The concept for the gathering came about because both men believed that with the Hobart race becoming more glamorous, so the spontaneous party and social scene in Hobart, which had been one of the race's great attributes, was disappearing. In its place was an increasing level of formality and lavishness which were tailored more for the yacht owners and their navigators than the crews in general. Cable later explained:

> We just wanted to recapture some of the old spirit that we found after our earlier races to Hobart. We reckoned that, with the pressure of bigger fleets and international competition, some of the after-the-race fun was squeezed out. So we wanted to put it back.

It worked...

On New Year's Day 1970, not long after opening time at the famous old Shipwright's Arms Hotel in Hobart, a few of the early starters at the bar watched a handful of sailors walk in. 'Obviously remnants of the race,' they no doubt thought, and they were right. The locals took no more notice until two of the yachties, Cable and Dawson, stepped away from their mates, walked up to the bar and ordered 200 beers! The stunned look on the young barman's face said everything: 'Two hundred! I'm sorry, sir, I've gotta go and ask my boss about this'. The hotel owner came out to the bar, and, after explaining how in his 30 years in the business, he had never heard of such an order (while looking at a group of grinning yachties in the corner) asked, 'Who is going to drink them?'

'Our friends and us,' the publican was advised. 'You see, we're having a party here today, so we just wanted to kick it off to a good start.'

'What party?' was the hotel owner's retort.

He soon found out, as over the next 15 minutes, an ever-increasing number of yachties, men and women, filed into the bar, and as they did the 200 beers on the bar started to disappear – rapidly. Not that this was of any concern; to keep ample beers on the bar, the crew of *Jisuma* stepped up and ordered another 200. Soon, more crews were following that lead (with the minimum shout being 100 beers), and as each order went across the bar a progressive tally was chalked onto a blackboard for all to see.

By early afternoon, Cable reminisced, it was time for some of the crews to deliver some spontaneous entertainment – performances that set a standard for the Quiet Little Drinks of the future – which were already inevitable.

> Some of the not internationally renowned entertainers you
> saw at the 'QLD' were worth paying Joan Sutherland
> prices for, the adults-only version of 'Old MacDonald had
> a Farm' was always a winner, and everyone loved the
> Japanese crews, especially when they sang their version of
> 'You are my Sunshine' in fractured English, or sang the
> special Japanese winch grinders song, complete with
> actions. They were hilarious.

Cable's more than appropriate – because his stature and physical features matched the title – song-and-dance rendition of the 'Short, fat, bald man' became another annual favourite.

A total of 1467 beers were consumed at that inaugural Quiet Little Drink – but the day wasn't all about beer consumption. A considerable amount of money was raised to support various local charities and to fund promising young Tasmanian sailors to attend international regattas.

The QLD as such disappeared into obscurity in 1980 after a huge gathering of sailors saw 20,197 beers (near 10,000 litres) consumed, and a lot of money collected for the youth sailing program.

Today the QLD takes the form of an annual fundraising cocktail party at the CYCA in Sydney, the profits from which still go to support that club's youth sailing program.

Col Anderson

SAILING BIO

My introduction to sailing came with the 4th Williamstown Sea Scouts, and my first big victory was in the International Cadet Australian Championship in Hobart 1963/64. I started ocean racing with Bernie Case on *Serifa*, and completed my first Sydney Hobart on *Banjo Paterson* with John Jarret in 1973. That was followed by two races aboard *Fantasy Rag*. I have now sailed in a total of thirty-five Hobart races. In 1979 I was aboard *Police Car* for the *Admirals Cup* in England. I then began a long relationship as crewman and sailmaker for the legendary Lou Abrahams, originally on *Vittoria*, then aboard *Challenge II* (winning the Hobart race in 1983). That was followed by *Challenge III* (*Admiral's Cup* in 1985), then *Ultimate Challenge* for the *Admiral's Cup* in 1987, and a win in the Hobart race in 1989. I also did a Hobart race with Syd Fischer on *Ragamuffin* in 2007, coming second on corrected time.

WHAT WAS YOUR BEST DAY SAILING IN THE SYDNEY HOBART?

A spectacular spinnaker run down the Tasmanian coast and across Storm Bay in the 1983 race aboard *Challenge II*. It was a rocketship ride that contributed greatly to us winning on handicap.

WHAT DAY OR EXPERIENCE WAS THE TOUGHEST OR MOST CHALLENGING?

Having a man overboard on the first night out of Sydney in 1998 on *Challenge Again* while I was on the helm. All I saw was a blur go across the boat in front of me – a body being hurled through the air. It was Garry 'Skippy' Schipper, a Victorian policeman. Fortunately, he had a waterproof torch with him when he went through the lifelines and into the water. We managed to get the mainsail and headsail down and headed back towards where we could see the torchlight. It was a miraculous set of circumstances that led to us getting him back aboard, virtually unharmed. If this had happened 24 hours later after the storm had struck, we probably would not have been able to recover him.

WHAT KEEPS YOU GOING BACK TO THE HOBART RACE?
The challenge and the satisfaction of finishing, especially when it's been a hard race.

WHAT ARE SOME OF THE BIG CHANGES THAT YOU'VE WITNESSED IN YOUR YEARS ASSOCIATED WITH THE RACE?
Safety systems are far better, and the boats are way faster.

CHAPTER 11

The Flying Footpath, Flat Bottoms & Foreign Invaders

The 1970s was the decade where a new trend began to appear in the world of offshore yacht racing. It was a trend that saw designs moving away from the robust, deep-keeled offshore racing yachts that had prevailed seemingly forever, to an era where the yachts in general were akin to lightly constructed, high-performance, flat-bottomed offshore-racing skiffs. Both sides of the design field had their merits, as they did when it came to their advocates and critics. However, there was one point everyone agreed on – when it came down to hard-nosed comparisons, there was probably no better testbed than the Hobart race. The reason was simple: the one thing about the Hobart that would never change was the weather! Its mood swings could be extreme; it could go from calm to calamitous in an hour.

That was certainly the case in 1970, as *Modern Boating* magazine's report on that year's race confirmed. Under the headline, 'Hobart Holocaust', the story declared:

It was no armchair ride this year. An ice-cold blast from the South Pole turned the race into one of the roughest in the classic's 26-year history. The big seas and the wind, which gusted to 60 knots, knocked out a record number of fourteen yachts, many others arriving at the finish with damaged hulls and rigging. Some planked yachts literally fell apart at the seams; some, including fibreglass entries, finished with splintered bulkheads and cracked deck beams.

The fleet size was down considerably on the previous year – sixty-one starters – but the public's fascination with the event remained undiminished. It was estimated there were more than 2000 small craft on the harbour following the yachts while the hills, headlands and bays were again packed with spectators.

A brisk north-easterly wind made the first 24 hours of racing a dream run downwind under spinnaker – perfect conditions for the 22-metre plywood Kiwi cutter, *Buccaneer* (Tom Clark) and the local fancy, *Apollo*. They were having a great race at the front of the pack, at times surfing down waves at 18 knots, but misfortune found *Apollo* as it began to cross Bass Strait; too much pressure was exerted on the boom to the point where it buckled like a bent straw. Then, a short time later, the crew heard a loud and disconcerting 'bang'. There was no immediate indication as to the source of the noise – until they looked aft and saw the rudder blade bob to the surface 50 metres astern. Their race was run.

The majority of interest then centred on whether or not the big, black-hulled *Buccaneer* would set a record pace for the course. That question was answered in a matter of hours when a savage southerly gale belted in from the Southern Ocean. The casualty list was increasing by the hour – broken masts, broken rigging, broken boats and broken hopes. One screaming squall targeted Graham Nock's 13.1-metre sloop *Rumrunner,* knocked it flat then, with the assistance of a large breaking wave, rolled it 360 degrees. To the amazement of the crew, the mast was still standing, but the two small stormsails the yacht had been carrying were nowhere to be seen.

The thoroughbreds of the fleet, Bob Crichton-Brown's *Pacha,* Syd Fischer's *Ragamuffin,* Arthur Byrne's *Salacia II* and *Koomooloo,* then owned by Norman Rydge, dealt with the challenge from the weather and locked into a fight to the finish for handicap honours. It was brilliant tactics and excellent navigation on the part of *Pacha*'s navigator, Stan Darling (his fifth overall victory – then a record), that led to it claiming the *Tattersall Cup. Pacha*'s corrected time resulted in it being declared the race winner by the narrowest margin ever: just 5 minutes and 41 seconds over *Ragamuffin.*

*

It was the 1971 Hobart race that left the world of ocean racing in no doubt that the Kiwis had arrived. Their ascendancy had begun with *Fidelis* taking line honours in 1966, then *Rainbow II* won on corrected time the following year. However, in 1971 the Kiwis came with the intention of dominating the race – beating some of the world's best yachts and thus going on to claim the *Southern Cross Cup* for New Zealand.

A quick scan of the list of entries confirmed the Kiwis' desired result was not going to come easily. Apart from Australia's best ocean racing yachts being part of that year's fleet of seventy-nine, the Brits were there in force, determined to win the *Southern Cross Cup* too. That team included Arthur Slater's exceptional sloop, *Prospect of Whitby*, *Cervantes IV*, and the then British Prime Minister's new 12.8-metre-long, *Morning Cloud*. Unfortunately for the PM, the pressure of office prevented him from being aboard his yacht for the race. Also in the fleet were the American maxis *Kialoa II* (Jim Kilroy) and *Ondine*, and the converted *America's Cup* yacht, *American Eagle*, sailed by young American media man, Ted Turner. The Kiwis arrived in strength with three very good and quite small yachts, *Pathfinder*, *Runaway* and *Wai-Aniwa*, along with the previous year's line honours winner, *Buccaneer*.

A problem caused by an oversight impacted the start that year – someone forgot to tell the wind that New South Wales had gone to daylight saving, so the sea-breeze would be required one hour earlier than in previous years.

Consequently, the start of the race was a drifter with the fleet barely making headway from the start to the harbour entrance. Also, the wash from the thousands of spectator boats did nothing to help the progress of the race yachts.

What followed was one of the easiest Hobart races on record. In the early stages it appeared that *Kialoa II* would better the record time of 3 days, 4 hours, 46 mins, 16 secs set by *Ondine* in 1962. But light weather across Storm Bay and on the Derwent destroyed any chance of that happening.

However, the weather pattern did suit the smaller Kiwi yachts. They made great speed down the Tasmanian coast under spinnaker, and by doing so ended what looked like a British domination of the handicap results. Instead, it was the Kiwi trio, *Pathfinder* first, *Runaway* second and *Wai-Aniwa* third. And on that result the *Southern Cross Cup* crossed the Tasman for the first time.

In Prime Minister Ted Heath's absence, his crew managed to secure a highly respectable fourth place on corrected time.

*

Having completed the Hobart race, Ted Turner, who was a high profile participant in the *America's Cup* in the 1970s, as well as ocean racing, decided to leave his yacht, *American Eagle* in Sydney after the Hobart race and return in December 1972 for another crack at winning top honours. Often referred to as 'The Mouth from the South', he was a very likeable and vociferous yachtsman from Atlanta, Georgia, who was full of fun and daring. His positive persona, dry sense of humour, skill as a sailor and ability to lead meant he was one of the best known and more popular owners on the international sailing circuit. In business he was recognised as the founder of the giant CNN communications network, but in the real world he, more often than not, just wanted to be one of the guys and go sailing. He also liked having Australians in the crew of his yacht – many of them expats living and sailing in California or Newport, Rhode Island.

Boxing Day 1972 was a grey day for the start of the 28th Hobart race, so the red-hulled *American Eagle* was the most conspicuous yacht among the seventy-nine starters. During the pre-race briefing all skippers had been requested, for safety reasons, to remain well clear of the spectator fleet lining each side of the harbour, but that request must not have registered with Turner. For him, getting the best possible start mattered more than dodging a few spectator boats, so, during the final countdown to the starting cannon being fired, Turner was heard shouting to his bowman using every possible decibel of his southern drawl to wave spectator boats away so he could manoeuvre the yacht into the most advantageous position.

At the Heads, the long and sleek *American Eagle* sliced its way into the lead over the considerably larger 72-foot Canadian maxi ketch *Graybeard*, the yacht most fancied for line honours. But with conditions forecast to be generally light for almost the entire course, the '*Eagle*' stretched her wings and showed the way.

The two leaders stayed in visual contact for almost all 628 nm. At times, when the breeze was at its strongest, *Graybeard*'s massive spread of sail was sufficient to power it into the lead. But just as quickly, when the wind went soft, *American Eagle* would be back in front.

In the hunt for the corrected time trophy, the *Tattersall Cup*, Gordon Ingate's ageing *Admiral's Cup* yacht, *Caprice of Huon*, which benefited greatly from an age-allowance handicap bonus, looked to be the boat to beat. However, as many observers predicted, with the wind having been so light almost the entire race, the final 11 nm up the Derwent would probably decide the results.

The conditions on the river certainly provided a scare for *American Eagle*'s crew as they made their last lunge for line honours. At The Iron Pot, *American Eagle* led *Graybeard* by 4 miles, then got parked in a calm, and were forced to watch the Canadians continue to glide towards them. After many nerve-racking moments, the faintest breeze finally came their way – sufficient to see *American Eagle* cruise across the finish line, a mere 15 minutes ahead of their rivals.

It was then late afternoon and quick calculations by race officials confirmed that *Caprice of Huon* had until midday the following day to finish if it was to beat *American Eagle* on handicap.

From the early hours the next morning, Turner, some crew and his supporters, stood at the finish line at Battery Point, watching *Caprice of Huon* in the distance moving ever so slowly.

Time, tide and breeze went in *American Eagle*'s favour; another glassy calm descended on Ingate's yacht, trapping it. It was a situation not dissimilar to the one that had almost cost *Eagle* line honours. This time, however, *Caprice of Huon* remained trapped.

When it became apparent that *American Eagle* could not be beaten and had therefore secured an historic double – line and handicap honours – jubilation filled the air and the celebrations began. It was only the second time since *Rani* that a yacht had scored the double.

*

An interesting aspect to this same race was the entry of a small, radical looking yacht named *Evolution*. The original concept was for it to be a low-cost, light-displacement Half Ton Cup class yacht about 9 metres in length. It was commissioned by CYCA member John Diacopoulos, but at some stage during the design process an error was made in the calculations – a mistake that wasn't realised until after the yacht was launched and measured. *Evolution* did not rate as a Half Ton Cup class yacht.

The yacht was built using the composite sandwich technique – fibreglass outer and inner skins with an end-grain balsa core sandwiched in between. Everything about this yacht was somewhat different, and basic: it had only one winch and that was mounted on the deck just forward of the cockpit; the stove was located in a drawer under the companionway stairs; the navigation table folded down from between the twin companionway hatches which gave access to the cabin; there were no floorboards (so the crew walked around on the keel bolts in the bilge). But it was the rating that was the problem, and this was where Butch Dalrymple-Smith (ex the British yacht *Prospect of Whitby* in the 1969 Hobart) stepped in. His calculations revealed that if *Evolution* was rigged as a ketch it would rate as a Half Tonner (apart from the fact that it would be unique by being the only Half Tonner in the world rigged as a ketch). Butch was sufficiently impressed by the yacht that he joined the crew for the 1972 race – and as it turned out *Evolution* proved to be remarkably fast in the conditions that prevailed. The little yacht was well placed on corrected time all the way to Cape Raoul, on Storm Bay – but that was where the shutters came down on what had been a following breeze most of the way from Sydney. From there it was a drifting match. *Evolution* eventually finished 33rd on corrected time, but the *Evolution* crew didn't really care. They had finished 25 minutes before midnight on New Year's Eve, and that meant they were able to join one very large dockside party.

*

The emergence of fibreglass as a material suitable for building ocean racing yachts started to happen in America around the time of the inaugural Hobart race. The major structural problem was to be able to create a hull that was light enough yet strong enough to be competitive. Even so, as such targets started to be achieved, the purists would not have a bar of it. 'If God meant for there to be plastic boats he would have made plastic trees,' was one common comment. Fibreglass boats were also referred to as 'Tupperware boats' and 'cocktail shakers'.

But there was more to come: Sydney yachting enthusiast Dr Tony Fisher literally 'rocked' the local and international ocean racing scene when he launched his maxi cruising yacht, *Helsal* – which was built from ferro-cement, the same material that Ben Lexcen experimented with in the mid-60s. It was designed by a former high school technical drawing teacher in Sydney, Joe Adams. And, while *Helsal* could not be described as a thing of beauty, it certainly showed a good turn of speed in early trials – so much so that the owner decided to enter it in the 1973 Hobart.

Much to everyone's amazement the 'rock boat' turned out to be a bit of a rocket; it completely outclassed the two line honours favourites, Jack Rooklyn's *Apollo* and Rolly Tasker's *Siska II*, especially when there was plenty of wind coming from astern. Not even a spinnaker wrap, when the giant downwind sail wound itself tightly around the forestay (an incident that took 3 hours to unravel), could stop *Helsal's* record-breaking run. It was 3 days 1 hr 32 mins after departing Sydney that the yacht, which had become a sentimental favourite with the public, reached Hobart. *Helsal* had broken the race record time for the course set by *Ondine II* 11 years earlier by more than 2 hours. It was dubbed 'the Flying Footpath'.

To rub salt (maybe even sand) into the wounds of their rivals, the crew of *Helsal* celebrated in grand style at the dock in Hobart – serving cocktails from a cement mixer standing proudly on the deck.

When it came to the corrected time result, there was cause for Ben Lexcen to enjoy his own celebration – the Hong Kong owned *Ceil III,* which he designed, survived a brutal nose dive in a 50-knot squall off Tasmania's east coast, and sailed on to claim the *Tattersall Cup.*

But it was *Helsal's* amazing achievement that had everyone talking, even Arthur Slater, whose *Prospect of Whitby* finished second overall and won Division A: 'I'm in the concrete business myself. I make about five million cubic yards a year, but I still wouldn't go to sea in a concrete boat.'

*

It was no surprise that Huey Long was not impressed by the news that he had lost his race record time to the Flying Footpath. It was also unsurprising that he returned the following year determined to regain his crown, this time with a new yacht, the 24-metre *Ondine III*, which was fresh from winning the Newport to Bermuda race. It was described as the most expensive, luxurious and innovative ocean racing yacht in the world.

As the fleet raced towards the Heads, spectators ashore and afloat expected a grand showdown between *Ondine III* and Jack Rooklyn's 2-week-old maxi, the Ben Lexcen-designed, *Ballyhoo*, but it was the 15-metre sloop *Bumblebee 3* that became the centre of attention. Despite being manned by some of Australia's best yachtsmen, the beautiful sloop slammed straight into Sow and Pigs Reef near the harbour entrance. Frantic efforts by the crew soon had the yacht back in deep water and sailing – the only reported damage being to the pride of those on board. However, the yacht's penchant for hitting things stayed with it for the race – a whale was the next victim off the New South Wales south coast.

With no *Southern Cross Cup* series associated with that year's race, the fleet size was down to sixty-three, but in that number there were seventeen brand new yachts.

The charge for line honours between *Ondine III* and *Ballyhoo* was dramatic, close and exciting, with both yachts surging across Bass Strait under spinnaker and at great speed. At that stage *Ballyhoo* was within sight of *Ondine III*, but in an instant its race took a dramatic turn for the worse – the yacht was hit by a sudden wind gust of around 40 knots, and before the crew had time to lower the spinnaker, *Ballyhoo* went out of control, did a spectacular pirouette and was knocked flat. It then went into wild gyrations before being knocked down again to a point where the mast was 20 degrees beyond horizontal. Two crewmen were hurled overboard only to be saved by their safety harnesses. It was 15 hellish minutes before full control was regained and the yacht could resume racing. Meanwhile, *Ondine III* continued to sail towards the southern horizon.

To the delight of many, especially members of the CYCA, it was Peter Kurts's beautiful sloop *Love & War* that went on to claim the *Tattersall Cup*. Full credit for this result went to the highly experienced crew, which included Magnus Halvorsen as navigator. This race was a remarkable achievement for the great sailor. It was his twelfth Hobart race start and in that time he had achieved a record of five wins and six second placings. *Ballyhoo* made a late charge in the race for line honours, but it was not enough to beat *Ondine III* home. For Huey Long, this was the sixth consecutive line honours victory for the new yacht in different races, but its time for the course was 12 hours outside *Helsal*'s record.

*

By the mid-1970s Ben Lexcen was having an obvious impact on the Australian sailing scene with his designs, and there was more to come.

For competitors and race followers alike there were many magnificent elements to the 1975 race, including the presence of American Jim Kilroy's grand maxi *Kialoa III* (which was billed as the world's fastest maxi), and fellow countryman Mark Johnson's legendary maxi *Windward Passage*, then holder of eleven course records worldwide.

The local hope to be first to Hobart was *Ballyhoo*, and it certainly got off to a good start; cheers could be heard filling the air as *Ballyhoo* led the record fleet of 102 yachts out through the Heads and onto the open sea.

The one historical feature to this year's race was the presence of the first ever all-female crew led by noted Sydney yachtswoman and dinghy sailor, Vicki Willman, skippering *Barbarian*. Unfortunately, the yacht became the centre of attention at the start for all the wrong reasons: a spectator craft strayed onto the course but went unnoticed by Willman and her crew. Consequently, the yacht ploughed straight into the small boat, literally cutting it in two. The first Vicki knew of the incident was when a man, dripping wet, and with a shocked look on his face clambered onto the deck of *Barbarian*. Incredibly, the always determined Willman had one response to this moment: 'Get him off. Get him off. We're racing!'

This was to be a Hobart race where dreams came true – it was a downhill sleigh ride to Tasman Island for almost all the fleet. *Kialoa III* and *Windward Passage* were locked into a dogfight where it was give-no-quarter racing. They had every possible square centimetre of sail set and surfed down wave after wave, and were sailing so impressively that it was apparent by the time they were mid-Bass Strait that the race record was destined to fall, but to whom was impossible to guess.

The 17-metre pocket maxi *Apollo*'s effort to stay in touch with the leaders and finish inside the existing record began to unravel when two of its largest spinnakers exploded into tatters within a very short time.

If there was a prize for the most unfortunate moment for any crew member during the race, it would have had to go to Peter Shipway, who was a crew member aboard the previous year's race winner, *Love & War*. Once in Hobart, he told of the incident:

I was on the toilet for the first time in the entire race when the yacht was knocked flat. I couldn't hang on to anything, so I went crashing through the toilet door. As I landed on the opposite side of the cabin, the entire contents of the toilet spilled out and landed all over me. All I could think was great fun, this ocean racing!

The line honours battle between *Kialoa III* and *Windward Passage* was as intense as it was exciting all the way to the finish line. *Kialoa III* got the gun 23 minutes ahead of its rival. Most importantly, Kilroy had achieved his goal and set a new course record with an elapsed time of 2 days, 14 hours, 36 minutes, slicing some 11 hours off the previous best time.

The race winner was the West Australian yacht, *Rampage*, another Ben Lexcen design, this one owned by Peter Packer. It was a hard earned and well deserved victory as the yacht's crew had to repair a broken boom mid-race and survive a serious dose of the death rolls (where the yacht rocks violently from side to side, always on the verge of going out of control).

*

The 1976 Hobart race confirmed that a revolution in yacht design had arrived – and there would be no turning back. It was the year that a lightweight, flat-bottomed, skiff-type yacht won the race on corrected time; a result that meant the transition from the centuries-old concept of deep hulls, deep keels and high displacement was complete.

The driving force behind this change was Kiwi designer Bruce Farr, who, in his younger years, had enjoyed a remarkably successful career designing highly competitive 12-foot and 18-foot skiffs. Now two of his ocean racing designs, *Piccolo* (John Pickles, New South Wales) and *Rockie* (Peter Kingston, New Zealand), were taking on some of the world's best yachts in the Hobart race.

The official program for the '76 race said of *Piccolo*: 'A big effort will be needed if this yacht is to do well.' Well indeed – and that's exactly what Pickles and his enthusiastic team did, beating the fleet on corrected time. Then, confirming this result was no fluke, Kingston and his Kiwis sailed *Rockie* into second place, beating Syd Fischer's highly fancied *Ragamuffin* and Peter Kurts's two-time Hobart race winner *Love & War* into third and fourth places respectively.

The ability of this design concept to sail extremely fast downwind was confirmed as both *Piccolo* and *Rockie* blasted across Bass Strait on the face of a powerful following wind. But what made their dominance even more stunning in the eyes of their detractors was that 70 per cent of the race that year was to windward, or with sails slightly eased. They also brought to an end the days of crews sitting in the cockpit and trimming sails from there. Now, body weight was considered moveable ballast, so the majority of the crew spent most of their time either perched on the windward side of the yacht or sleeping in bunks, again on the windward side.

*

As if to level the playing field between the old and new design concepts, the weather gods delivered a howling weather system for the 1977 race – a system so powerful that the light-displacement yachts were put to the test more than thoroughly. One person very much on the receiving end was world champion, Harold Cudmore, from Ireland, who brought his Half Ton Cup class *Silver Shamrock* to Sydney for the big race south. Designed by Ron Holland, this was a lightly constructed skiff-type yacht which had an unballasted retractable centreboard (like an off-the-beach sailing dinghy) and internal ballast.

'We got very bad conditions in the Hobart race that year,' Cudmore recalled:

> The weather was far worse than we ever anticipated – so bad, in fact, that the boat started falling apart around us. The initial front came in at more than 50 knots and settled down at around 40, so we decided the only thing to do was to abandon the race and head back to shore as quickly as possible. I took over the helm because I reckoned that if I was sailing for my life, then I wanted to do it myself!
>
> Initially, we started running downwind on a course towards Sydney, but suddenly we were overwhelmed by a massive wave that capsized us so badly that the mast was in

the water. It was a wild and frightening situation. Fortunately, the boat came back upright, so we then decided to forget Sydney and just track towards the coast. As soon as we had things settled down and were confident it was safe to do so, we had Killian Bushe – who built the boat – go below to check things out. When he went to check the engine he noticed the oil dipstick was missing and that there was oil splashed on the underside of the cockpit floor – that told us how extreme the knockdown was. We had obviously gone well beyond horizontal!

The hair-raising ride continued, but fortunately we managed to reach Ulladulla and shelter there. All the time we were at sea I was reminding myself that having no external ballast and just a simple centreboard was not the smartest decision we ever made. It was the worst Hobart race I have experienced, but I have to say it wasn't as bad as the horror Fastnet race in 1979.

Following this and other incidents in this race, many experienced offshore sailors labelled the light-displacement, skiff-type yachts as being death traps. The CYCA had no option but to take immediate action – it drew up new regulations that imposed far more stringent stability rules for all yachts entering the classic in future years. Even so, in time these new rules would prove to be not rigorous enough.

There was a record number of 130 starters in 1977's race, but within 24 hours the gale which had capsized *Silver Shamrock* had wreaked havoc across the fleet. The toll was alarming: within a very short time fifty-eight yachts had been forced to retire through structural or rig damage, sea sickness, injury, fatigue and fear. Also, the case against the light-displacement yachts was coming through loud and clear – only one of the seven that started reached Hobart, and even it suffered structural damage to its hull.

The gale also took the gloss off the fact that the two American glamour maxis, *Kialoa III* and *Windward Passage* – which had competed in the 1975 race – were participating this year. The pair had enjoyed a neck-and-neck charge down the New South Wales coast until the southerly buster arrived unannounced. Both had spinnakers set at that time, but in a matter of minutes they went from racing south at around 10 knots to heading north back towards Sydney at a similar speed. The *Kialoa III* crew handled the situation in a superior fashion and consequently had their yacht back on course for Hobart much sooner than their rival. By next morning *Kialoa III*'s lead had opened up to a whopping 26 nm. The big ketch also won on corrected time from Syd Fischer's *Ragamuffin*, with *Windward Passage* third.

*

If there was an award for the greatest ever line honours achievement in the Sydney Hobart race then the late Jack Rooklyn's 17.8-metre-long pocket maxi, *Apollo*, would have to be a leading contender.

It started with a 16,000 nm loop around the Pacific and culminated in an amazing result.

Over Easter in 1978, *Apollo* – which was designed by Ben Lexcen and built for Alan Bond 9 years earlier – claimed yet another line honours in the Brisbane–Gladstone race. After that satisfying result Rooklyn directed his boat manager, the well-respected and very capable yachtsman Duncan Van Woerden, to sail the yacht to Hawaii to contest the international *Pan Am Clipper Cup* series. That was a successful mission, so *Apollo* was then sailed to California to compete in the high profile Big Boat series on San Francisco Bay. With Rooklyn being the head of the Bally poker machine organisation in Australia, the yacht was also used for corporate hospitality purposes in association with the American parent company.

With those tasks complete, and the Hobart race being next on the yacht's agenda, Van Woerden and four crew, including one woman, set sail from Los Angeles on 20 August, bound for Sydney.

'Our schedule for getting to Sydney in time for the big race looked good,' Van Woerden explained:

It meant we would have a few weeks up our sleeve in Sydney to get the yacht race ready. But that wasn't to be the case; light winds slowed us dramatically on the 2300 nm stretch from Fanning Island to Samoa, but even so our schedule was still looking okay.

However, the next leg over the 600 nm between Samoa and Fiji changed all that. We were hit by winds of 50 knots and copped an absolute shellacking. Worse still, two of our mast stays began to fail. I immediately radioed Sydney and arranged for replacement rigging to be airfreighted to Suva. We lost 13 days in Suva while we waited for the new rigging to arrive and be fitted.

When we finally left Suva we were confronted by an absolute glass-out – zero wind day after day. All we could do was keep motoring towards Sydney and hope that the breeze would soon arrive – but it didn't. We then knew we would almost certainly run out of fuel so we diverted to Lord Howe Island. The locals floated three 44-gallon drums of diesel out to us in the lagoon and we were able to lift them aboard using a halyard and our spinnaker pole as a 'crane jib'. That exercise cost us another two days so it wasn't until 23 December – just three days before the start of the Hobart – that we departed. And, wouldn't you know it, we found ourselves in another calm.

I was sending progress messages to Jack Rooklyn on a regular basis so he and the race crew knew our whereabouts.

At that time things were very much against us making the start, but then 'bingo', a howling 25-knot north-easterly wind arrived on the scene. Up went the spinnaker and off we went, aiming straight for Sydney; it was make-it-or-break-it sailing. Then came another problem – we lost all communications which meant I couldn't advise Jack by radio of our stroke of luck – that there was then a remote chance we would make it!

About 200 nm out of Sydney we saw a ship heading in the same direction as us. Fortunately we were going faster than it was, so after a while we were able to sail up alongside it and shout to the captain, asking him if he would advise Sydney radio of our position. Obviously the ship's crew were impressed by how fast we were going because the radio officer, when he contacted Sydney radio, reported: 'We are doing 14.5 knots and we have just been passed by a yacht under spinnaker heading for Sydney'.

The nor'east wind continued unabated so *Apollo* surfed through Sydney Heads under spinnaker at midnight on Christmas Day. As relieved as the crew was, they realised they faced an immediate problem – there weren't enough crew on board to lower the spinnaker in such windy conditions. So, Van Woerden steered the yacht straight ahead into Middle Harbour so the sail could be lowered in the lee of a headland.

Apollo then began motoring towards the CYCA marina in Rushcutters Bay where it arrived at 3am – just 10 hours before the start of the Hobart!

The race crew and other supporters, who were waiting on the dock, immediately went about the task of converting a yacht that was in cruising mode into an all-out race boat.

Van Woerden recalled:

Everyone – the delivery crew included – went about what was an incredibly well orchestrated plan. Even the Customs guys were there determined to make things as easy as they could for us.

We all worked right through the night. We made some essential repairs while new racing sails and deck equipment went on board, as did the food needed for the race. While this was all happening in the darkness there was action underneath the boat; a scuba diver replaced the cruising propeller with a racing model then scrubbed the bottom of the hull.

Everything went as planned so, quite understandably, a massive cheer went up from supporters, spectators and rival crews as *Apollo* pulled away from the dock mid-morning and headed for the start line.

'It was almost as though we didn't stop in Sydney,' Van Worden said later. 'We arrived at 3am and were racing at 1pm.'

After such a Herculean effort there was little wonder that *Apollo* went into the race as a crowd favourite among the ninety-seven starters. And soon after the gun sounded there was a fitting reward for the efforts put in by the yacht's team – *Apollo* led the fleet out of the harbour!

An unstable and very light weather pattern off Gabo Island, at the northern edge of Bass Strait, split the fleet. The seven leading yachts escaped its clutches and continued to progress south while the rest were trapped by a calm for up to 15 hours.

In the words of Van Woerden:

The race was a drifter, but we didn't mind because *Apollo* was good at drifting. At one stage we could see seven yachts around us, including *Anaconda*, *Helsal*, *Love & War* and *Margaret Rintoul II*.

After we crawled across Bass Strait we opted to stay well offshore while the race leader, *Helsal*, was about six miles inshore of us. Our tactic paid off. We found the breeze and *Apollo* went on to be first into Hobart. It was a wonderful reward for everyone who had been associated with this effort from the moment we arrived in Sydney just those few hours before the start of the race. But more than anything, it was a big thank you to Jack Rooklyn who was on board with us. From that moment on Jack and I became mates for life.

The 34th Hobart race would prove to be the slowest in 10 years. But more importantly it would confirm what a great yacht *Love & War* really was. For the second time in 4 years owner Peter Kurts stood atop the podium and was awarded the *Tattersall Cup*. This outstanding achievement was thanks in no small way to exceptional crew work, coupled with a bold move they made in near-drift conditions at Tasman Island. The yacht was guided to a point where it was just metres from the rocky shore, a position where it was able to benefit from the downdraught coming from the imposing 250-metre-high cliffs and thus make solid gains over its rivals while heading for the finish.

*

A number of sailing tragedies in Australia and the UK in the latter half of 1979 saw the sport of ocean yacht racing end the decade with its back to the wall. The worst incident occurred during the Fastnet Race in England in August that year. Fifteen sailors perished, twenty-four yachts were abandoned, five yachts sank and 125 crewmembers were rescued during a storm that quickly grew to become a near hurricane that roared across the Irish Sea and battered the 303 competing yachts.

That disaster rang alarm bells for the highly respected yacht designer, builder and Hobart race competitor, Magnus Halvorsen. Of particular concern to him was the continuing trend towards light-displacement yachts, a concern that caused him to go on record with a warning that there would be a disaster in the Hobart race if standards weren't improved.

Around that time, the CYCA was analysing all the information relating to the causes and consequences of the Fastnet tragedy, along with Halvorsen's alert. Also taken into consideration were concerns expressed by club member Gordon Marshall, who had reviewed yacht construction, stability and safety issues for many years.

*

It was obvious that the Fastnet Race disaster earlier in the year did not deter entries in the 1979 Hobart – 147 registered for that year's race, thirty-seven more than the previous best in 1977.

When it came to the race start, it was only the second time in the classic's thirty-five-year history that spectators on shore and afloat were treated to the sight of a downwind spinnaker start. As the race gun fired, spinnakers burst open in a blaze of colour. Two yachts towered above the rest: Bob Bell's magnificent maxi *Condor of Bermuda,* and the new local hope *Bumblebee 4*, owned by John Kahlbetzer. Much to the delight of the locals *'The Bee'* stole *Condor*'s thunder.

Within 24 hours the wind had gone around to the north, a change that gave the yachts a dramatic spinnaker ride down the coast and into Bass Strait. In those conditions the crews needed to stay on high alert as it was easy for a yacht to go into death rolls. The consequences of this situation can be dire, as two crews were to discover when the yachts *Moonshadow* and *Regardless* rolled so severely to windward that their spinnaker poles and part of their spinnakers plunged into the water. With that, the masts and rigging became so overloaded that the masts failed. They buckled in half and crashed over the side of the boats in a tangled mess.

For much of the passage down the Tasmanian coast, the wind went soft and the air soggy, the latter situation being due to a fog which at times was so dense that visibility was as little as 75 metres. This made for anxious moments for crews as they probed their way through the gloomy grey environment towards an unseen Tasman Island. The pressure on each yacht's navigator was intense as they checked and rechecked their plots. Phil Eadie, navigator aboard Graham Lambert and John Crisp's *Impetuous*, did a masterly job during its approach to the island in darkness. Every crew member on deck was peering ahead, looking for any sign of the loom from the lighthouse until someone realised it wasn't ahead of them; it was actually above them – 300 metres up! The powerful beam from the light was barely visible because the fog was so thick. This situation also meant that *Impetuous* was only a few hundred metres from the island's vertical cliffs.

Condor of Bermuda proved to be no match for *Bumblebee 4*, which, after taking line honours in Hobart, looked to be the yacht to beat on handicap. But the whim of the wind put an end to that hope and instead brought about what was the biggest upset in the race's history. Conditions rapidly turned in favour of the smallest yachts near the tail of the field. They sped into Hobart so fast that they completely dominated the corrected time results – the top nine place getters were all less than 10.3 metres in overall length. And, much to the delight of the Tasmanians, the winner on corrected time was Bob Cumming's 9-metre-long sloop, *Screw Loose* – the smallest yacht ever to win the Hobart classic.

On a sad note, this 35th edition of the Hobart race was marred by two offshore tragedies. Leading Hobart yachtsman and business identity Charles Davies and his crew of four disappeared without trace when their new yacht, *Charleston*, foundered in a Bass Strait gale while sailing to Sydney for the race start. A similar fate beset the New Zealand yacht, *Smackwater Jack* and its crew, which was led by promising young yacht designer Paul Whiting. It disappeared without trace somewhere between Hobart and Auckland after having finished 38th on corrected time in the race. These tragedies, along with the warnings from Halvorsen and Marshall, led to the CYCA introducing new standards relating to the structural integrity of hulls and the stability of race yachts.

Damien Parkes

SAILING BIO

I've sailed over 250,000 miles here and overseas. Unusually, all my races have been either as a watch captain or as skipper. The 1976 Hobart was my first. I've also sailed in two *Clipper Cups* in Hawaii and contested over twenty races to Lord Howe Island, Southport and Brisbane.

WHAT WAS YOUR BEST DAY SAILING IN THE SYDNEY HOBART?

Standing on the foredeck of *Vengeance* in Constitution Dock having won line honours in a boat I had sailed from Perth to Sydney, then raced as watch captain with Dave Kellett in the Hobart. He came up and gave me a hug ... we were both a bit teary. My other best sailing day was when my son and I sailed our first race together on a Sydney 38 with some sailing school students. We came third overall and my son came up to me and said, 'You do know how to do this Dad, don't you!'

WHAT DAY OR EXPERIENCE WAS THE TOUGHEST OR MOST CHALLENGING?

Breaking the inner forestay on the famous 12-metre *Gretel* just after we rounded Cape Raoul. Kellett tried to get me to steer conservatively while he fixed the problem. It was so frustrating knowing that until that point, we might have won the race. From that moment on, we couldn't push the yacht to its full potential as we stood the chance of losing the rig. We finished up losing the race on handicap by just seconds. Another testing day was when I had to retire my boat, *Freight Train*, and go to the assistance of a yacht in distress in the '93 race.

WHAT KEEPS YOU GOING BACK TO THE HOBART RACE?

The camaraderie before, during and after the race, along with the sight of The Iron Pot at the entrance to the Derwent.

WHAT ARE SOME OF THE BIG CHANGES THAT YOU'VE WITNESSED IN YOUR YEARS ASSOCIATED WITH THE RACE?

The changes in the design and structure of the yachts will hopefully mean that we won't see dramatic events like those that came in 1998, 1993, 1987 or 1977 again.

CHAPTER 12

Alan Payne's Crystal Ball

In the wake of the Fastnet Race tragedy in 1979, and the loss of Hobart race entrants *Charleston* and *Smackwater Jack,* alarm bells were ringing across the sport of ocean racing, and nowhere more so than in Australia. This was a considerable problem for the CYCA as the club was recognised the world over for its leadership in all corners of the sport. However, the advent of the light-displacement yachts, and the fact that there were few rules in place governing their structural integrity and stability, created a dilemma. Whereas in the aviation industry new aircraft concepts had to comply with rigorous design standards and the test pilots had to be highly qualified, there were no such controls within ocean racing, which, after all, was a sport. It was a situation where the crews were at times pilots without parachutes aboard test craft that would, in a severe storm, be exposed to incalculable stresses, strains and dangers.

In reality it was baptism by fire.

This situation had been gnawing away at designer Alan Payne's conscience for some time, until he could not stand back any longer. He felt compelled to do something about it: he had to speak out.

That opportunity came in December 1981 when he was invited to be the guest speaker at a dinner for prominent offshore racing sailors. The venue was a penthouse, owned by *Ragamuffin*'s Syd Fischer, which was located atop the Gazebo, a high-rise hotel in Kings Cross.

Despite his great talent as a yacht designer, Payne was a very modest man, so it was no surprise that he explained to the guests that he wanted to put something before them – but at the same time he had no desire for it to go into the public domain. The subject, which he had researched extensively, dealt with what could confront a race yacht in the worst case scenario in Bass Strait. In essence it was a warning – his case study analysed what could be expected should race yachts be confronted by a 35-knot gale in the Strait. He based much of his findings on wind and wave height data gathered from offshore oil rig platforms located in Bass Strait. He also researched what adverse influence a fast-flowing southerly current would have on wave heights in a strong southerly gale along with the frequency of rogue waves, which can be twice the height of the average wave in a storm.

Highly experienced offshore racing yachtsman John Stanley, who was at the dinner, said Payne told the guests they would have to do 1000 Hobart races to be certain of seeing a rogue wave, and while that was of little worry for competitors, race administrators should be concerned. When it came to wind strength Payne argued that, in general, the stability of the current crop of racing yachts was insufficient for the conditions that could be expected in a Hobart race. He referred those present to the design of the classic Bristol Channel Pilot Cutter in England – a deep-keeled sailing vessel with no engine that had proved itself capable of riding out any sea conditions, and even more impressively, sail away from a lee shore. He added that in his opinion none of the current crop of ocean racing yachts was seaworthy enough to achieve this.

Then, in closing, Payne made what would, in 1998, be seen as a hauntingly accurate prediction: he hypothesised that in a storm three yachts would completely disappear, taking twenty-two people with them; six crew would be lost overboard; three life rafts containing twelve people would never be found and a rescue helicopter would crash while on a mission. The warning was there for all to consider.

*

The 1980 race was a whitewash for the Kiwis – thanks primarily to the legendary round-the-world yachtsman Peter Blake, and his impressive 21-metre sloop, *New Zealand*. The expertly crewed maxi was under spinnaker and on record pace from the start all the way to Tasman Island and on into Storm Bay, to a point where it had 6.5 hours to cover the remaining 40 nm. That would normally be easy pickings for such a yacht – but this was a Hobart race, and nothing is ever certain. Sure enough, the wind died and *New Zealand* virtually became glued to the sea; it covered less than 2 nm in the next 7 hours! After much frustration a gentle puff arrived, enough for *New Zealand* to break free from the shackles of the calm. It glided into the Derwent and 11 nm up the river to the finish sufficiently far ahead of the fleet to secure both line and handicap honours – only the fourth yacht in race history to do so.

*

By the time the '81 race was completed one could have been forgiven for thinking there was some form of annual rotation happening within the classic. In 1979 the smallest entries filled the major places on corrected time, then in 1980 it was the big boats, and in 1981 the little boats were back in force.

Certainly for the race followers in Sydney, and probably for the majority of the crews, the most spectacular and exciting part of the 1981 race was the fact that it was a wonderfully colourful downwind spinnaker start. It was noted: 'As the start gun sounded, billowing multi-coloured spinnakers popped open like blossoms in spring, delighting the hundreds of thousands of spectators on and around the harbour, and those watching on national television.'

It was an easy race – almost a cruise – as light headwinds prevailed for the majority of the near 600 nm to Tasman Island. Then, once around that corner and into Storm Bay there was a minefield of calms that trapped many of the competing yachts.

This writer, who was aboard Syd Fischer's *Ragamuffin* that year, well remembers the frustration associated with the yacht being 'parked' in a windless hole when tantalisingly close to the entrance to the Derwent. After battling fitful breezes all the way across the bay to that point where the wind shut down, *Ragamuffin* then became a beacon for those crews aboard yachts approaching from behind. It was obvious to all – with

Ragamuffin rocking like a giant pendulum in the gentle swells and the sails flapping uselessly – that there was no wind where we were. It was a 'no-go zone'. We were stopped there for more than 3 hours with the sun belting down on us, watching our rivals picking up streaks of breeze all around us. What made it even worse was that on too many occasions we had to endure the sight of yachts that had been many miles behind us pick up puffs that enabled them to glide past us a few hundred metres away, enter the Derwent then beat us to the finish by hours. We could only remind ourselves: 'That's ocean racing', or as others might suggest: 'The joy of ocean yacht racing is one of the world's best kept secrets!'

One interesting result in the race was that Bernard Lewis's latest acquisition, the sleek, red-hulled maxi *Vengeance* (nee *Siska*), with long-time Hobart racer Dave Kellett at the helm, did much better than the 'experts' predicted. The line honours challenges expected from Bob Bell's visiting maxi, *Condor*, plus *Helsal* and *Apollo*, never really eventuated. *Vengeance* sailed across the finish line off Battery Point more than 4 hours 30 minutes ahead of *Condor*, but its elapsed time for the course was more than 36 hours outside *Kialoa III*'s record time. The mid-sized yachts, which were the most fancied for top honours on corrected time, hit the wall when the wind evaporated in Storm Bay. The winner of the *Tattersall Cup* was Jim Dunstan's 10.1-metre-long fibreglass production yacht, *Zeus II*. There was an additional record for the books – the fleet of 159 was the largest in the race's thirty-seven-year history.

*

The 1982 Hobart was the year of the grandstand finish. In a scene that was akin to the closing stages of the Melbourne Cup where two favourites go to the line nose-to-nose, two of the line honours contenders in that year's Hobart race went to the line bow-on-bow. The atmosphere was electric as thousands of spectators gathered onshore at the finish cheering, clapping and shouting encouragement while willing their favourite home.

The two combatants were the maxi yachts *Condor of Bermuda* (Bob Bell) and Jack Rooklyn's new *Apollo*.

There were another three maxis in the fleet of 119 that year, the others being Bernard Lewis's *Vengeance*, Tony Fisher's *Helsal II*, and the South African downwind flier *Rampant II*, owned by Alan Tucker.

Legendary navigator Stan Darling, who at age 75 was competing in his 27th Hobart, knew how best to describe the 1982 Hobart: it was 'a gentleman's race'. Wet weather gear and seaboots were not called for over the entire distance; and it was easy, exhilarating sailing almost all the way. Still, there was a dramatic man overboard situation that could well have changed the outcome of the race.

The five big boats were within sight of each other for the entire distance from Sydney to Hobart, and at some stage each one was either in the lead or close to it. Even as they approached the entrance to the Derwent River they were still within sight of each other. The one thing no one knew, either on the water or onshore, was that they were setting themselves up for the greatest finish ever seen in ocean racing anywhere in the world.

When *Condor of Bermuda* rounded The Iron Pot and entered the Derwent, it held a 1.5 nm advantage over *Apollo* with

Helsal II very much within striking distance. *Condor*'s crew chose to stay close to the eastern shore while the *Apollo* and *Helsal* crews knew if they were to have any chance of gaining the lead over the final few miles, then they should sail down the western shore in the hope of finding better breeze – and that's what happened. A sea breeze fanned across the glassy river and favoured the pursuers first. Lightweight spinnakers were set immediately to capture every puff. It was late morning when *Condor* and *Apollo* converged just 4 miles from the finish – and *Apollo* had its bow in front! From that point it was a tense and tactical bow-on-bow battle all the way to the line. Onshore, while all this was unfolding, the atmosphere within the huge crowd of spectators was electric – and they were cheering themselves hoarse. It was *Apollo, Condor, Apollo, Condor,* in slow motion all the way to the line. Just a couple of boat lengths from the line, the breeze faded to almost nothing, and it played into the hands of the *Condor* crew. Their yacht's considerably heavier displacement gave it better momentum, which was enough for it to glide past *Apollo* and claim line honours by a mere 2 metres. The official margin was just 7 seconds.

No previous race anywhere in the world had seen such a close finish.

*

Prior to the race starting, Sir James Hardy's already successful offshore racer *Police Car* was the favourite to win on handicap. The yacht, which took its name because 'no-one passes a police car', looked as though it would deliver the goods until the schizophrenic nature of Storm Bay's weather intervened yet again — and showed that this particular *Police Car* could be overtaken when nature chose.

A southerly blow, with gusts of 40 knots, suddenly appeared and immediately brought a near calm to an end. At this stage the crew of Ray Johnston's 11.5-metre sloop *Scallywag* could see *Police Car*, which meant that their yacht was very much in the hunt when it came to winning the *Tattersall Cup*. With this added incentive to keep the yacht at maximum speed, the crew worked hard trimming the sails until a wave suddenly surged along the deck of the heavily heeled yacht, picked up crewman Richard Kilkelly and washed him through the safety rails and over the side. Amazingly Kilkelly, who fortunately had managed to grab a rope on his way overboard, somehow held on until three of his crewmates could grab him and drag him back on board.

It was a race-winning save; when *Scallywag* reached Hobart it was declared the *Tattersall Cup* winner by a mere 1 minute 43 seconds!

Michael Spies

SAILING BIO

I have chalked up five world championship wins, forty-two Sydney Hobart races and countless Australian, state and regional championship victories.

WHAT WAS YOUR BEST DAY UNDER SAIL IN THE SYDNEY HOBART?

Skippering *Nokia* up the Derwent, early morning in a fresh southerly at full speed in 1999. Not only did we get line honours but we smashed the race record by 19 hours.

WHAT DAY OR EXPERIENCE WAS THE TOUGHEST OR MOST CHALLENGING?

The whole of the 1993 race. It was the Hobart that everyone referred to as 'the low blow' – a southerly gale blew for almost the entire distance. At the time, it was considered to be the roughest and toughest Hobart ever.

WHAT KEEPS YOU GOING BACK TO THE HOBART RACE?

It is something I have done all my adult life. It is all about the people, not the boats.

WHAT ARE SOME OF THE BIG CHANGES THAT YOU'VE WITNESSED IN YOUR YEARS ASSOCIATED WITH THE RACE?

The boats have obviously got faster and faster. The whole race is a lot more professional which is not a bad thing though it has impacted the Corinthian spirit.

CHAPTER 13

Incidents, Arguments and a Cracking Sound

In the three months preceding the 1983 Sydney Hobart race, Australia's international profile had never been higher — thanks to the Alan Bond owned/Ben Lexcen designed *Australia II* winning the much coveted *America's Cup* in Newport, Rhode Island. It was a victory that ended the longest winning streak in all forms of international sport. Until that moment, on 26 September, the superb, hand-crafted silver ewer had been successfully defended by the New York Yacht Club on twenty-three occasions over the 132 years since they first won it in England in 1851.

There is no doubt that *Australia II*'s success had a positive impact on the number of entries in the Hobart race that year: the fleet was huge — 172 yachts from across Australia and yacht clubs all over the world.

Among those entrants was one of the key players in Bond's remarkable campaign, Sir James Hardy. He was back for another tilt at top honours on corrected time after finishing a highly creditable third with *Police Car* in 1982.

Experts predicted there would be a titanic struggle for line honours between Bob Bell's *Condor* and American Marvin Green's stunning, blue-hulled maxi *Nirvana*. It was, but no one could have anticipated the actual outcome. While competitors and spectators alike believed they had seen it all after the remarkably close finish between *Condor* and *Apollo* the previous year, the finish in 1983 was considerably more dramatic.

Once outside Sydney Harbour the armada of race yachts was greeted by a freshening southerly wind and boisterous seas – the ingredients for a tough, upwind slog. At the front of the pack *Apollo* showed it was no match for its two rivals and fell off the pace while *Condor* and *Nirvana* locked into a duel that lasted all the way to Storm Bay. The wind strengthened to 25 knots and the seas became steep and nasty – a circumstance that soon took a toll on the boats as well as the bellies of those who had overindulged on Christmas Day.

By next morning, ten yachts had been forced out of the race due to rig or hull damage.

Condor and *Nirvana* charged through the night in give-no-quarter racing. By the time the pair reached Tasman Island *Condor* led by just 6 minutes and then by a mere 150 metres soon after the pair entered the Derwent. This scene had the hallmarks of being another grandstand daylight duel, and the spectators in Hobart responded accordingly. There was a frantic rush to get to Battery Point to watch the action.

Out on the river a light breeze soon filled in from the south, so spinnakers were hoisted on both yachts. *Nirvana* got the early advantage and glided past *Condor* then, 4 miles from the finish line, a slightly stronger breeze favoured *Condor* – enough to create the opportunity for it to overtake *Nirvana* via a 20-metre-wide gap that existed between that yacht and the eastern shore of the river. The distance was barely wide enough for the manoeuvre to be executed, so the *Condor* crew exercised their rights and called on *Nirvana* to change course and provide sufficient room for their yacht to overtake unimpeded and not run aground.

Crash!

Condor hit submerged rocks and stopped! The two yachts then made slight contact, but *Nirvana* escaped the situation unscathed. As it had not run aground and stopped, it was able to continue. It took the *Condor* crew 5 minutes of manoeuvring and changing the sail trim to free their yacht from the rocks while *Nirvana* sailed to the finish and secured line honours by just 2 minutes and 16 seconds.

But it didn't finish there. The race's Protest Committee intervened and, after analysing the circumstances around the incident, disqualified *Nirvana* for not allowing *Condor* sufficient room to pass and awarded line honours to *Condor*.

In the race for the big prize, the *Tattersall Cup*, the batch of light-displacement designs from New Zealand's Bruce Farr had been living up to expectations. Progressive handicap calculations confirmed they had been dominating the corrected time placings since the start, especially *Pacific Sundance*. However, the race took an interesting turn when the mid-size yachts entered Bass Strait and Victoria's favourite son in offshore racing, Lou Abrahams, found ideal conditions for his 14-metre yacht *Challenge II* and gained a valuable jump on the opposition.

At Tasman Island the smaller *Pacific Sundance* still looked the likely winner until a Storm Bay calm shattered its crew's dream. *Challenge II* maintained speed all the way to Hobart and became a very popular race winner. Abrahams had been trying to win the Hobart for 20 years, and finally he had cracked it.

*

For New Zealand's famous around-the-world race veteran Peter Blake, the most memorable thing about the 1984 Sydney Hobart was finishing. The race was, as some people put it, a horror show. A savage southerly gale hammered the fleet within 24 hours of the start and lasted for 2 days. The wind, which was howling through the rigging at up to 50 knots generated ugly, breaking seas up to 8 metres high. All too often yachts speared off the crests of the waves and into mid-air, a prelude to a thumping, bone-jarring crash into the trough that followed.

The same storm brought great sadness: for the first time in the race's forty-year history, a competitor lost his life.

The Lake Macquarie yacht *Yahoo II* was one of the many that found the going too tough and turned back for Sydney during the second night at sea. Soon afterwards, seventy-year-old Wal Russell, a veteran of fifteen Hobarts, was moving out of the cockpit to go below deck when the yacht was overwhelmed and flattened by three huge waves. When it eventually came upright, Russell was missing – he had been washed overboard. The crew soon spotted him 30 metres away, face down in the water. Sadly though, all attempts to rescue him failed.

A cloud of grief hung over the fleet.

Little wonder that year's Hobart was likened to the tragic 1979 Fastnet Race out of England.

*

For Peter Blake and his Kiwi crew, this Hobart race was a perfect opportunity to prepare his latest yacht, the 24-metre maxi *New Zealand*, for the following year's around the world challenge. By race end, after the yacht had reached Hobart and secured line honours, the skipper declared he had encountered conditions comparable to the worst he had ever experienced in all his years of ocean racing. 'Sailing to windward felt like you were driving a truck off the top of a three-storey building and landing on concrete,' the weather-beaten sailor announced in Hobart. 'The conditions were terrible.'

The fact that Blake was aboard the biggest boat in the race reinforced how bad the blow had been. The point was emphasised even more at the finish when only forty-six of the 152 starters reached Hobart. Broken boats, rigs and sails, coupled with seasickness and fatigue, brought the race to a premature end for many. Some crews that reached the finish had been forced into survival mode for some of the distance. The highly experienced team aboard the Gunter Heuchmer/ John Eyles entry, the 12-metre-long Bruce Farr designed *Indian Pacific*, had been able to press on. That crew realised through experience that they should set a course offshore in search of a favourable windshift towards the south-east. They did just that and, when the yacht was near 130 nm east of Gabo Island, they were rewarded superbly. *Indian Pacific* had made huge gains on the fleet, so much so that at one stage it was lying second behind *New Zealand*, which was twice its length. Race organisers plotting fleet positions back on shore refused to recognise *Indian Pacific*'s position, so, much to the disgust of the crew, moved the yacht one complete degree (60 nm) back to the north on the official race position map.

But the *Indian Pacific* crew had the last laugh: they received a huge welcome when they sailed into Hobart and were declared the winner of the *Tattersall Cup*.

*

The ensuing 9 years leading up to the 50th anniversary Hobart race in 1994 were not free from arguments or incidents, starting with the 1985 race. During that period more than 1100 yachts crossed the start line and headed for Hobart. The total participation by men and women sailors was in excess of 11,000.

What was arguably the worst controversy the race had seen came in 1985 – the year where it could be said the winner didn't win. It came about because of a minor incident at the start line in Sydney, and wasn't resolved until after *Drake's Prayer*, sailed by the successful and very popular offshore racing enthusiast Peter Kurts, was stripped of its corrected time victory after reaching Hobart.

Being protested out of a win in the classic was not new – it had happened back in 1953. This year, however, the circumstances were very different. The post-race protest came from a third party – some crew of the then second–placed

Sagacious. It was alleged that during the crush on the start line, a *Drake's Prayer* crewman innocently touched *Ragamuffin's* side rails. If the protest was upheld then it was possible that *Drake's Prayer* would be stripped of its victory and *Sagacious* installed as the corrected time winner. The race's Protest Committee had no option but to uphold the protest because any contact between vessels during a race, no matter how minor, must be reported. In this case neither the *Ragamuffin* nor *Drake's Prayer* crews had advised the Race Committee of this extremely minor incident.

Drake's Prayer and *Ragamuffin* were subsequently relegated to 37th and 111th places respectively. However, in an unexpected twist, *Sagacious* was not declared the race winner. Instead, the yacht was simply recorded as having the second-best corrected time, while no winner was declared.

This race was another tough one; a southerly buster swept up the coast like a northbound locomotive and once again created havoc. The wind built in strength throughout the night and started to generate steep, punishing seas. The next day the sea's state became even worse when the wind switched direction towards the west and settled in at a very testing 40 knots.

It was the steepness of the waves, which were often as sheer at their backs as they were at their fronts, which caused most of the damage to the yachts. The crew of the British entry *Panda* had to react very quickly to save their yacht after the hull split in three places following a jaw-jarring drop into a wave trough.

The final tally in Hobart saw thirty-three yachts forced out; five of those had been dismasted and four had severe structural damage.

In the race for being first to Hobart, smart tactics by the crew of *Apollo* on the first day at sea made it possible for them to take full advantage of the change in wind direction when the southerly buster hit. *Windward Passage* (then owned by Sydney's Rod Muir) could not recover the ground it lost, so trailed *Apollo* into Hobart by 3 hours.

*

Following the controversial corrected time result the previous year, race organisers were forced to confront the fact that the starting line could not accommodate large fleets. It was also obvious there was not sufficient room within the harbour to start so many yachts on a single line: the waterway was just too narrow. An alternative had to be found.

Initially, the thought was that the starting line would have to be relocated outside the harbour, a move resisted by almost everyone because the race would be robbed of one of its many magnificent attributes: the spectacle each Boxing Day of hundreds of thousands of people watching a fleet of ocean racing yachts cutting a path down one of the world's most beautiful harbours towards the open sea.

After considering the problem for some weeks, Sydney Hobart Race Director and Cruising Yacht Club of Australia Sailing Committee chairman, Gordon Marshall, produced a unique solution – the creation of two parallel lines within the harbour, set about 400 metres apart, with the largest yachts starting from the front line and the smaller yachts from the rear. Then, to equalise the distance sailed to the finish by each group, rounding marks would be set a similar distance apart at the entrance to Sydney Harbour. Those yachts starting from the front line would sail to the more distant buoy at the Heads, while the starters on the other line would round the closer mark.

The concept was put to the test in the 1986 race and it proved to be a world first that worked!

The fleet of 123 that year was visually impressive as it contained a striking array of maxi yachts. The stand-out was the recently launched Sydney yacht *Sovereign*, owned by Bernard Lewis and skippered by David Kellett. Measuring 25.6 metres overall, this American design was the world's largest offshore racer, but it was destined to face stiff competition in the form of the world's original maxi, the mighty *Windward Passage* and, from Bermuda, Bob Bell's *Condor*.

Southerly busters were becoming a tradition of the race and this year was no exception. During the first night at sea, a 30-knot change made conditions very testing, so testing that some impressive scalps were claimed, most notably *Sovereign*, which suffered serious rig damage.

By the time the fleet was mid Bass Strait the wind had switched to the west and increased in strength to a howling 50 knots. But despite this and the enormity of the waves, it was Tony Dunn's little 10.9-metre sloop *Ex-Tension* that made the race-winning move. Dunn recalled a tough time where the wind was blowing the tops off the waves and shot-blasting the crew with horizontal spray. Knowing by then they were in the hunt for the *Tattersall Cup*, the *Ex-Tension* crew refused to let the conditions beat them. They went without sleep and stayed on deck around the clock, driving the yacht hard and always opting to set the maximum amount of sail the conditions would allow.

The effort was worth every second as *Ex-Tension* went on to win on corrected time by little more than 8 minutes. It was also a close race for line honours: *Condor* beat *Windward Passage* into Hobart by only 21 minutes.

*

During the first 36 hours of the 1987 race — which boasted a fleet of 154 — there were growing signs that *Kialoa III*'s eleven-year-old race record time would finally be bettered. On the approach to Bass Strait, Bernard Lewis's maxi *Sovereign*, again with David Kellett at the helm, was leading the charge in grand fashion. Riding on the front of a 25-knot north-easterly breeze, the big red boat was surfing down powerful, full-bodied waves at better than 10 knots and was soon 24 nm ahead of *Kialoa III*'s record pace. But then the seemingly magical ring of defence *Kialoa III* held around that record prevailed once more — a gale-force southerly headwind arrived and slowed every yacht's pace towards the finish to a crawl. *Sovereign*'s charge south was hindered in those conditions, and by dawn on the 28th the crew had given up all hope of claiming the race record, although they knew their yacht was still a chance to win on corrected time, as well as in the hunt to be first home, along with Syd Fischer's maxi *Gazebo* and Jack Rooklyn's *Apollo*.

In their wake, two of the more fancied international entries, *Sidewinder* and *Highland Fling*, had been dismasted. Unbeknown to the crew of Peter Kurts's entry *Madeline's Daughter*, the outer skin of its composite sandwich construction hull had suffered a metre-long split due to the pounding it had endured in the big seas. Fortunately the damage did not deteriorate, and it wasn't until after the yacht docked in Hobart that the crew became aware the problem existed when someone on another yacht pointed it out to them.

More than 3000 people cheered *Sovereign* into Hobart for her line honours triumph, but crew members were not confident of winning on corrected time unless the weather changed in their favour – and it did. The wind faded to a pant, and with that the chance improved by the minute. Still, it was an agonising wait, the crew was clock-watching, calculating if any yacht still out on the course could beat their corrected time. Everything went in *Sovereign*'s favour and it became the first Australian owned and built big boat to take the elusive double.

*

Windward Passage was one of the world's truly great maxis and, having enjoyed the excitement and satisfaction of owning that yacht, Rod Muir decided to step up and build a spare-no-expense, state-of-the-art maxi which he would name *Windward Passage II*. With the decision made, he declared that his intention was to claim Hobart race line honours in Australia's Bicentennial Year, 1988. However, this yacht made its mark on the international scene even before it was launched, though not in the yachting arena. It was brought to the attention of the yacht's project manager for the build, Duncan Van Woerden, that NASA in America was claiming that the doors of the space shuttle were the largest composite structures in the world. Van Woerden promptly brought to NASA's attention that *Windward Passage II* was a composite structure and considerably larger than their shuttle doors! With that, NASA dropped its claim.

While that futuristic, 22.5-metre-long sloop was perhaps the centre of attention for the classic that year, there was another interesting participant. The weakening of the post-war Iron Curtain allowed Russia to make its first foray into the international ocean racing scene, and it did so with the entry of the sloop *Veter* from Vladivostok.

An estimated 200,000-plus spectators (more than twice the capacity of the Melbourne Cricket Ground) were either on or around the harbour to watch the 119 yachts head for Hobart on a perfect summer day. It was a magnificent sight as a sea of white sails zig-zagged away from the start and towards the Heads in a gentle northerly breeze. The twenty-five-man *Windward Passage II* crew was not holding back; they had their yacht in full flight right from the gun, and were untroubled when it came to winning the honour of being first out of the harbour in a stunning time of just 14 minutes. Once on the open sea, and with the spinnaker aloft, *Windward Passage II* set a cracking pace, averaging near 12.5 knots for the first 4 hours. Syd Fischer's maxi *Ragamuffin* and Arthur Bloore's *Hammer of Queensland* were in pursuit.

True to the adage that 'It's not a Hobart race unless you get a Southerly Buster', a powerful front swept up the coast and bowled into the fleet as though they were skittles. It was an alarming time for some crews as sails flogged and masts whipped around with such force that it felt as though the yachts were being shaken to pieces. Within minutes of this blow arriving, three yachts were dismasted and there was more carnage to come.

A deteriorating sea state and unrelenting wind continued to take a toll, causing the retirement of thirty-eight yachts, nearly half due to broken masts or damaged rigging.

The new *Windward Passage II* was more than impressive during this rough time; it maintained a record-breaking pace throughout the second day, even though it was sailing upwind under greatly reduced sail. However, unfortunately for the owner and crew, this amazing yacht soon revealed a weak spot with a sickening cracking sound. The source was located almost immediately; a hole had been cut in the aft deck to accommodate a small compass but the area around the hole with its space-age, composite structure had not been properly reinforced. There was a real threat of extreme structural failure should the yacht continue to pound its way upwind. *Windward Passage II* headed for home.

Finishing is what matters in any ocean race and when the going gets tough, seamanship, boat preparation and great sailing skills combine to deliver victory. To that end, nothing could be taken away from the effort by veteran Syd Fischer and his team aboard *Ragamuffin*. He pushed the big boat (formerly *Bumblebee 4*) to its maximum and was suitably rewarded. After twenty-one attempts, Syd scored a win in the Hobart race – the line honours trophy. However the sailing conditions, which included a calm patch on Storm Bay, were not conducive to a fast passage, so *Ragamuffin* finished more than a day outside *Kialoa III*'s 1975 time.

On handicap, one of the smallest entries, Gino Knezic's 10.3-metre-long *Illusion*, was sailed superbly in the rough weather and went on to beat all comers, only the second yacht from Victoria to achieve the honour.

*

After becoming a national hero when he won the *America's Cup* in 1983 and being welcomed at the White House by President Reagan, the heady world of multi-millionaire Alan Bond was unravelling while he participated in the 1989 race.

Bond was back for another tilt at line honours that year with his impressive maxi *Drumbeat*, a yacht that had already proven itself against top-class competition in the Mediterranean.

The scene on the harbour for the start was unprecedented. It was estimated that more than half a million people watched the 126 yachts set sail and there was a huge national television audience as well.

A westerly wind made it an unusual start; it meant that the yachts reached across the wind from the start to the Heads, where spinnakers were set for a short but spectacular leg to the seaward mark from where they turned south. Syd Fischer cared nothing for the much-touted form of *Drumbeat* and showed he meant business with his maxi *Ragamuffin* by charging away from the start line at full speed.

However, while *Drumbeat* trailed *Ragamuffin* out of the harbour, it took off once clear of the Heads, running down the coast before a strong north-westerly wind. The anticipated announcement next morning that *Drumbeat* was a clear leader didn't come. Instead, the ten-year-old *Ragamuffin* had averaged better than 10 knots during the night and was more than 1 nm ahead of the favourite. Arthur Bloore's *Hammer of Queensland* was also right up there.

There was a tragedy early the next day as the bulk of the fleet belted into the teeth of a 30-40 knot south-westerly gale which had swept across Bass Strait overnight. The Melbourne yacht *BP Flying Colours* thumped off a big wave and the resulting shock load tore a pulley supporting the mast away from the deck. The pulley hit crewman Peter Taylor in the temple with enormous force as the yacht's mast crumpled over the side. Eight race yachts, the radio relay vessel and a helicopter with a doctor aboard all rushed to the crippled yacht, but sadly Taylor failed to respond to treatment.

Back on the race course *Hammer of Queensland* caused another surprise for the *Drumbeat* crew when it sailed ahead of them. But once *Drumbeat* tasted the rough going it charged forward. With sails slightly eased, it generated amazing power and speed in the big seas. By the third morning at sea, Bond's boat had opened up a 50 nm lead over *Ragamuffin* and from there was unbeatable in the race for line honours.

Drumbeat sailed in to Hobart at 7.20pm on 29 December and Bond received a huge welcome from the thousands of people lining the shore at the finish line and at the dock. However the gloss quickly came off his victory; when Bond stepped ashore he was hounded by the media after having been advised that his international commercial empire was collapsing.

Throughout the race the doyen of ocean racing in Victoria, Lou Abrahams, had his yacht *Ultimate Challenge* at or near the top of the progressive handicap list. He maintained this advantage all the way to the finish and went on to score a very popular win. His win in the 45th Hobart race was his second.

*

Corporate sponsorship was a delicate issue in the sport in the late 1980s and early 1990s, so the CYCA knew it had a problem when the British around-the-world race yacht *Rothmans* arrived in Sydney for the 1990 race – namely cigarette advertising. After much debate, the yacht was cleared to compete, but prior to the start, skipper Lawrie Smith was advised that he could not fly any spinnakers bearing a Rothmans logo.

There were two firsts of note associated with the race that year: gambling on the result was legalised via the TAB (Totalisator Agency Board) and the race was started from land when the New South Wales Premier, Nick Greiner, fired a replica of an 18th-century cannon.

It was all about *Rothmans* at the start. The British yacht led the other 104 yachts out of the harbour with *Condor of Currabubula* (Tony Paola), *Ragamuffin*, *Brindabella* (George Snow), *Freight Train* (Damien Parkes) and *Bobsled* (Geoff Bush and Nick Feros) in its wake.

It was a fast ride down the New South Wales south coast, so fast that the big yachts were ahead of the record pace set by *Kialoa III* back in 1975. *Rothmans* maintained its lead and made an even more impressive charge under spinnaker in the middle of Bass Strait when the wind strengthened from the north-east. The crew later revealed in Hobart that the yacht was being pushed so hard at times it was almost completely submerged under a mass of foaming white water. The conditions were so demanding that fourteen yachts turned for home before reaching the halfway mark.

Rothmans' blistering run ended off the north-east corner of Tasmania when the wind went light. It was out of sight of land and, with its lightweight racing spinnaker in shreds, skipper Smith decided to risk setting another spinnaker – the one with the company logo. Soon after, though, a media helicopter flew out from the coast and surprised the *Rothmans* crew ... snap, snap, snap ... pictures of *Rothmans* carrying the spinnaker that should not have been set.

Back in Bass Strait the smaller yachts were still enjoying a hard and high-speed run before the powerful nor'easterly wind, none more so than Gary Appleby's *Sagacious V* which, while being handled by one of the race's most experienced crews, was out of control as often as it was under control.

Soon after 8am on 29 December, *Rothmans* sailed in to Hobart to hear the gun signalling line honours; but race officials had already seen the images of 'that' spinnaker. *Ragamuffin* finished two hours behind *Rothmans* and was followed by *Condor of Currabubula*, *Brindabella* and *Bobsled*.

The Race Committee quickly drew Lawrie Smith's attention to the fact that he had set an illegal spinnaker and was then advised there was no alternative but to apply a penalty, albeit the minimum penalty. *Rothmans* was replaced as line honours winner by *Ragamuffin* and given twelfth position across the line – a placings penalty of 10 per cent of the number of yachts in the race.

Meanwhile, back on the course, *Sagacious V* sailed on to a hard earned and well deserved victory on corrected time. After his controversial 'win' in 1985, this was the sweetest possible reward for its popular owner, Gary Appleby.

*

A win is a win, be it by a minute or a mile. And, as the crew of Australian-owned *Atara* (formerly *Madeleine's Daughter*) would tell anyone who wanted to listen, to win the 1991 Hobart race by just 2 minutes, 20 seconds after racing for 3 days and 10 hours, and thus secure Ireland's first-ever victory on the international sailing scene, was sweet pickings.

By winning the Hobart race, the yacht contributed greatly to Ireland securing the *Southern Cross Cup* – the appropriate reward for a remarkable team effort.

'Team work and total dedication was what won it for us,' said Bill Sykes, who was a member of the syndicate that chartered *Atara* for the Cup series, along with the yacht's actual owner, John Storey, and Irish sailing legend Harold Cudmore. 'No-one tried harder to win than us,' he added, 'and we were rewarded for our effort.'

Soon after the race started, Peter Walker's pocket-maxi *Amazon* had charged down the New South Wales coast under spinnaker while Peter Sorensen's 15.2-metre yacht, *2UE/Mitre 10* was in hot pursuit. The skiff sailors aboard Sorensen's yacht revelled in the hard downwind conditions, to the degree where 24 hours into the race, they were leading the fleet of ninety-nine and more impressively, were ahead of *Kialoa*'s record pace for the course.

Around 200 nm down the coast, a typical southerly buster with 25-knot winds impacted the fleet and brought a new look to proceedings. Sykes later explained:

We were well positioned for the change and settled ourselves down as quickly as possible for what was going to be a long and hard slog south. When it came to being off watch, if you didn't want to sleep, you stayed on deck where your weight made the greatest contribution towards stability.

Maintaining crew morale was essential and we had no problem because Irishman Gordon Maguire – a brilliant helmsman – kept the jokes running. At the same time, everyone was always mindful of boat-speed – thinking ahead and discussing what our next sail change might be.

By the time we reached mid-Bass Strait, it was obvious the race [on corrected time] was going to be between us and Lou Abrahams with *Ultimate Challenge*. It was there that we got our break. The wind kept changing in direction, by only a few degrees, and each time it did, Harold (Cudmore) ordered a tack to ensure we were on the gaining leg towards Hobart. We must have tacked 40 times over the next few hours, because we soon opened up a gap over Lou.

We raced hard all the way to the Derwent and even harder after that. We did more sail changes over the final 11 miles than we did all race, trying desperately to catch

321

every change in the breeze. It was the middle of the night and a few metres from the line when we ran out of breeze and stopped. Then a faint puff moved in, so we set our lightest headsail and glided across the line, then waited for *Ultimate Challenge* to arrive to see if it could beat us on corrected time.

With *Amazon* out of the race due to a broken forestay, and *2UE/Mitre 10* uncompetitive when sailing to windward, *Brindabella* scored line honours by 1 hour and 16 minutes from *Hammer of Queensland*.

*

Sailmaker and top-level ocean racing yachtsman Bob Fraser put the 1992 Hobart race into perspective with just a few succinct words: 'It was a windy, wet, cold, never do another one sort of Hobart race.'

It was Fraser's 14th Hobart but certainly not his last.

In reality, this was what might be seen as a typical race to Hobart: there was the colourful and easy start on Boxing Day (for which many were thankful as it let the Christmas Day lunch settle), a brick wall midway in the form of a strong southerly change, a challenging section around Tasman Island and across Storm Bay, and the usual game of chess with the weather in the Derwent.

The star attraction in the fleet of 110 was the ultra-modern Kiwi maxi, *New Zealand Endeavour*, which well-regarded international yachtsman Grant Dalton and his crew brought to the race so it could be put to the test as part of their preparation for the next Whitbread round-the-world race. And put to the test it was.

This race was historic as for the first time two handicap winners were declared. One came from the International Offshore Rule (IOR) division, which had delivered the race winner for many years, and the other from the new International Measurement System (IMS) division, the emerging handicap formula for ocean racing yachts worldwide.

The IMS handicap rule was adopted by the CYCA as a result of the high number of retirements in the 1989 race, which wasn't considered to be a tough test. The retirement rate for IOR yachts that year was twice that of IMS yachts.

The move towards the introduction of this new rating rule was driven by prominent and highly dedicated CYCA club member Gordon Marshall who, over the previous decade had applied considerable influence on all matters relating to offshore racing, safety and ratings.

Marshall's blunt report to the club read in part:

One's chances are 3 times greater of getting to Hobart in an IMS yacht than in a Grand Prix IOR yacht. So much for the development and 'progress' in ocean racing under the IOR… Committees responsible for administration of the rule over the past 10 to 15 years may begin to see that they have produced a camel instead of a horse. With any luck, the animal may die, and then we could start again.

IOR yachts are now difficult – read dangerous – to sail without crew perching [high on the windward side]:

skippers demand 'no more than one crewman below at any one time'. This may be exhilarating for 20-mile triangle courses in bright sunshine just outside a port for shelter, or in enclosed waters, but we are talking about ocean racing – out at sea for days on end.

New Zealand Endeavour, which represented the very latest thinking in maxi yacht design, was a short-priced favourite for line honours, and it didn't disappoint its supporters. However, much credit for that result was given to the considerably smaller and older *Amazon*, which kept the pressure on and rounded Tasman Island just 2 hours behind the Kiwis.

The previous year's race winner, *Atara*, and Syd Fischer's *Ragamuffin*, were battling for the ultimate prize in the IOR division until a few miles north of Tasman Island. That was where a wind change howled in from the south and blew *Atara*'s mainsail apart. It had already been an eventful race for the *Atara* team, with owner, John Storey, being swept overboard by a huge wave that buried the yacht mid Bass Strait. Two crewmen grabbed him as he went over the lifelines and managed to hang on to his jacket until more crew arrived and helped drag him back aboard.

Fischer was certainly the sentimental favourite for a win on corrected time that year. Incredibly, the man who had contributed so much to offshore racing in Australia had not won a Hobart in twenty-four attempts, but during the latter stages of the race there were signs that suggested he might break the drought. *Ragamuffin* had its share of problems as well but Fischer and his team, showing great experience and tenacity, sailed on to a magnificent and well deserved victory in the IOR Division.

Robin Crawford's well-prepared 12.2-metre yacht *Assassin* lived up to expectations and was declared the race's first ever IMS winner.

Iain Murray AM

SAILING BIO

I began sailing on Middle Harbour, in Sydney, as a ten-year-old in the Flying Ant class. Subsequently, I have enjoyed a tremendous career as an offshore racer. In my teenage years, I graduated into 18-foot skiffs and won a record six consecutive 18-foot skiff world titles from 1977 to 1982. I've logged twenty-five Sydney Hobart Races, including three overall victories and nine line honours aboard the supermaxi, *Wild Oats XI*. We have broken our own race record on numerous occasions. Beyond ocean racing, I have been involved with four America's Cup campaigns and represented Australia in the Star class at the 2008 Olympic Games. I am currently the Performance Director of the Australian Olympic Sailing Team.

WHAT WAS YOUR BEST DAY SAILING IN THE SYDNEY HOBART?

The second day of the 2005 race on *Wild Oats XI* sailing across Bass Strait and down the Tasmanian coast in a strong north-east breeze. It was our first race in the *Oats* and we had no idea what we were doing other than sailing the legs off the boat. We approached Tasman Light with a top speed of 39 knots.

WHAT DAY OR EXPERIENCE WAS THE TOUGHEST OR MOST CHALLENGING?

Day two of the 1977 race aboard *Knockout*.

WHAT KEEPS YOU GOING BACK TO THE HOBART RACE?

I line up for my twenty-sixth this year and the last sixteen have been continuous. After the first race, I doubted whether I would participate again. I think sailing with Peter Kurts changed my perspective and introduced me to the teamwork required to ocean race. Since then, being in great teams has been the motivation to return year on year.

WHAT ARE SOME OF THE BIG CHANGES THAT YOU'VE WITNESSED IN YOUR YEARS ASSOCIATED WITH THE RACE?

Firstly, the speed of the race: my first race took 6 days; in 2017 we took 1 day 12 hours on *Wild Oats XI*. Then there's the size of the yachts: big used be 60 feet, now the limit is 100 feet. Finally, the technology: yachts used to be primarily sailcloth, timber, aluminium and composite. Now it seems that everything is carbon fibre.

CHAPTER 14

Miracle Man

The 1993 Sydney Hobart was a curtain raiser: the penultimate event before that historic milestone, the 50th anniversary edition of one of the world's great sporting challenges.

Without doubt, the Hobart race was recognised as a thorough test of sailing skills, tactics and navigation, as well as the design of the yacht, its equipment and crew. Accordingly, for the majority of observers and participants, to win a Hobart race was confirmation that the yacht and team on board could stand among the best in the world.

However, the 1993 race had another element to it; one that showed how a remarkably well coordinated search and rescue mission could deliver a miracle – one so amazing that it was headlined worldwide.

Hobart race history now recognises the '93 race as being 'the year of the low blow' when nature unleashed a storm so furious that many of the participants would remember it for a lifetime – if they survived. There was no doubt it was one of the worst.

In the days leading up to the start, highly respected yachting meteorologist Roger Badham – a weatherman of international fame – announced it would probably be the roughest race ever; not because of the strength of the wind, but due to the fact that the wind would blow horrendously hard out of the south for the entire distance.

How right he was!

When the 104 yachts set sail from Sydney in idyllic conditions – clear skies, a warm sun and a light north-easterly breeze – Australia's sailing knight, Sir James Hardy, who was among the more than 300,000 spectators watching proceedings on the day, summed up the situation perfectly: 'Oh how the children play, oblivious to their fate.'

Within hours of the start, the dream run under spinnaker that all crews had been enjoying after clearing the Heads came to an abrupt end when the anticipated southerly change hit like a sledgehammer. The seas were on the up-and-up while the wind howled through the rigging, every yacht was in the middle of a maelstrom and there was still 600 nm to go! The first retirements came almost immediately and continued. Within 48 hours, broken rigs, broken boats and broken spirits led to almost half the fleet being forced to head for safe haven on shore.

The second night at sea was the most dramatic: two yachts sank and another was rolled 360 degrees by one mountainous wave. Hobart race veteran Peter Joubert went to the rescue of the crew of *Adjuster* after it sank. He spotted them in the middle of the night more than 20 nm offshore, clinging for life to an upturned life raft.

'I just remember their eyes,' Joubert said later. 'Our spotlight illuminated them; the eyes were haunting. That sight of their eyes and the look of panic on their faces will stick with me forever.'

The same night proved to be one of miracles, the most amazing of all being the rescue of yacht owner John Quinn, after he somehow survived for more than 5 hours in the turmoil of the monstrous and frighteningly turbulent seas, some 50 nm offshore.

Just before midnight a breaking wave of mesmerising proportions – more than 10 metres high – came out of nowhere and loomed over Quinn's 10.6-metre sloop *MEM*.

The overwhelming force of the water that broke over the yacht almost submerged it, bulldozing *MEM* onto its side. The motion was so violent that Quinn was hurled overboard into the wildly turbulent ocean. He had been steering at the time and was wearing a safety harness that was attached to a strong-point in the yacht's cockpit, but the shock load exerted onto the harness when his body hit the water was so powerful that the webbing strap which was his lifeline to the yacht snapped like it was a piece of cotton.

When Quinn came to the surface he faced the terrifying realisation that the harness had parted and he was no longer in contact with the yacht, a situation made more dramatic by the fact that in the darkness and amid the raging seas, he could see *MEM*'s white stern light disappearing into the distance.

Knowing that his chances for survival were down to him, he set about doing everything he could to remain afloat. His crew sent out a distress call and turned the yacht back so they could initiate a search. Fortunately Quinn's ocean racing experience over many years – he had thirteen Hobart races to his credit – meant he was wearing oversized seaboots and could immediately discard them with relative ease. Should he have not been able to do this he might as well have had house bricks tied to his ankles.

With *MEM* turned back and headed towards the point where they believed Quinn was lost, the shocked crew probed as deeply as possible into the darkness, desperate to see some glimpse of their skipper. But the odds were against them; for a start they had no exact point for a target, and by being at sea level in huge rough seas it was quite likely that, even if they did sight him, it would be very brief. As it turned out, *MEM* was within 200 metres of him at one stage, but while Quinn could see them the crew had no hope of spotting him because of the size of the seas. He shouted his lungs out in the hope that he might be heard, but there was no way his shouts could carry above the roar of the wind and waves.

Within minutes of the crew having sent out a mayday message, all race yachts in close proximity to *MEM* changed course so they could assist with the search. At the same time, back at the CYCA, race organisers contacted maritime authorities and activated a greater search effort that involved any commercial shipping in the area. However, while they were doing everything possible to rescue him, they knew deep down that Quinn had virtually no chance of surviving in those conditions.

An added concern was that those crews aboard the yachts involved in the search were themselves exposed to greater danger. Every 15 minutes or so they would probably have to contend with a rogue wave more than 12 metres in height, a wave almost certainly capped by an avalanche of white water.

After four hours of searching, it seemed increasingly likely that Quinn had perished. Race officials even discussed writing his obituary.

But, at that moment Quinn, aided by the light buoyancy vest he was wearing, and backed by an incredible will to survive, was still alive. To his own amazement, he devised a technique of duck-diving as each huge and churning wave charged towards him, thus escaping its full fury, then surfacing on the other side frantically gasping for air. As he later explained:

> The only time I really started to get a bit desperate was right at the end, but that was only for a very short period of time. At that stage the buoyancy vest I was wearing was losing some of its buoyancy, so I was starting to swallow water and get tired. Then it happened...
>
> A short while later as I rode to the top of one big wave, I saw it – the most beautiful Christmas tree you have ever seen. It was a bloody big ship with all lights blazing coming ever so slowly towards me.

In what was a stroke of profound good fortune, it happened that the oil tanker *Ampol Sarel* was about 30 nm from *MEM*'s position when Quinn went overboard. The captain, on hearing the mayday call, changed course and headed for the search area. He decided that the most effective contribution that his ship could make would be for it to steer a course to the exact spot where Quinn was lost, then shut down the engines and drift downwind on the path he assumed Quinn would travel in those conditions. He called all available crew to the ship's bridge, which was the highest point of the superstructure and near the stern. Once at the desired spot, *Ampol Sarel*'s powerful searchlights were turned on so the crew could scan the storm-driven seas. At the same time, four of the race yachts which were already in the search area were requested to fall in behind the ship and follow it on the drift.

For Quinn, the elation that came with sighting the ship soon disappeared. The huge waves were actually moving the ship away from him. His emotions dropped to a new low: by then he had survived more than five hours in the stormy seas, but he knew that his one chance for being saved was beginning to disappear.

Quinn continued:

I thought the ship was going to pass me without anyone spotting me because it was coming down the drift at an angle, and the stern – where all the lookouts were gathered on the bridge and using the searchlights – was the most distant point from me.

My heart began to sink, but then a huge wave picked up the ship's stern and washed it sideways towards where I was. Suddenly the ship was right there, just metres away. I started to yell my lungs out, 'Hey, hey, hey,' I shouted.

Brent Shaw, who was the guy manning the searchlight, heard my yells then spotted me. He was fantastic. After hearing me shout, he locked the beam of the searchlight onto me and started to shout out, 'I've got you. I can see you.'

Shaw held Quinn in the full glare of the searchlight while the crew of the race yacht *Atara,* which was immediately astern of the ship, was advised that the target, i.e. Quinn, was in the water right where the beam of the light was hitting the surface of the sea.

Atara accelerated to that spot and sure enough, there was an exhausted Quinn struggling to believe his luck. Conditions were so rough however that the crew were unable to drag him aboard, so two of them donned safety harnesses, leapt into the water and put a line around him. The others on deck then dragged him to the side of the boat and completed the recovery.

Quinn, who was suffering from severe hypothermia, had been stung badly by bluebottles, particularly on his face, but right then he could cope with that. He was immediately helped below, stripped of his wet and heavy clothing, dried off and put into a bunk. Having been trained in emergency procedures to be followed in such a situation, the *Atara* crew knew that the quickest way to get heat back into Quinn's body was to share their own body heat with him, so they took it in turns to crawl into the bunk and help keep him warm.

The effort by the *Atara* crew in the search and recovery mission received high commendation as it was only realised later that the yacht had itself been in survival mode when it turned to search for Quinn. Not long before Quinn went overboard from *MEM, Atara* was dismasted and subsequently suffered considerable structural damage. For one, the broken mast had punched a hole through the hull with such force that the topsides were bulging inwards. To save the vessel, the bunks in the area where the damage had occurred were ripped out so six of the 12 crew became human wedges – they locked their backs against sail bags that were put over the damaged area, just to ensure that the hull did not cave in.

This caused one of the crew to joke with Quinn that while he had been rescued there was still a chance *Atara* would not reach shore. 'Do you realise that you might have to be rescued for a second time?' the crewman asked.

'No,' Quinn replied. 'If I'd known this ambulance was sinking I wouldn't have got aboard.'

By the time *Atara* arrived in Eden, Quinn had completely recovered.

When the remnants of the 1993 fleet reached Hobart there was a belief among some of the competitors that on the night Quinn went overboard, a single rogue wave of enormous proportions had swept through the fleet and delivered much of the carnage. Of the 104 starters, sixty-seven failed to reach the finish.

There was an ironic twist between this incident and the inaugural Hobart race in 1945. John Quinn's father, Harry, bought *Rani* from Captain John Illingworth soon after it won that first Hobart race. Not much later Quinn Snr took John and two family friends on the yacht for a fishing trip from Sydney to Port Stephens, 90 nm to the north.

A storm moved in while they were there, so they anchored *Rani* off the deserted Broughton Island and went ashore to spend the night sheltering in an old fisherman's hut. Unfortunately *Rani* dragged its anchor overnight and was wrecked on a coastal beach a few miles away. There was no sign of survivors when the wreck was found, and the worst was feared. However an aerial search for them eventually spotted the four on Broughton Island, but the conditions were so severe they had to wait there another 4 days before they could be rescued by a boat.

*

Yachts reported wind gusts of nearly 80 knots and the attrition rate continued to climb. Even maxis like George Snow's new glamour boat, *Brindabella*, were forced out.

Andrew Strachan's 14.3-metre sloop *Ninety Seven* pushed on through the gale and took line honours in a well-deserved fashion. It was an incredible effort as *Ninety Seven* was the smallest yacht in 40 years to be first to Hobart. Equally commendable was the effort of Nigel Holman's considerably smaller yacht *Cuckoo's Nest*. It was second to Hobart and a deserved winner on corrected time in the IMS division. A Hobart race stalwart, the ever-popular Roger Hickman, won the IOR division with his yacht *Solbourne Wild Oats*.

After many years of relatively easy rides to Hobart, the 1993 race was another powerful reminder as to why the Sydney Hobart had always held a reputation for being one of the world's toughest ocean racing encounters, and must always be respected.

Ian Davis

SAILING BIO

I learned to sail in Cadet Dinghies at Royal Melbourne Yacht Squadron when aged 10, then moved on to keelboats in time for the 1977 Sydney Hobart. I was aboard *Lowana II* and we, along with everyone else, sailed into the eye of a storm. It blew in excess of 50 knots and the seas were massive. After that experience, I became an apprentice sailmaker and this led to me being invited to join the crew racing offshore with Lou Abrahams. I was aboard *Challenge*, *Challenge II* and *Ultimate Challenge*, winning the Hobart in 1983 and 1989. I also represented Australia at two *Admiral's Cups*, the *Clipper Cup* in Hawaii and the *Southern Cross Cup*. I have competed now in twenty-seven Sydney Hobarts, two Fastnets, three China Sea Races, three Around the State Races in Hawaii, three Hong Kong–Vietnam races and a Middle Sea Race.

WHAT WAS YOUR BEST DAY UNDER SAIL IN THE SYDNEY HOBART?

It was aboard *Ultimate Challenge* in 1989, two-sail reaching across Bass Strait in 20 to 25 knots of breeze, side by side with *Sagacious V*. The lead changed numerous times. *Sagacious* beat us across the line by 6 minutes and we beat them by 6 minutes on corrected time to be first overall.

WHAT DAY OR EXPERIENCE WAS THE TOUGHEST OR MOST CHALLENGING?

Sailing up the river on *Challenge II* to the finish in 1980. It was late evening and the wind started to go soft when we were abeam of the casino. We had 45 minutes to cover the two miles to the finish – if we could do that we would be the outright winner. Two hours later we crossed the line to finish third on corrected time behind *New Zealand* and *Gretel*.

WHAT KEEPS YOU GOING BACK TO THE HOBART RACE?

It's all about the people. I have been lucky enough to sail with some of the greatest owners and learn from some of the best sailors in the world, and now I am sailing against their kids. You turn up to do the race but it's great to catch up with friends. It's also great to sail with my son. I like the longer races such as the Sydney Hobart because you get into the rhythm of watch-keeping that shorter races don't allow.

WHAT ARE SOME OF THE BIG CHANGES THAT YOU'VE WITNESSED IN YOUR YEARS ASSOCIATED WITH THE RACE?

The boats have got bigger and faster. The parties in Constitution Dock aren't like they use to be. People stay in hotels and not on their boats, nor do they hang around in Hobart as long as they used to – or maybe it's just that I'm getting old!

CHAPTER 15

Fifty Years to Hobart

Sydney Harbour was almost covered by a spectacular canopy of white sails on Boxing Day 1994 as a vast fleet of 371 yachts and more than 4000 participants set out in the 50th anniversary edition of the Hobart race.

The scene was almost beyond comprehension. It was as if a massive maritime evacuation of the harbour was under way as, apart from the race yachts, there was a monumentally large fleet of spectator boats on the water to share in the atmosphere accompanying this historic moment. And, as was always the case for the start of a Hobart race, countless thousands of spectators were on every vantage point around the foreshore to witness the spectacle.

There were many outstanding elements to the day, including the fact that the fleet represented the largest gathering of Category One ocean racing yachts, including maxis and pocket maxis, the world had seen. Adding to this spectacle was an amazing cluster of vintage yachts entering for the challenge, like *Winston Churchill* and *Archina*, which were among the nine yachts that had participated in the original race in 1945.

The CYCA's Race Committee had undertaken a mountain of

planning to get the historic event to that point, but the effectiveness of those plans couldn't be known until Boxing Day. In a bid to have the entire fleet exit the harbour as quickly and safely as possible, it had been decided to set three parallel starting lines, and introduce a staggered start. The 30-year and 20-year division yachts would start from the northernmost line (closest to the Heads) at 12.30pm and 12.35pm respectively while the bulk of the fleet, which had been assigned to the two other lines according to their size or racing division, was scheduled to start at 1pm.

The start was only part of the final plan. An enormous safety net had to be created, one that could cover the fleet for every one of the 628 nm. This involved having two large sail-training vessels, including the Royal Australian Navy's *Young Endeavour*, shadowing the fleet all the way.

Remarkably, two of the 'old salts' who participated in the inaugural Hobart race – CYCA founder Peter Luke, and club member Engelbert 'Boy' Messenger – signed up to race; Luke was aboard the powerful sloop *Charisma*, while seventy-year-old Messenger was the designated skipper of *Musket Cove Resort Fiji*. Two other veteran race competitors, Norm Hudson and Ray Richards (who sailed aboard *Rani* in 1945), would fly to Hobart to be part of the post-race celebrations.

Spice was added to the mix pre-race with race sponsor, Kodak, offering $100,000 to the line honours yacht should it better *Kialoa III*'s race record time of 2 days, 14 hours, 36 minutes and 56 seconds set in 1975. And, with the IOR handicap category being replaced by IMS that year, the Marine Board of Hobart announced it would present the corrected time winner with a $10,000 cash prize.

Fancied for being first to Hobart was the maxi ketch *Tasmania*, formerly the 1992 line honours yacht *New Zealand Endeavour*. It had been purchased by prominent Tasmanian shipbuilder and yachtsman Bob Clifford and renamed. Its most likely challengers were seen to be *Congere VII* (formerly *Drumbeat*) and *Brindabella*.

The cross-section of participating yachts would have impressed even the most experienced of old sailors, especially when the yachts were there for all to see on the harbour at the same time.

One of the classic standouts was the 1950 race winner, Sir James Hardy's 13.7-metre-long *Nerida*, with its traditional gaff rig, long bowsprit and sweetly curved hull lines. The spectacle was not lost on Sir James:

> There were seventy-six items on my to-do list which I drew up after the crew and I decided we should get into the spirit of the race and enter *Nerida*. Somehow we got through it, and I'm so glad we did, because to be part of that start on the harbour was something one will never forget.
>
> We sailed through the Heads and out to sea in grand style – with a jackyard topsail set at the masthead. It worked a treat for us; to the degree where classic old *Nerida* embarrassed a number of more modern yachts by sailing past them.

The wall of sail that stretched across the harbour as the 371 yachts glided downwind towards the Heads en masse was a sight to behold. However, as each division converged on their respective turning marks at the Heads it was increasingly obvious that they were heading for a logjam. That was especially the case for the Grand Prix division yachts. The scene that unfolded was almost unbelievable. At one stage the number of yachts trying to round their designated buoy simultaneously was near 20-wide, gunwale to gunwale. Consequently, gunwales were bumping and sails were thumping in response to the gentle swell, while vociferous crews were either shouting at each other or laughing loudly at the ridiculous nature of the scene. Making matters worse was the number of yachts that had done a U-turn and sailed back through the oncoming fleet after failing at their first attempt to round the buoy.

It took an hour before the entire fleet had cleared the Heads and turned to starboard into a gentle southerly. *Brindabella* made the best of the situation and was soon leading the fleet.

With the benefit of the south-flowing current and a favourable wind, the majority of the yachts were either in Bass Strait or beyond it, when the weather alerts started coming through via radio.

Sure enough, when crews cast their eyes to the south-west they could see a sausage-shaped, long grey cloud emerging over the horizon – a 'grey roller' – which heralded the approach of a powerful and menacing gale that was destined to impact the rear half of the fleet. It was time for the crews of those yachts to consider their options. As Sir James recalled:

We were two-thirds of the way across Bass Strait when we heard the forecast. At that stage we were having some problems with broken halyards, so I decided we should have a vote – push on or turn back. Everyone agreed that Eden sounded like a nice destination, so we, along with many others, did a 180 degree turn and headed in that direction.

The weather front proved to be a monster. Some crews reported wind gusts of around 70 knots and breaking seas up to 6 metres high. Not surprisingly, discretion was the better part of valour for many – sixty-three yachts retired, three of those as a result of being dismasted.

The battle between the ketch *Tasmania* and *Brindabella* for the honour of being first to Hobart in this history-making race turned into a slugfest all the way to the line. They went tack-for-tack in the Derwent with the local heroes covering every move *Brindabella* made. Those tactics, and a dose of local knowledge, led to *Tasmania* claiming line honours by a mere 7 minutes. Unfortunately though, the crew had to pay for their own party: there was no $100,000 bonus to collect as *Tasmania*'s elapsed time was a little more than 2 hours outside the race record.

Raptor, an Australian designed and built yacht owned by Germany's Andreas Eichenauer, went on to take first place in the IMS division from *Ninety-Seven* (Andrew Strachan). Peter Kurts's *Love & War*, winner of the 1974 and 1978 races, won the 20-year Veterans' Division, and Don Mickleborough's sloop, *Southerly* (aka *The Southerly Floating Hotel*) won the 30-year Veterans' Division.

*

Love & War's imposing result in that historic event confirmed that the 14.3 metre Sparkman & Stephens design, which was launched in 1973, was one of the most outstanding yachts in the fifty-year history of the classic. Twelve years later, in 2006, this superbly maintained yacht stepped up another notch in Hobart race history, this time with long-time navigator Lindsay May at the helm. The solid upwind conditions that prevailed for much of the race suited 'the old girl' immensely, so much so that May, backed by many of the yacht's usual crew, sailed the then thirty-three-year-old *Love & War* into Hobart and claimed the *Tattersall Cup* by an hour on corrected time over *Bacardi* (J. Williams). It was a historic victory, after the Halvorsen brothers' all-conquering *Freya*, *Love & War* became only the second yacht to win the Hobart race on three occasions.

*

For 46 consecutive years, Christmas Day was more Boxing Day Eve – the day before the start of the Sydney Hobart race – for Lindsay May. It only meant he was once again going sailing as a specialist navigator.

In early 2019 he put pen to paper for the CYCA and noted some of his memories spanning all those years. Apart from skippering *Love & War* to victory in 2006, he won as navigator aboard *Indian Pacific* in 1984 and *Atara* in 1991.

> I realised just how much, and how fast, things had changed over that period when I gave my grandson a book as a birthday present – only to be stunned by the sight of him trying to turn the pages by swiping them, just as you do with an iPad.
>
> In 1973 I was a 24-year-old ex-surf swimmer from Wollongong who somehow jagged a for'ard-hand position

aboard Peter Rysdyk's *Onya of Gosford*, which he built himself. He was a fascinating Dutchman; larger-than-life, who loved his sailing. In every race we did we had Happy Hour at 1700; that was when he would enjoy a Scotch and *hors d'oeuvres* with the crew gathered in the cockpit. We always ate well, until the late '70s when the need was to make boats as light as possible, and that meant a minimalist approach to provisioning.

The crew were experienced and competent sailors. I learned about the howling nor'easter that funnels down the Tassie coast, and the venturi effect over Tasman Island – a phenomenon that took me years to completely understand.

In 1974 Peter built another *Onya of Gosford*, a tiny Cole 31 class yacht that had a crew of five. Our crossing of Bass Strait in that year's Hobart was terrifying. We must have had 50 knots from the south-west with huge waves bearing down on us. The challenge for the helmsmen was to try to steer around the cresting ones, but all too regularly a wave would swamp the boat, which meant if you were the guy on the wheel you would be crushed to the deck under the weight of the water.

Peter didn't spend a lot on fittings and equipment for the yacht; for example a safety harness was a rope you tied around your waist and secured to a cleat, while the topping lift which supports the boom was secured to the boom by a piece of string. One race, when we were reefing the mainsail that string broke, and Peter, who was leaning on the boom at the time, was launched over the side to the extent where his 'safety' line had him half in the water and half on-board. Three of us scrambled to him and tried to haul him aboard. It was a tough task, however it's surprising how much strength one can muster in such a situation, so we soon had him back on deck, wet but okay. I was soaked through as my sailing attire wasn't quite up to the task – my wet weather jacket was a Wollongong City Council plastic smock with air holes under the arms and a lace up neck. I stayed wet for the rest of the race.

That was when I decided to become a specialist navigator.

It was all very basic in those early days. Initially the weather forecasting for a race meant you collected newspaper weather chart cuttings each day for weeks prior to the race, and then from those, predict what would happen over the coming days. We also got radio forecasts and recorded all the weather station air pressure readings, wind direction and plotted these on a map of Australia. From that we drew our own synoptic charts.

Whilst progress since that era has been revolutionary in design, hull construction, navigation equipment, sailcloth, clothing, etcetera, the most significant advances have been in safety. Even before the tragic 1998 race, the CYCA had led the world with hull, rudder and deck specifications, hull stability, communications and crew capability requirements. The pivotal 1998 race allowed much of this early work to be seen for its merits, and I have no doubt many potential deaths have been prevented due to the foresight and passion of a dedicated group of volunteers and staff. They worked together to bring about changes that have helped make a dangerous but exhilarating pastime one where we can expect to arrive safely, albeit exhausted, smelly and weather-beaten, but with outrageous smiles and wonderful stories that will last until the following 26 December.

*

In 1996, *Kialoa III*'s Hobart race record time of 2 days 14 hours 36 minutes and 56 seconds had stood for an astonishing 21 years, so that fact was enough for the 1996 race sponsor, Telstra, to offer a $300,000 prize should any yacht break the record that year. Whether it was that incentive, or simply the appeal of the Hobart race, is unknown but German billionaire Hasso Plattner, the co-founder of SAP SE software, was in Sydney with his magnificent maxi *Morning Glory* for the Hobart that year. It turned into a great race against the clock where, for much of the time, it appeared that the record would stand for another year. In fact, nothing was certain until the finish line was in sight. *Morning Glory* glided across the line 20 minutes inside the long-standing record. Quite understandably, Hasso Plattner and his crew had a large celebration in Hobart that night, as did Victorian Giorgio Gjergja and his crew as they took out corrected time honours with the Farr 47 design, *Ausmaid*.

*

This last decade of the 20th century was seeing perhaps the greatest evolution in yacht design and construction in the history of international ocean racing. Not surprisingly, the annual Hobart race became the ultimate testbed for these trends and, as a consequence, the Cruising Yacht Club of Australia pioneered many of the regulations, safety practices and communication networks needed to keep the sport as safe as possible.

Prominent Kiwi offshore racing sailor and design consultant, Geoff Stagg, declared at the time that he did the Hobart race as often as possible 'for a personal reality check' and to be at the battlefront when it came to assessing hull structures and the all-round performance of new design concepts.

'The Hobart is a bloody great race,' Stagg said. 'I think it's actually tougher than an around-the-world race because I don't think the around-the-world racers get anything like the extreme conditions you get in a Hobart race. The Hobart race also demands a good all-round boat. One-way machines rarely do any good – in fact very few of them actually finish.'

For local and international yacht designers, to have one of their latest designs win line and/or handicap honours in the Hobart race was like winning the lottery – such success would place them at or near the top of the list for yacht owners who were considering who should design their next yacht.

Not surprisingly then, many designers pushed every parameter to the limit, as if it was a Formula One race car. This included the type of construction (usually composite), the hull form (generally wide, fat and flat) and the yacht's stability factor (a figure influenced by the fact that a considerable number of crew would be positioned on the windward side of the yacht and contribute significantly to the 'righting moment' – in other words, a form of moveable ballast.

Ed Psaltis

SAILING BIO

I've been involved with offshore sailing since I was 2 months old. I've done thirty-eight Sydney Hobarts, twenty-eight as owner/skipper. Over the years, my crew and I have won, overall, every offshore race out of Sydney. This includes the Sydney Hobart, Mooloolaba, Gold Coast, Cabbage Tree Island, Lord Howe Island, Bird Island and Flinders Island races. I'm proud of the fact that now three generations of Psaltis' have or are competing in the Sydney Hobart – Bill Psaltis, then his three sons (all competing in the 75th), and now my son Ben, with three under his belt going into the 75th race.

WHAT WAS YOUR BEST DAY SAILING IN THE SYDNEY HOBART?

Rounding Tasman Island aboard *Midnight Rambler* at dusk in the hellish 1998 race in close company with two very well-sailed and much bigger boats, *Quest* and *Industrial Quest*. We had raced hard going into, and especially after, the dreadful storm. It was through great crew work and seamanship, that we had survived the worst of the storm. At 4 am that next morning on the Derwent, we got a new line of breeze after being becalmed. From that moment we knew the breeze would get us over the line before the deadline and therefore see us claim overall victory from *Ausmaid* and *Ragamuffin*. None of us had slept for days, but the adrenaline kept us going.

WHAT DAY OR EXPERIENCE WAS THE TOUGHEST OR MOST CHALLENGING?

Mid-storm in the 1998 race. I've seen many gales but none before or since have gone anywhere near the ferocity and unbridled power of that system. For at least 12 hours it was very much touch-and-go as to whether we would get through alive. The conditions remained extreme for the next 12 hours. In most other gales if you were good enough / tough enough, and worked hard enough as a crew, you could establish a level of control over the boat and how it was taking on the extreme conditions. In '98, no matter how hard you tried, nature certainly let you know that it very much had the upper hand. But for us, it was a very proud moment witnessing how our seven-man crew worked together to beat the odds and survive aboard a small and light racing boat.

WHAT KEEPS YOU GOING BACK TO THE HOBART RACE?

Its aura – the Hobart race is like no other. The mates I've raced with are life-long friends. When you go through extreme conditions like we have over the years, you form intensely close bonds with those who toiled with you. There's also the challenge of taking on rivals who you know are among the best in the world. On those occasions where we have beaten them, it is extremely rewarding. Finally, the Hobart gets me away from the realities of day-to-day business life. Out at sea you realise all the problems you thought you had back on land are not really big problems at all ... nature humbles everything. I couldn't survive in this world without getting out on the oceans.

WHAT ARE SOME OF THE BIG CHANGES THAT YOU'VE WITNESSED IN YOUR YEARS ASSOCIATED WITH THE RACE?

The standard of professionalism and safety in those entering the race has increased. This is good but the downside with it is that, due to time and cost, the average owner now finds it very hard to put a campaign together for a Hobart race. I miss the older days when the average Aussie and his mates would have a go, and where the comradeship among boats post-race was huge. Constitution Dock ain't what it used to be ... but that's progress I suppose. These days more than ever, winning in your division is what you strive for – where you are racing in roughly the same conditions as your competitors. That fact is enough to keep me and others interested in continuing to 'have a go'.

CHAPTER 16

The Fatal Storm

The spectacular success of the 50th anniversary race in 1994, and *Morning Glory*'s record time for the course 2 years later, contributed significantly towards the Hobart race maintaining an unprecedented level of prominence in the media, nationally and internationally.

Unfortunately, 4 years later the 1998 race brought the classic into news headlines worldwide for the worst possible reason.

It was a maritime tragedy of horrendous proportions.

There had been a widely held belief, since the first race in 1945, that the Hobart had seen the complete range of weather conditions that could be expected – from 'glass-out' calms where the yachts lay motionless for hour after hour as if glued to a mirror-like sea, through to powerful storms where howling winds generated waves that resembled liquid mountains capped by an avalanche of thundering white water.

Still, given the unpredictable nature of Bass Strait and the Tasman Sea, many seasoned sailors believed that the worst weather might not yet have been seen; that one day the ultimate storm and the Hobart race might intersect. And that is what happened in 1998. The raging tempest Alan Payne had alluded to some years earlier became a reality.

*

Since its inception, the Hobart has stood as a unique experience and a symbol of excellence in Australian sport. The reason is easy to understand: the race is a boundless challenge within the realms of nature that fascinates everyone – sailors and followers alike. Each Boxing Day the Hobart race takes people from all walks of life on an exciting journey, where nothing is certain.

The waters of the Tasman Sea and Bass Strait form the arena for this experience. It is a stadium where the participants are like gladiators pitched against a controlling and often invisible force, the weather. It is a playing field that can be blissfully benign and a thing of beauty one day, and one step from hell the next – a combination of factors that is very much part of ocean racing's appeal, and which brings participants back year after year.

*

At the compulsory pre-race weather briefing that skippers and senior crewmembers attended 48 hours before the start of the 1998 race, the Bureau of Meteorology representative declared that it was difficult to provide an accurate forecast due to the unstable nature of the developing weather pattern. However, it was almost certain the fleet would be confronted by a storm out of the south during the first night at sea. In addition, there was a low-pressure system lurking off the New South Wales coast that might move south.

While this briefing was taking place, internationally acclaimed yachting meteorologist Roger 'Clouds' Badham, who had enjoyed a long association with the Hobart race, issued his own warning, reminding competitors that during the previous 6 weeks there had been intense and sometimes cyclonic low-pressure systems active in the Tasman Sea. Then, on the eve of the race, he also advised those skippers who subscribed to his forecast service that a strong southerly change would emerge out of the darkness during the first night at sea. He added: 'I am beginning to wonder how God knows it's time for a Hobart race.'

As was always the case on Boxing Day morning, Badham travelled to the CYCA to deliver his final race forecast to his many clients then headed back to his home south of Sydney. When he got there, he went straight to his office and within minutes was alarmed by the weather models unfolding on his computer screens. The pattern developing over Tasmania was turning ugly; during the few hours he was away at the CYCA, the low-pressure system had become a very worrying storm of near cyclonic proportions.

Under race rules, competing crews were not permitted to receive any outside assistance regarding the weather during the race, so Badham, knowing he couldn't issue any warning to his clients competing in the race, decided the next best thing to do was to contact a media reporter who was covering the race:

I have just looked at all the latest weather models and there is only one thing I can say. If I were on half those yachts out there this afternoon, I'd be taking my spinnaker down right now and turning back to Sydney. They are going to get hammered. There's a bomb about to go off in Bass Strait. A low is going to develop and intensify. They are going to get 50 knots, maybe more, and huge seas.

His prediction was that the worst of the weather would strike the majority of the fleet at around 2.30pm the following day, and this would prove to be correct. Unfortunately, under the existing race rules, the competing yachts could not be warned of this development until the official weather forecast was issued at 10pm – 9 hours after the start. By then many of the yachts would be 100 nm south of Sydney or more.

When this official forecast was broadcast to the race yachts that night some crews elected to retire immediately and head home, but for many others it was considered to be too late to turn back, so they pressed on.

By next morning, Badham's worst fears were realised. The weather station at Wilsons Promontory in Bass Strait was already reporting wind gusts of 92 knots. Bringing additional drama to this already grim piece of information was the knowledge that the confluence of the howling wind from the south-west and a fast-flowing southerly current was generating the worst imaginable conditions. The most worrying feature was the magnitude and sheer might of the seas. By 2.30pm on 27 December the majority of the fleet was trapped by the storm, and as conditions deteriorated SOS calls started to fill the radio waves.

The response from AMSA (Australian Maritime Safety Authority) based in Canberra was immediate. The emergency rescue procedure it was about to coordinate would, within 48 hours, become Australia's largest peacetime search and rescue effort. It involved the Royal Australian Navy, the Police Air Wing, helicopter rescue services, media helicopters, light aircraft and private vessels.

For the next 48 hours across Australia and around the world the developing disaster became headline news; it was a rescue mission that was almost beyond comprehension, one that covered hundreds of square kilometres of savage ocean off the south-east corner of the Australian mainland.

Tragically, by the time the storm began to abate, six sailors had perished while fifty-five were winched to safety, some in remarkable circumstances. Of the fleet of 115 starters, five yachts sank and only forty-four reached Hobart.

Many of the rescue stories reflected the sheer bravery of the rescuers, or how a miraculous level of good fortune led to sailors surviving the heinous conditions.

One such story involved American John Campbell, who was lost overboard from the yacht *Kingurra* when it was rolled 360 degrees by a mighty wave well to the east of Gabo Island. Fortunately he had been able to remove his wet weather gear and seaboots while in the water, boots he had deliberately bought oversize so they would be easy to remove in such a circumstance.

His rescue came at the hands of the crew of a Victoria Police Air Wing helicopter led by pilot Darryl Jones. The chopper reached the scene from the mainland in a remarkably short time thanks to a 70-knot tailwind. But the return leg against the wind would be far more challenging.

Jones told his story in the book *Fatal Storm*:

As soon as we knew we'd located Campbell, I said to the
blokes; 'We'd better do this as quickly as we can. I need
to make sure we have as much fuel as possible for the leg
home.'

We put Keysie [David Key] on the wire and lowered
him into the water. That wasn't easy to start with because
of the strength of the wind – he was blowing out behind
the chopper instead of going straight down. The winch
man, Barry Barclay, guided me forward so we could move
Keysie towards the target – and that was when the big
wave arrived on the scene.

Jones then told how, when hovering at 100 feet, a gargantuan
wave almost claimed the chopper:

When I looked ahead, as I began to fly forward, I saw
another massive wall of water coming at us. It was a
huge wave building in the windscreen, and I said to
Barry 'Play out some cable, I have to climb'. So I
climbed up to 150 feet and when this thing went
beneath us, the radio altimeter needle was showing 10
feet clearance.

It was a mountain of water and we actually dragged
Dave straight through it – it was so huge and came at us so
suddenly, there was no way we were going to get him up
and over it.

After some considerable effort, Key got to Campbell and
secured him in the rescue harness, then the two men were

winched up to the helicopter. That done, Jones set a course towards the nearest airport, Mallacoota.

His calculations revealed that in the prevailing conditions, the chopper had 80 minutes of fuel remaining and the flight time to Mallacoota was 40 minutes – but the instruments didn't take into consideration the 115-knot headwind!

> After a while, when checking my gauges, I noticed that I had flown for about 40 minutes, and the GPS was still telling me I had 40 minutes to get back to Mallacoota. Basically, it meant that while our airspeed was 120 knots, there were times when I had a ground speed of about 5 knots.
>
> I could see land about 25kms ahead but even so, I was starting to sweat a bit about fuel – and sure enough, a short while later the low-fuel warning lights came on. I was doing my best to wean the chopper while thinking 'Maybe we won't make it to land'.

Without saying anything to Campbell, Key and Barclay began preparations for a ditching, including attaching themselves and Campbell to the helicopter's life raft. At the same time, Jones knew that if they had to ditch, there was no way he would be able to escape from the cockpit. Still, he had not given up hope that a miracle might occur and they would be able to make it to land.

> I started flying towards the nearest point of land I could see and incredibly, we got there. From that point I just

kept stretching it and stretching it, all the time looking for a landing location if I needed one.

The moment I got over the inlet at Mallacoota and saw the football oval I knew that was where I was going to land. I put the thing on the ground as quickly as I could – nothing fancy and certainly not a full and proper procedure. It had taken one hour and 22 minutes to get back to shore.

Once you have landed a helicopter, the procedure is to pull the engine throttle levers back to ground idle position, and let them run for a minute so the temperatures and pressures in the engine settle down. I pulled the first one back; hit the stopwatch and 40 seconds later, it stopped on its own. It had run dry! Then I pulled the second lever back, hit the stopwatch again and that lasted 20 seconds before it ran dry!

Without hesitation, Jones, Barclay and Key stepped out of the helicopter, walked a few metres away and stood in a huddle; a slight tremor passed through all their bones while they looked at each other in total disbelief.

*

Still the storm raged, causing grief and mayhem on the waters of Bass Strait and off the south coast of New South Wales. Incredibly though, while lives were being lost in terribly tragic circumstances, more miracles were occurring.

Aboard Stephen Ainsworth's 13.5-metre-long sloop *Loki*, Michael 'Zapper' Bell was one of three crewmembers on deck when, while some 70 nm offshore, the yacht was overwhelmed by a rogue wave of monumental proportions. Incredibly, *Loki* headed up the vertical wall of water and flipped over backwards, upside down. Bell recalled:

> What followed was the most amazing experience I've ever had at sea. There I was, underneath this upturned yacht in the most incredibly serene situation. I could have been swimming in the fishpond; in fact it was like swimming in the Caribbean – clear and warm. Everything was still and beautiful. I saw my glasses get washed off my face and had time to simply reach out and grab them. I remember all the coloured halyard tails and lines just wafting through the water like colourful sea snakes. I was amazed that I felt no panic. I knew I had to release my safety harness at my chest to get out. There was no gasping for breath or panic, just deliberate movements to escape. Then, all of a sudden, the yacht righted itself with the rig and everything still intact.
>
> With that, all hell broke loose again. We were back into the real world. Not surprisingly, we decided that was enough. We set a sea anchor from the stern and ran under bare poles, still doing 7 knots. Some of the crew wanted us to head towards Eden – 70 miles upwind. 'Bugger that,' I said. 'We're heading for New Zealand. It might be 1200 miles away but I know I can catch a jet back to Australia from there. We are not going upwind in this weather.'

The 12.5-metre yacht *B-52*, owned by Wayne Millar from Townsville, was also overwhelmed by a rogue wave, but remained inverted for some considerable time with two crewmembers outside and eight trapped in the air bubble inside the cabin. Crewman John Byrne still remembers 'the eerie emerald-green light filtering into the cabin through the windows and the deathly quiet despite the chaos outside'. He also explained that those inside the hull were understandably disoriented as debris was floating all around.

> Even simple things, like the engine, became confusing because it was upside down, and I couldn't work out what had happened with the stove. I thought the round methylated spirits tank on the stove was the engine filter, until I realised the engine was now actually above my head. Fortunately fuel and oil didn't pour out of the engine and also, the fact that we had gel batteries meant that we didn't have battery acid going everywhere.
>
> It's amazing what you do in such a situation. Ray LaFontaine grabbed the microphone on the two-way radio and said, 'What about a mayday?' One of the guys turned to him and said something like, 'I'll attend to that when it's appropriate.' Ray then let out a textbook perfect mayday call. We all just looked at him bemused, as if asking; 'Who are you calling, Flipper the dolphin? Mate, we're upside down!'

About four minutes later, without warning, the ghostly silence was broken by an almighty whoosh. With that, all hell broke loose in the cabin yet again: *B-52* was upright with two crewmen still attached and alive on deck.

While *B-52* headed for Eden, the enormous search and rescue effort continued. Many yacht owners and crews decided that, regardless of the cyclonic weather, they were trapped by it whether racing or retired, so opted to press on south towards Hobart, albeit with great caution.

*

It was around 8am on 29 December when *Sayonara*, then the world's greatest maxi yacht, owned by American billionaire businessman and co-founder of Oracle Corporation, Larry Ellison, came into view from the finish line on Castray Esplanade.

As expected in these circumstances, there was no great level of excitement being exhibited aboard the yacht or onshore. The scene was solemn. Hobart was a city in mourning.

Neither the 5000 plus people there to welcome the line honours winner, nor *Sayonara*'s crew knew quite how to handle the situation when the yacht crossed the line and docked. There was a distinct air of discomfort.

The media throng descended on a sorrowful Ellison as he stepped onto the dock, but instead of taking questions he made a declaration:

> Never again. Not if I live to be 1000 years old, will I do a
> Hobart race. This is not what it's supposed to be about.
> Difficult yes, dangerous no, life threatening – definitely
> not … It was by far the toughest race I've ever done in my
> life. It was horrible. The crew work was inspirational.

Very bad things could have happened to us out there and these guys got us through. Guys were knocked down but they just kept getting up and back to their jobs. They kept doing what had to be done to keep the boat in one piece — and keep all of us alive. It was truly extraordinary. Anyone who signs up for this race expects a difficult race but no one expects a dangerous race. The seas were enormous and the wind made sounds I've never heard before.

Rupert Murdoch's son, Lachlan, who was a member of *Sayonara*'s crew, was similarly contemplative: 'I think a lot of the guys in this crew have very strong and mixed feelings about even finishing in this race at all. You needed to be out there to know just how bad it was. If you imagine any disaster movie you have seen before, you have to double it or treble it.'

Meanwhile, off Tasmania's east coast something quite remarkable was in the making; one of the smallest yachts in the fleet, the 10.6 metre Hick 35 design, *AFR Midnight Rambler*, owned by Ed Psaltis and Bob Thomas, was emerging from the worst of the storm and looked to be the yacht to beat for victory on corrected time, and thus claim the *Tattersall Cup*.

Through great skill the yacht had survived the 80-knot weather bomb in Bass Strait, thanks to Psaltis' helming technique throughout the night, and the determination of the crew to survive the storm.

At the height of the tempest some crews had opted to go into survival mode with their yachts, either setting storm sails or running downwind with no sails aloft. However, Psaltis and Thomas devised a different tactic. It was imperative that they avoided steering the yacht directly up the front of the worst of the monster waves because of the risk of the yacht being flipped over backwards. Instead Psaltis steered a course up and across the face of the waves at a 60 degree angle. It proved to be a remarkably safe option, one where the yacht was still sailing quite fast and not spearing into mid-air off the wave crests.

AFR Midnight Rambler sailed across the finish line in Hobart in 10th place – a remarkable effort for a yacht that size. The height of the bar for victory on corrected time had been set and would prove insurmountable for what remained of the fleet.

Meanwhile, the massive air and sea search for missing sailors continued, particularly in the northern waters of Bass Strait where the oldest yacht in the fleet, *Winston Churchill*, had sunk. It was 20 nm south-east of Eden when it burst through the crest of a mammoth wave and dived into the trough that followed. The subsequent impact was so great that hull planks burst open and water poured in.

The crew barely had time to issue a mayday call and scramble into two life rafts before the classic old yacht – a participant in the inaugural Hobart in 1945 – disappeared before their eyes. Six of the crew were eventually rescued in miraculous circumstances, but sadly three perished.

Following a coronial enquiry conducted by the New South Wales government, and an extensive investigation by CYCA officials, considerable changes were made in relation to the conduct of the race, crew and yacht eligibility, race safety equipment and search and rescue techniques. As a result of these findings many changes were introduced to the sport, while the magnitude of the rescue effort led to improvements in search and rescue procedures nationally and internationally.

*

Considering the enormity of the disastrous 1998 race, no one was surprised when entries for the following year's Hobart were down by more than one-third – seventy-five as against 115. The spectacular celebrations planned to mark the end of the millennium in Sydney were another reason sailors were staying home.

Of those who did race, many chose to be there as a mark of respect for the sailors who had lost their lives while enjoying their chosen sport.*

George Snow's maxi *Brindabella* was odds-on favourite for line honours, but there was a sheep in wolf's clothing in the pack in the form of the Danish Volvo 60 class yacht *Nokia*. It had been entered by Stefan Myaralf and local yachting identity Michael Spies. At 22.5 metres, *Brindabella* was 3 metres longer than *Nokia*, but the *Nokia* team hoped that the 4 tonnes of water ballast they were permitted to carry (amid considerable controversy) when needed during the race would at least level the playing field, if not create an advantage.

That amount of water ballast pumped into tanks built into the hull was akin to having as many as forty extra crew sitting

---

* The six sailors who died were: Phillip Charles Skeggs (*Business Post Naiad*, drowned, 27 December); Bruce Raymond Guy (*Business Post Naiad*, heart attack, 27 December); John Dean, James Lawler and Michael Bannister (*Winston Churchill*, all drowned, 28 December); and Glyn Charles (*Sword of Orion*, drowned, 27 December).

on the windward side while sailing upwind in heavy conditions. Then, when sailing downwind the water was no longer an advantage, so it was pumped out – and the yacht then became significantly lighter and therefore faster.

The race proved to be a bitter-sweet experience for the crew of *Brindabella*.

Twenty-four hours into the charge south, both line and handicap honours were still up for grabs. Six yachts were then inside the record pace required to set a new mark for the distance, and most importantly, it appeared that the fast running conditions would hold. *Nokia*, which had been averaging more than 16 knots, surfed to the head of the pack and went on to surge across the finish line after just 1 day and 19 hours of sailing. By doing so, it lopped more than 18 hours off the previous race record. *Brindabella* was about an hour astern in second place, and on corrected time was just seven minutes off topping *Yendys*, sailed by the by every-popular Geoff Ross. However, all was not lost: *Brindabella* was recognised as the race record holder for conventionally ballasted yachts.

*

It was almost two years after the calamitous 1998 race before the coroner's report on the tragedy was handed down. It was a document eagerly anticipated by the sport in general as much as the CYCA membership, as the findings could mean the end of the Hobart race as it was known. However, the club put the time taken to prepare the report to good use, developing new rules and regulations all designed to make the sport safer.

The club was fortunate to have life member Gordon Marshall still within its ranks, a highly dedicated member who over the years had served the club as Rear Commodore, chairman of the Sailing Committee, Race Director for the Hobart race and Chief Measurer.

Marshall's engineering and sailing expertise led to him being a strong advocate against the trend towards less stable, lightweight hull construction. This led to the club's Sailing Committee developing, under his guidance, a stability/self-righting factor for all competing yachts based on a possible knockdown/stay-down situation occurring while crossing Bass Strait. This was a well-calculated, but in some quarters, controversial, move where the owners of yachts of questionable stability were required to have their yacht undergo a physical haul-down/capsize test, a procedure that would confirm if the design had the righting moment needed to return the vessel to upright following a knockdown in a storm.

*

While this procedure was being developed, there was considerable uncertainty within the club as to how many yachts would compete in the 2000 Hobart race, because many potential participants were waiting for the release of the coroner's report before deciding whether to race; they wanted to make sure their yacht could comply with any proposed rule changes.

The eagerly anticipated document was delivered just two weeks before the race start, and if there was one piece of good news within its pages for both organisers and participants, it was that very few yachts would be impacted by proposed new requirements. Also on the subject of safety, CYCA officials were pleased to note that the new set of safety requirements they had already introduced sat comfortably with the Coroner's recommendations. Those rules included a requirement that at least half the crew of each competing yacht must attend a special course relating to yacht safety at sea, and that at least two crew had to be qualified in advanced first-aid. An additional safety measure – one that would make the progress of the race more media friendly – required that all yachts were required to carry a satellite transmitter so the progress of the fleet could be monitored '24/7'.

When it came to the actual sailing instructions for race, there was one significant new rule: when a competing yacht was abeam of Green Cape (on the New South Wales–Victoria border), each skipper was required to report back by radio that the yacht and its crew were in good shape and capable of crossing the challenging stretch of water that lay ahead.

*

The start of the race on 26 December 2000 capped off what had been a dazzling year for Sydney. It had been the city's Olympic year, an event recognised worldwide as a spectacular success.

After the yachts cleared the Heads and turned south, it was easy going for the first 400 nm. But true to the long-standing adage that it was not a Hobart race unless you experienced a blow, the fleet had to contend with a howling gale-force wind during the final stages. It was sufficiently powerful to force 24 yachts retire, some of those retirements coming when the crew considered their situation, and the weather outlook, on reaching Green Cape.

The Swedish maxi, *Nicorette* (Ludde Ingvall) claimed line honours that year while the Tattersall Cup went to South Australia's Kevan Pearce with his Farr 47 design, *SAP Ausmaid*.

*

Nicorette's success brought into the limelight a young lady who would go on to become one of the female greats of the sport – the yacht's navigator, Adrienne Cahalan.

Adrienne started sailing as a youngster in small dinghies on Sydney Harbour then graduated to the high-performance and highly spectacular 18-foot skiffs. By 1984 she had developed the desire to go ocean racing, so did her first Hobart that year aboard *Mystic Seven*. It would prove to be 'the slow boat to Hobart' as it took the yacht six days to complete the course. More than three decades later, on the eve of the 75th anniversary race, Adrienne – by then a qualified maritime lawyer – could stand proud as one of the world's leading female offshore sailors. She had competed in 27 Hobart races (a record for a woman) and could boast a record that included six line honours, three second places across the line, two victories on corrected time, two race record times and three division wins. Of note, she was navigator aboard *Wild Oats XI* in 2005 and 2012 when it scored the treble – line and handicap honours and a race record time.

Beyond the Hobart race, Adrienne was a member of the crew of the giant American catamaran, *Cheyenne*, when it broke the round the world non-stop speed record in a time inside 64 days. She also has round the world races to her credit – and in that same time managed to become a mother of two!

*

The 2001 Hobart was destined to be a 'no-frills' race for the CYCA as Telstra had stepped away from being the event sponsor after six years. This caused the club considerable concern, especially when entries closed on 2 November and there were fewer than forty-five yachts on the list. Fortunately, though, as the weeks rolled on so the number continued to grow until it reached the final figure of seventy-five. It was a line-up that had an interesting international flavour to it – the eight yachts contesting the Volvo Round the World race were among the entries as the Hobart race was made part of their circumnavigation. *Nicorette* was also in the line-up, owner Ingvall no doubt hoping for second consecutive line honours.

When it came to the start there was a pleasantly historic moment associated with that year's race for competitors and spectators alike – Peter Luke, a founder of the CYCA and competitor in the inaugural Hobart race – fired the cannon that got the fleet underway.

The race had been going only a few hours when remarkable natural phenomena, a water spout, led to *Nicorette* making the headlines. The spiralling twister formed when the leading yachts were off Nowra and quickly swept across the course, directly towards the Swedish yacht. While some crew dived below deck, or hung on in the hope they would not be blown overboard, Ingvall, who was on the helm, had nowhere to hide. His only option was to wedge himself inside the ring of the large diameter steering wheel and try to minimise the chance of being injured by the force of the twister. Fortunately, the incident lasted less than a minute and no one on board was hurt, so with that *Nicorette* was back on track to Hobart in a matter of minutes.

The high-performance Volvo 60 class yachts were manned by some of the world's best offshore sailors, so few were surprised when another Swedish entry, and Volvo race competitor, *Assa Abloy*, skippered by Englishman Neal McDonald was first across the line, some 20 minutes ahead of *Nicorette*. That year the Tattersall Cup was claimed by John Kahlbetzer's stylish, Murray, Burns and Dovell design, *Bumblebee 5*.

Bruce Taylor

SAILING BIO

I've enjoyed ocean racing for forty years including thirty-eight Sydney Hobart Races, thirty-five as owner/skipper, (*Chutzpah* and *JLW Chutzpah*). I've taken second place overall twice, plus ten divisional wins. Additionally, I've won the Sydney–Gold Coast Race (2018), represented Victoria and Australia in the *Kenwood* and *Southern Cross Cups*, won multiple Victorian ocean races as well as the Sydney 38 state championship. I also participate in ocean racing from Royal Hong Kong Yacht Club aboard my son's yacht, *Ambush*.

WHAT WAS YOUR BEST DAY SAILING IN THE SYDNEY HOBART?

The second day of the 2017 race – extremely hard and fast downwind sailing in warm weather.

WHAT DAY OR EXPERIENCE WAS THE TOUGHEST OR MOST CHALLENGING?

Attending the mayday distress call from *Kingurra* when American, John Campbell, was lost overboard during the height of the storm in the 1998 race. The conditions could not have been worse and we held little hope that he would be rescued, but thankfully he was saved in miraculous circumstances.

WHAT KEEPS YOU GOING BACK TO THE HOBART RACE?

You might call it a pathological obsession! But the best part is sailing with a fantastic crew who are as dedicated as I am – many of whom have sailed with me as part of the team for more than thirty years.

WHAT ARE SOME OF THE BIG CHANGES THAT YOU'VE WITNESSED IN YOUR YEARS ASSOCIATED WITH THE RACE?

The ever-increasing downwind speed of the 40-foot yachts, GPS navigation, the internet, and significant improvements in weather forecasting.

CHAPTER 17

Keels that Cant

The first few years of the new millennium saw the Sydney Hobart race gain an even higher profile nationally and internationally due to two developments – one commercial, the other a revolution in yacht design.

In 2002, the international standing of the race was confirmed when one of the sport's greatest supporters, Swiss watchmaker, Rolex, became Title Sponsor for the event. This endorsement placed the Hobart alongside the world's greatest offshore events, like the Rolex Fastnet and the Rolex Middle Sea races.

Similarly, on the design front, there are few if any test tracks better than the course between Sydney and Hobart.

For example, it was the Hobart race that exposed the design and structural shortcomings of the light-displacement skiff-type yachts. The storm in 1998 led to significant advances in many facets of the sport and also contributed to the improvement of search and rescue techniques.

In general though, the desire to win the Hobart race, be it line honours or on corrected time, sees yacht owners and designers coming together under the umbrella of a common goal – to go one better than the rest. Consequently, the Hobart race has been a proving ground for many innovations over the past seven decades, none more so than the canting keel, a concept that impacted the sport worldwide.

It was a pioneering innovation that came to the attention of international ocean racing primarily through the open-minded thinking of three men: the late Bob Oatley (as owner of the most successful yacht in the 75-year history of the Hobart race, the 30-metre supermaxi *Wild Oats XI*), his eldest son Sandy, and the yacht's highly talented skipper Mark 'Ricko' Richards. The concept was developed in association with the *Wild Oats XI* design team Reichel/Pugh, located in San Diego.

Today this revolutionary appendage is to be found on a wide range of high-performance offshore racing yachts, including round-the-world racers.

*

It was 1939 when Bob Oatley, then aged 11, became a sailing enthusiast. He had purchased a canvas-covered canoe for 2 shillings and 6 pence, fitted it with a broomstick for a mast and a cut-down bedsheet for a sail then set off on adventures on Sydney Harbour.

After leaving school in his early teens and starting work as an office messenger boy in Sydney, his astuteness and diligent work ethic saw him enjoy considerable success in the coffee and wine-producing industries over the ensuing decades.

By the early 2000s, he was in a position to return to enjoying sailing. His first move was to purchase a partially completed 18.2-metre-long Reichel/Pugh design on the Gold Coast, then soon after – with input from his son Sandy and yacht builder Mark Richards – he set about creating the next generation of ocean racing yachts.

'Bob always wanted to explore new ground, so when he heard about the concept for the canting keel it really sparked his interest,' Mark Richards explained.

> We went to San Diego to evaluate the idea with Reichel/Pugh and to sail a 12-metre-long yacht that had a crude version of the canting keel which was operated by a pulley system. The yacht was an absolute pile of junk, and it had weed growing on the bottom, but that didn't stop Bob from seeing its potential. When we got back to the dock after our sail we discussed the keel, then Bob simply said without hesitation, 'Well, let's have a go.' It was as simple as that. He called it an 80/20 chance back then – an 80 per cent chance it would be a lemon and a 20 per cent chance it would be an absolutely sensational breakthrough in yachting. Fortunately, it was the latter.

By having the keel swing out to windward, the increased leverage delivered meant the yacht required considerably less ballast than one with a conventional fixed keel to achieve the same level of stability. That meant the yacht would be lighter and therefore faster. In aviation parlance it was like going from propeller-driven aircraft to jets.

The mechanics of the canting keel proved to be a huge design and engineering challenge based around the need for a powerful hydraulic ram to swing the keel from one side to the other when the yacht tacked or gybed. But everything fell into place and the yacht that emerged through this effort, named *Wild Oats*, was remarkably successful from the outset.

Wanting to then test the concept on the international stage, Oatley and Richards decided in 2003 to form a two-yacht Australian team to challenge for the *Admiral's Cup* (recognised at the time as the world championship in offshore racing) in Cowes, England. Sailing friend Colin O'Neil chartered a competitive yacht and it became the second yacht in the team. After a series of hard-fought races the Australians won the Cup, beating the Spanish team led by King Juan Carlos into second place.

*

The concept for the keel soon became a focal point for offshore racing sailors in Australia and around the world. Some sailors developed their own version of what would become a revolution in the sport. This was the case in 2004 when Melbourne yachtsman Grant Wharington entered his supermaxi, *Skandia* – which had been fitted with a canting keel – in the Sydney Hobart race. Unfortunately, the keel failed when *Skandia* was some 80 nm offshore and, as a consequence, the yacht went upside down. The response from rescue organisations was swift and the entire crew was saved. The yacht was salvaged and competed again the following year.

Skandia's problems were only part of what would prove to be a dramatic Hobart. Race legend Syd Fischer saw his highly fancied Farr 50 design, *Ragamuffin*, dismasted when the yacht crashed off a huge wave and into the following trough. But circumstances were even worse for one of the line honours' contenders, the New Zealand entry, *Konica Minolta*, owned by Stewart Thwaites. His hopes for being first to Hobart were literally crushed when the yacht was struck by a monster wave. 'Just before 6am we barrelled off the top of a gi-normous wave and crashed down the other side,' Thwaites reported by radio. 'I was below deck when it happened. I heard the wave, then I heard the foam in the deck crushing. It was all hands on deck. The helmsman was keeping the boat under control and trying to slow it down. This wave was twice as big as any others we've seen during the race'. It was soon realised that the structural damage to the yacht was so bad it could not continue racing.

Conditions were so rugged that year, near 50 of the fleet of 116 were forced to retire. The race was won on corrected time by *Aera*, owned by Englishman Nick Lykiardopulo.

*

Back at home, Oatley already knew that well-known Kiwi yachtsman Neville Crichton was building an all-carbon-fibre 30-metre canting keel supermaxi in Sydney (30 metres being the maximum overall length accepted for yachts contesting the Sydney Hobart race). It too had been designed by the Reichel/Pugh group in San Diego. That project excited Oatley immensely, so he decided to follow suit and build a similar yacht for the Hobart race that year.

What followed was possibly one of the most amazing building programs ever seen in the yachting industry anywhere in the world. *Wild Oats XI* was built in just 9 months and launched less than 4 weeks prior to the start of the classic that year.

With Crichton's yacht, *Alfa Romeo*, already in the water, the 2005 Hobart race had all the hallmarks of becoming one of the world's greatest ocean racing showdowns – a drag race under sail over 628 nm.

'Neville's boat was clearly the one to beat,' Richards later recalled.

However while Bob never put any pressure on us, the words he said to me as we left the dock on Boxing Day really stuck. He said, 'Ricko, we've got her to the start line and that in itself is a huge achievement. There's no pressure, just go out there and do the best you can.' Then, with a little grin on his face he added, 'but if you could just lead the fleet out through the Heads for us, it would be fantastic.' We ended up doing exactly that!

*

The two supermaxis raced bow-on-bow down the New South Wales south coast all the way to Bass Strait. At that point *Alfa Romeo* held a narrow advantage, but then Crichton opted to break the cover he held over his rival and head off on a different course out to the east. It was a move that proved to be an expensive mistake. By morning *Wild Oats XI* led by near 30 nm.

Wild Oats XI went on to take line honours by more than an hour from *Alfa Romeo*, but the overall result was far greater than just being first home. Oatley's supermaxi wrote its name into the history books by taking the race's Triple Crown – line honours, the race record time and first on corrected time. It was the first time a yacht had achieved this since *Rani* in the first Hobart race in 1945. Amid the dockside euphoria, Bob Oatley declared: 'I believe that the Hobart is the greatest ocean yacht race in the world, and to achieve what we have in our first attempt is very, very special. It's the ultimate reward for the ultimate effort. It is beyond a dream.'

Oatley's focus then turned to the 2006 race.

*

A quality fleet of seventy-eight, including Sean Langman's magnificently restored seventy-eight-year-old, 9.01-metre-long gaff cutter *Maluka*, faced the starter in 2006. Other yachts of interest included the Kiwi supermaxi, *Maximus* (Charles St Clair Brown and Bill Buckley), which was making its Hobart debut; supermaxi, *Skandia*; the two-time handicap winner, *Love & War*, and the 1968 corrected time winner, *Koomooloo*. Also of note was the presence of Lou Abrahams from Melbourne, himself a two-time corrected time winner who, by participating that year, equalled the record of Tasmania's John Bennetto, who had started in forty-four Hobarts.

That race was packed with high drama and excitement. The fleet had a rapid ride down the New South Wales coast until the seemingly inevitable southerly change arrived. With that, the sailing conditions turned nasty – powerful and large seas generated by a chilly wind that topped 35 knots.

Until then the supermaxis were having a great battle for the honour of being first to Hobart; *Wild Oats XI* was leading *Maximus* by less than 3 nm while *Skandia* was only a short distance astern of the Kiwis.

However, it wasn't long before the might of the storm began taking a toll, and consequently the radio waves were being filled with drama-laced calls relating to injuries and carnage. At 3:30am an emergency call from *Maximus* advised that the yacht had been dismasted 10 nm east of Batemans Bay and five of the crew had been injured when the huge carbon fibre wing-mast crashed to the deck. Three of those injured were airlifted to hospital at Moruya — one suffering a broken leg plus pelvis and rib injuries. Two other crew members were taken ashore by police launch.

Mid-morning on 27 December, there was a mayday call from Mike Freebairn's beautiful sloop, *Ray White Koomooloo*, the 'floating Steinway', advising that for an undetectable reason the yacht was taking water so rapidly that the crew were preparing to board life rafts. They were rescued soon after the yacht sank about 60 nm east of Narooma.

The loss of *Koomooloo* — which won the Hobart in 1968 and twice represented Australia in the *Admiral's Cup* — came as a shock for competitors who knew the yacht. It was considered to be superbly built and well maintained. It could only be assumed that there was a structural failure in the hull, or more probably, the yacht had struck a semi-submerged object.

Back in the race *Wild Oats XI* was 7 nm ahead of another supermaxi *Skandia*, with Matt Allen's *Ichi Ban* in pursuit. *Skandia* was back to top-flight racing mode after a major rebuild over the preceding months. It had capsized in the 2004 race when its canting keel failed off Flinders Island and the crew abandoned ship.

The fleet had been racing for 47 hours when *Wild Oats XI* surfed into Storm Bay, sailed on into Hobart and secured back-to-back line honours – the first yacht to do so since *Astor* in 1963.

This achievement was one of two historic moments that year: the other was when the beautifully proportioned sloop *Love & War*, then owned by Simon Kurts and skippered by Lindsay May, became the only yacht after the Halvorsen brothers' legendary *Freya* to win the coveted *Tattersall Cup* three times. However, there was one significant difference: *Freya's* victories were consecutive.

∗

History was made in the race the following year – 2007 – when American yacht *Rosebud*, an STP65 design owned by Roger Sturgeon, won the *Tattersall Cup*. Most impressive though was the achievement of Sydney yachtsman, eighty-five-year-old John Walker, who, sailing his yacht *Impeccable*, became the oldest skipper ever to complete the race. Similarly, the yacht *Phillip's Foote Witchdoctor* bettered its own record with an unmatched 27 starts in the great race.

That same year, *Wild Oats XI* claimed its third consecutive line honours, equalling the record set by *Morna/Kurrewa* in 1946, 1947 and 1948. 'Oats' faced stiff competition from Mike Slade's new *ICAP Leopard* which had come to Australia from England after smashing the 2007 Rolex Fastnet race record in

379

August. Oatley's yacht would claim another line honours in 2008, but the following year its run came to an end when it was led into Hobart by Neville Crichton's *Alfa Romeo II*.

Two very different yachts with one thing in common were the winners of the *Tattersall Cup* in 2009 and 2010 — one a production yacht and the other a Grand Prix level racer — but both from South Australia. In '09 orthopaedic surgeon, Andrew Saies, took the honours with his Beneteau First 40 *Two True,* while the following year Geoff Boettcher finally achieved his goal after twenty-two attempts when he triumphantly held the *Tattersall Cup* aloft to the delight of an admiring crowd.

His victory didn't come easily. He told the media that while the 1998 race was the worst imaginable, the 2010 experience was a tough one.

> About half-way to Hobart we began to realise we were in the hunt for first place so we pushed the boat to the absolute limit, knowing that even the slightest mistake could cost us the win. At one stage we thought it was all over when the bowman, who was on the foredeck lowering the headsail, disappeared over the side. Fortunately, he was wearing his safety harness so was being dragged along in the water at the side of the yacht. Still, it took five guys to pull him back on to the deck.

Boettcher, a Vietnam vet, went on to liken his experience in both the 1998 and 2010 races to being on the battlefield — 'You just never knew what was going to come at you next and what the consequences might be.'

If nothing else, Boettcher's success was the reward for persistence. Over the years he had become known as the 'Mayor of Eden' due of the number of times he had been forced to retire from the race and head to that port.

*

A sombre mood prevailed over the 2011 Hobart race. Four months earlier one of the stalwarts of the classic, Gary Ticehurst, was killed in a helicopter crash at Lake Eyre in the centre of Australia. For 27 years Ticehurst had been an 'aerial angel' for competing crews as he flew his chopper from Sydney to Hobart. His primary purpose was news gathering for the ABC national television network, but on many occasions he became involved in search and rescue efforts. In the infamous 1998 race, Ticehurst was credited with contributing to the rescue of more than twenty sailors thanks to his flying skills in heinous conditions. His ashes were scattered by the crew of the supermaxi *Wild Oats XI* as that yacht crossed the finish line in Hobart.

*

Over the years former Tasmanian, Roger Hickman, had become something of a legend in the Hobart race by his participation and dedication to the sport.

In 2014 there was a touch of irony in the race when Hickman's yacht, the 43-foot *Wild Rose*, was declared winner of the *Tattersall Cup*. He had purchased this yacht some years earlier from supermaxi owner, Bob Oatley, who had competed in the Hobart race with it 21 years earlier.

Twenty-nine hours prior to *Wild Rose* crossing the line, Oatley's *Wild Oats XI* had reached Hobart at the head of the fleet, claiming a record eighth line honours trophy.

*

The first two decades of the 21st century saw some hard-earned and well-deserved victories achieved in the race for the *Tattersall Cup* and the line honours trophy. Across the race's 75-year history, it is the high-speed charge south by the largest yachts that has attracted almost all the interest for the general public. However, for the sailing community, the true champion is the claimant to the *Tattersall Cup* – the winner on corrected time – and that can be the largest yacht in the race, the smallest or anything in between.

In today's era of the big boats, where *Alfa Romeo* (Neville Crichton), *Wild Oats XI* (the Oatley family), *LDV Comanche* (Jim Cooney/Samantha Grant), *Perpetual Loyal* and *Investec Loyal* (Anthony Bell), have staged epic battles in the bid to be first to Hobart, there have been some classic clashes among the smaller, but similarly high-tech, contenders for handicap honours.

Of note are Bob Steel, from Sydney, who claimed the Tattersall Cup with his yacht *Quest* in 2002 and 2008, *Loki* (Stephen Ainsworth, New South Wales, 2011), *Victoire* (Darryl Hodgkinson, New South Wales, 2013), *Balance* (Paul Clitheroe, New South Wales, 2015), *Giacomo* (Jim Delegat, New Zealand, 2016) and *Ichi Ban* (Matt Allen, New South Wales, 2017). Also, there was the very popular corrected time win in 2018 by Hobart's own Philip Turner with his superbly sailed, 20-metre long yacht, *Alive*. It was the first Tasmanian yacht to win the *Tattersall Cup* in 40 years.

Still, Turner and his team almost didn't get it all their own way. Stacey Jackson and her very experienced all-female crew aboard *Wild Oats X* – which is almost identical to *Alive* – were second on corrected time.

That year 80 women competed in the 74th Hobart race.

*

The year 2015 was *Wild Oats XI*'s tenth birthday, and over the preceding decade the supermaxi had become the most successful big boat in the history of the Hobart race. Its impressive tally was line honours on eight occasions and two victories on corrected time, but new challengers were looming, particularly American Jim Clark's radical sloop *Comanche*, which had been dubbed 'The Aircraft Carrier' because its extremely wide and flat design was unlike anything else. This yacht was the holder of the world 24-hour sailing record for monohull yachts – a remarkable 618 nm at an average speed of 25.75 knots. For locals there was a particular point of interest relating to this achievement: the distance *Comanche* covered was just 10 nm shorter than the course for the Hobart race, and this translated to the chance that, in absolutely ideal conditions, *Comanche* could go close to completing a Hobart race in one day!

That news was enough for the Oatleys to decide they had two options if they wanted to remain competitive: give *Wild*

Oats XI a birthday present in the form of a $2 million makeover, or spend $25 million building a new yacht.

A think tank comprising the designers, plus the builder John McConaghy, skipper Mark Richards, and the Oatleys, was assembled to consider all options. It was soon agreed that if a new yacht was built it would not be significantly different from *Wild Oats XI* as it was. This thinking was based on the fact that the yacht in its current form was a good all-round performer – it was fast in light winds and strong both upwind and downwind. The only significant design difference between the existing yacht and a new one would be that the hull shape forward of the mast would be longer and made more buoyant, changes that would decrease the chance of nosediving when sailing downwind at 30-plus knots. Such design improvements would mean the yacht could be pushed harder, while the longer foredeck would also allow for larger headsails to be set – a bonus in light weather. It was also realised that it would take only a few months to suitably modify the existing hull forward of the mast, while to build a new yacht would take a year.

So, out came the chainsaws and soon after a 14-metre-long carbon fibre section of *Wild Oats XI*'s bow had been lopped off. A new 16-metre-long section was then prefabricated in Sydney and moulded onto the remainder of the hull. Simultaneously, to keep *Wild Oats XI*'s overall length within the 30 metre limit for the Hobart race, 2 metres had to be lopped off the stern and a new flush transom fitted.

When relaunched, the new-look *Wild Oats XI* proved to be faster than the original. Despite this, the next three Hobart races did not go in its favour. In 2015, the yacht was forced out with a damaged mainsail and *Comanche* took line honours. Only a few weeks later a gaping hole was left in the Oatley family, and for all who knew him, when Bob Oatley passed away at his home in Sydney aged eighty-seven.

Misfortune again dogged *Wild Oats XI* in the 2016 Hobart. Anthony Bell's supermaxi *Perpetual Loyal* was first to the finish in race record time after '*Oats*' was forced to retire into Eden due to a failure in the canting keel system. The 2017 race was an intensely exciting battle all the way from start to finish between the renamed *LDV Comanche* (which had by then been purchased by Sydney yachtsman Jim Cooney and Samantha Grant) and *Wild Oats XI*. *Oats* was first home in an impressive race record time, 26 minutes ahead of *LDV Comanche*. But a protest lodged by *LDV Comanche* against *Wild Oats XI* over a right-of-way incident soon after the start was upheld by the Race Protest Committee. As a consequence *Oats* was penalised one hour on its elapsed time, which meant line honours and the race record were officially awarded to *LDV Comanche*.

That same year Australia's most successful ocean racing yachtsman, Syd Fischer, aged eighty-eight, became the oldest skipper to sail the race. Three months later around the time of his eighty-ninth birthday and after contesting the classic on forty-seven occasions, he declared it was time to hang up his seaboots.

*

It had been 3 years of tough times for the crew of *Wild Oats XI* and its many supporters. But the 2018 race saw the team back on top of the podium after a grandstand finish. It was a real nail–biter over the final 40 nm; the most exciting finish since the 7–second margin between *Condor of Bermuda* and *Apollo* in 1982. This time though there were more elements in play for the honour of being first to Hobart – four supermaxis had been locked in an amazing contest all the way from Sydney, with the lead changing continually and just 4 nm separating them for much of the race. By the time the four reached Tasman Island, line honours was still for the taking until a carefully calculated change of course towards land saw *Wild Oats XI* break from the pack and gain what proved to be a winning advantage.

In a fitting tribute to Bob Oatley, as the yacht neared the finish, skipper Mark Richards handed the helm to Bob's grandson Daniel, who had been a member of the yacht's crew for three Hobarts, so he could steer the yacht over the final few miles to the line.

The moment the cannon boomed out its signal that *Wild Oats XI* was first into Hobart for the ninth time, there were scenes of great jubilation among the impressive flotilla of spectator boats on the river and the thousands of people gathered on the shore. Adding to the excitement was another Sydney Hobart first: never in the race's long history had four line honours contenders been seen in close formation on the river racing to the line.

Peter Harburg's supermaxi *Black Jack* from Queensland, which went gybe-for-gybe with *LDV Comanche* over the final 11 nm from The Iron Pot, was second home just 28 minutes behind *Wild Oats XI,* and a mere minute ahead of *LDV Comanche* which in turn was only 13 minutes ahead of Christian Beck's supermaxi *InfoTrack*.

Wild Oats XI's ninth line honours put its name on another page of Sydney Hobart history: it had bettered the record of seven line honours held by *Kurrewa/Morna*.

*

While the race to be first to Hobart is the contest much of the media and the mass of non-sailing race followers best comprehend, it is the race for the *Tattersall Cup* that matters most to the vast majority of race participants. To win that ornate trophy means the yacht has won on corrected time – it has sailed better than all others competing within the ICR handicap classification. Simply put, through the application of handicaps, the smallest yacht can outsail the largest and fastest yacht in the race and have its name engraved on the baroque trophy; regardless of size, age, rig configuration or construction, that yacht has out-performed all others. That's the Grand Prix level of the race, but there are also handicap divisions for yachts that are more cruising oriented.

Going into the 2018 race, former CYCA Commodore Matt Allen was expected to be the claimant for the *Tattersall Cup* for a second consecutive year, an achievement that would make his yacht *Ichi Ban* become only the second to do so since the famous *Freya* in 1963/1964. Should that occur, *Ichi Ban* would be in the running in the 2019 75th anniversary race to match *Freya*'s three consecutive wins. But in 2018 the weather gods did not go in *Ichi Ban*'s favour; it finished fifth on corrected time in the Grand Prix fleet. And, by comparison, the line honours yacht, *Wild Oats XI*, finished eleventh in the same division on corrected time.

It was the Tasmanian 60-footer *Alive*, owned by Philip Turner, that claimed the *Tattersall Cup* by winning the Grand Prix division that year. However, this well-deserved victory was almost eclipsed by the international all-female crew led by Australia's Stacey Jackson. The women were aboard *Alive*'s near sistership, *Wild Oats X* (which had been loaned by the Oatley family) under the banner of Ocean Respect Racing, an organisation dedicated to creating awareness of the growing level of plastic pollution in the world's oceans. Jackson and her crew were well qualified for the Hobart; she had completed two round-the-world races while the rest of the team had some twenty circumnavigations to their credit. *Wild Oats X* missed top honours on corrected time by little more than one hour. *Ichi Ban* was fifth on corrected time, behind *Voodoo* (Hugh Ellis, Victoria) which was third, and *Winning Appliances* (John Winning Jr, New South Wales).

Julian Freeman

SAILING BIO

I was lucky enough to come from a family with a strong sailing background. Born in Hobart, I started sailing when my parents bought me a sabot to race when I was eight years old. My first racing success came in the International Cadet Australian championships at Geelong, but my real passion was to sail larger ocean-racing yachts. This inspiration came from when I was a child watching my uncle Graeme 'Frizzle' Freeman come up the Derwent at the end of each Hobart Race – it didn't matter what time of the day or night it was, my dad would always take me out on his boat to watch him finish. Frizzle invited me to help him deliver *Bumblebee 4* back to Sydney after they won the 1979 race and that was it for me, I was hooked! This passion has taken me all over the world competing in *America's Cup* campaigns, *Admiral's Cups*, Fastnet races, Bermuda races, Maxi Yacht World Championships etc. It's been a sensational journey, where I have met some equally sensational people who have become life-long friends. I can't wait to compete in the 75th race. It will be my thirtieth start on Boxing Day 2019.

WHAT WAS YOUR BEST DAY UNDER SAIL IN THE SYDNEY HOBART?

No doubt, crossing Bass Strait in the 2017 race aboard *Concubine*. The breeze was pretty much north-east–north ranging from 25 to 38 knots and I'm pretty sure our average speed for the day was around 20 knots, at times reaching 30 knots on waves that famous Hawaiian surfer, Eddie Aikau, would have been more than happy to see! It only took us around 8 hours to cross the Strait. It was a very wet ride, but the sun was shining on an awesome day that was shared with some great blokes. I'll never forget it.

WHAT DAY OR EXPERIENCE WAS THE TOUGHEST OR MOST CHALLENGING?

I don't believe I've ever really had a bad day in the race, but I had a bad night once! Pretty sure it was the 2009 race aboard *Secret Men's Business*. The race started in a typical north-east sea breeze with a southerly buster forecast to hit the fleet just after dark on the first night. Well it hit and it hit pretty hard, probably around 30 to 35 knots. I awoke at around 2am to discover the boat was full of smoke, toxic smoke! I scrambled out of my bunk got the gear back on as quickly as possible and noticed a pizza sitting on the galley bench. I managed to scoff one piece down before heading out through the companionway and then a second piece before it got washed out of my hand during my scurry aft to check on our progress. I soon discovered that somebody (I won't mention any names) had cooked the pizza in an oven full of oven cleaner from the previous days' attempt at cleaning it before the race. Subsequently I (along with everyone else that had a go at the pizza) lay on the cockpit floor feeling violently ill for around 3 hours.

WHAT KEEPS YOU GOING BACK TO THE HOBART RACE?

I'm an extremely competitive individual – I like to go hard and leave nothing in the tank once I cross that finish line in Hobart. The race can be challenging, frustrating, cruel and at times very dangerous, but it can also be rewarding, satisfying and above all, great fun. I have some great mates that I love to share these experiences with each year. I guess all of these elements keep you going back, not to mention the annual debriefing at 'Shippies' (The Shipwright's Arms Hotel) and The Customs House. Many years ago, I set some guidelines for myself that I have always followed, and they are: 1) that I would only ever go on a boat that was in with a chance of winning; and 2) that I would never approach anyone for a ride in the race – if I don't get asked I don't go. So far so good!

WHAT ARE SOME OF THE BIG CHANGES THAT YOU'VE WITNESSED IN YOUR YEARS ASSOCIATED WITH THE RACE?

Obviously, the boats are much lighter, faster and easier to sail, but the biggest change for me is from a strategic point of view with both the accuracy of the weather routing and modelling and, more than anything, the introduction of the yacht tracker and being able to pinpoint your main competitors' locations at all times. It wasn't that long ago that we had to rely on radio skeds to check on how the race was unfolding, the early morning sked was always the most interesting and important one. Now you can run the tracker for the whole race if you have an owner that's happy to cop the data cost for the sat phone!

CHAPTER 18

Historic Hulk for 75th Hobart

While the spectacular supermaxis were destined to be centre stage at the start of the 75th Sydney Hobart race, it was one of the smallest entries – *Katwinchar* – sailing in the shadows of these leviathans that reminded everyone of the spirit that had led to the foundation of the race and guided its evolution over the decades.

This particular little yacht linked the early years of the race with the 75th anniversary milestone while paying homage to the English influence in its origins – primarily Captain John Illingworth and his small yacht, *Rani*.

At just 9.75 metres in overall length, *Katwinchar* is similar in size to *Rani* – just one metre shorter – and has a canoe stern. Also, like *Rani*, it competed in the 1951 Hobart race under the burgee of an English yacht club.

One significant difference was that while *Rani* was a locally built yacht, the tiny *Katwinchar* cruised 15,000 nm from its then home port of Christchurch in southern England to Sydney before racing to Hobart.

Through a remarkable set of circumstances and good fortune that unfolded nearly 70 years later, the same yacht was destined to be on the start line in 2019.

The relationship between *Katwinchar*'s extraordinary voyage and the 75th Hobart was strong: it embodied the challenge and spirit that has always been fundamental to the great race, a spirit that budded in 1945 via *Rani*, was reflected in *Katwinchar*'s participation in 1951, and resurfaced again in 2019. During the 2 years preceding the historic 75th event, family ties caused a derelict *Katwinchar* to be located then resurrected from its graveyard and set on a course designed to have it join the 2019 fleet.

The story started in England in 1904 – 41 years before the inaugural Hobart – when Ricardo Gilbey Watney, owner of the famous Watney Brewery, cleared out part of his brewery building located at Wandsworth, in London, so he could build the gaff-rigged cutter that became *Katwinchar*. It took its name from his three children – Katherine, Winifred and Charles. Once launched, it was based out of Cowes on the Isle of Wight, and sailed extensively on the Solent.

In early 1946 the then forty-two-year-old *Katwinchar* was bought by Eddie Mossop, a thirty-eight-year-old professional fisherman who, with two male friends, had a dream to sail to Australia and set up home in Hobart post-war '... because we can see no future in this life, so we intend to start a new life in Tasmania'. His crewmates were Dennis Tanner, 29, a fisherman, dental mechanic and bricklayer and Bill Bartlett, 27, a Flight Officer with RAF Bomber Command during the war and later a navigator with BOAC (British Overseas Airways Corporation).

When they set sail on the 15,000 nm passage in 1951 they had only one target date – to be in Sydney before 26 December that year so *Katwinchar* could be part of the fleet in the Sydney Hobart race.

The voyage in itself was a huge undertaking for such a small yacht; its beam was a mere 2.6 metres and the draught was little more than a metre. Below deck, the accommodation was barely better than living in a small, dark, cramped box. It was sitting room only as the headroom was just 1.45 metres. Some of the cabin space was also taken up by the engine, a chugging 7 horsepower petrol motor taken out of an Austin 7 motor vehicle, a model that went out of production in 1939.

The one significant modification Mossop made to *Katwinchar* for the voyage was to change the rig from a gaff cutter to a ketch so the sails would be easier to handle. The gaff yard from the old rig made an ideal mizzenmast.

On 15 April 1951 – 8 months before the start of that year's Hobart race – *Katwinchar* made an unassuming departure from Christchurch. Among the small crowd there to farewell the adventurers was Mossop's wife, who was intending to migrate to Tasmania via Sydney so she could be there for the start of the race, then travel to Hobart by ship. When Mossop was asked prior to departure by a newspaper reporter when he expected to reach Sydney he replied:

We have entered for the annual Sydney Hobart race in December and are hoping not to lose our two guineas entry fee. We have no idea what we're going to do in

393

Tasmania, but we are three healthy young men and willing to do anything.

He added that he and the crew 'expect no riches' and would probably seek jobs linked with yachts and the sea. He referred to their probable future being, 'fresh work among new friends'.

From southern England they sailed *Katwinchar* 1500 nm to the island of Madeira and then a further 3000 nm across the Atlantic to the Panama Canal. On transiting through the canal, it was realised that their tiny yacht was the smallest vessel ever to pass through. From there they sailed across the Pacific, stopping only briefly at numerous destinations so they would be in Sydney in time for the race. En route they were confronted by twelve storms, the worst of which was encountered just 200 nm from Sydney.

After a 196-day voyage, *Katwinchar* sailed into Sydney Harbour on 20 November 1951, just 5 weeks before the start of the big race. The yacht came through the passage unscathed but their catering for the trip was a bit light on: when they docked at the CYCA they had only three tins of food remaining – a can of sardines, one of potatoes and one of plums. This was a somewhat embarrassing circumstance for Mossop and Tanner – these professional fishermen trolled lures behind the yacht for the 15,000 nm from England and did not catch one fish! Mossop wanted to claim it as a world record.

Near penniless, the trio quickly found jobs in Sydney to replenish their funds and spent their spare time preparing their yacht for the next challenge – the Hobart race. Tanner and

Bartlett also planned ahead for their arrival in Tasmania: they placed an advertisement in the *Hobart Mercury* which read:

> Two Healthy, Single Englishmen, arrive in Hobart on completion of Sydney Hobart race, from Christchurch, England, require employment in Tasmania. Willing to do anything where initiative and resources are assets and reasonable prospects of advancement exist.

When the Hobart race started, *Katwinchar* was conspicuous among the fleet of fourteen for two reasons: its tan-coloured sails and the fact that it was already a considerable distance behind the other yachts by the time the fleet had reached the Heads. It all went downhill from there.

When Austin Edwards' *Margaret Rintoul* claimed line honours just over 4 days after departing Sydney (a new race record), *Katwinchar* was still in Bass Strait. That was when all hell broke loose in the form of a powerful south-easterly gale so strong that the little yacht could not make headway. Mossop elected to lower the sails, set the sea anchor and ride out the storm. When the gale abated 18 hours later, *Katwinchar* had been blown more than 20 nm off-course. The crew then realised that their desire to be in Hobart for New Year's Eve celebrations had gone with the wind. They adopted the only alternative, started the small Austin 7 engine, motored into the tiny township of Triabunna on Tasmania's east coast and joined the party there. It was a party which Mossop described as the best welcome they had received during their entire voyage.

The following day *Katwinchar* sailed from Triabunna and set on a course that would take it through the canal at Dunalley then onto the Derwent River and Hobart. Once there, the trio were treated like heroes, while their incredible voyage and amazing yacht made headlines across Australia and back in England. One of the many remarkable elements of this history-making voyage was that, after sailing all the way from England, *Katwinchar* had arrived in Hobart without breaking one piece of equipment, and with the dinghy still lashed on the cabin roof just as it was when they left their home shore.

The fact that *Katwinchar* had been registered as a retirement from the great race didn't matter to the three English adventurers. By sailing safely all the way from their home port then racing to Hobart, they had achieved their goal. With that, they were looking forward to a wonderful new life.

*

The three sailors, and Mrs Mossop, settled into their new world remarkably well. *Katwinchar* was also put to good use cruising on the Derwent and along the coast until 1960 when Mossop offered it for sale. It was subsequently purchased by three Sydney yachtsmen – Frank Barry-Cotter, Bob Chapman and Eddy Shaw – and delivered to its new home port of Sydney. Over the next 5 years, *Katwinchar* was sailed regularly on the Harbour and Pittwater. In 1965, it went back onto the market and was sold.

Forty-two years later, in 2007, Frank's son, well-known Australian luxury motor yacht builder Bill Barry-Cotter, decided to try to trace the yacht with a view to purchasing it and doing a restoration. A business associate, Peter Jenkins, lent a hand by having a letter published in *Afloat*, a monthly boating magazine, requesting that if anyone knew the whereabouts of *Katwinchar*, would they please contact him. Nothing of substance was forthcoming until – incredibly – a decade later. In 2017 Jenkins was contacted by an obviously alert chap, Alex Harper, who recalled the request all those years earlier. He advised Jenkins that the yacht was in Newcastle, north of Sydney, and in a sad state of disrepair. Bill Barry-Cotter traced the owner and confirmed the yacht's existence before heading to Newcastle the following day. The woman who then owned *Katwinchar* advised him that it was her late husband's wish to restore the yacht, but sadly he had passed away soon after beginning the project. Barry-Cotter offered to buy what was little more than a hulk there and then, only to be told by the woman, 'You can have it as it is, for nothing, but only if you are going to restore it'. Within days the 113-year-old remains of *Katwinchar* were trucked to Barry-Cotter's boat building facility on the Gold Coast, where, over the next 2 years, it underwent a spare-no-expense re-build from stem to stern, gunwale to gunwale, keel to masthead, all with the intention of it being on the start line for the 75th Sydney Hobart race!

It was a fitting tribute to the race, the CYCA, and its founders.

GLOSSARY

abaft – towards the stern of a ship; 'abaft the beam' means aft of abeam

abeam – a point 90 degrees out from anywhere along the centre-line of a vessel

athwartship – across the vessel at a 90 degree angle to the centreline

backstay – a part of the standing rigging of a sailing vessel that supports a mast in the fore-and-aft line; a forestay supports the mast from forward and backstay supports it from aft

bare poles – the condition of a yacht when all sails have been taken in

beam on – 90 degree angle to the fore-and-aft centreline of the vessel

Bowsprit – a spar running out from a yacht's bow from which sails are set

Broach – a rapid and dramatic change of course towards the wind due to the mainsail being overpowered by a gust of wind and the rudder not being able to maintain the yacht's course

canoe stern – double-ended – a boat where the stern profile and waterlines resemble or even duplicate the shape of the bow

Centreboard – a retractable keel which pivots out of a slot in the hull of a sailboat

Cutter – a fast sailboat with one mast that carries several headsails

death rolls – rolling severely from one side to the other

dog-house – a raised area at the aft-end of a yacht's coachhouse roof

draught – the measurement from the waterline to the deepest point of the vessel in the water

flogging sails – sails flapping violently in strong winds

gaff cutter – a gaff-rigged yacht with two or more headsails and often a long bowsprit

gaff rigged – gaff rig is a sailing rig (configuration of sails, mast and stays) in which the sail is four-cornered, fore-and-aft rigged, controlled at its peak and, usually, its entire head by a spar (pole) called the gaff

gaff yard – the gaff yard is the highest spar on the mainsail of a gaff-rigged boat

gybe – changing from one tack to the other away from the wind, turning the yacht's stern through the wind

heave/hove to – slowing a vessel's forward progress by fixing the helm and foresail so that the vessel does not need to be steered: a procedure usually applied in very rough weather

heel/ed over – lean/ing over at a dramatic angle

ketch – a two-masted, fore-and-aft rigged sailing boat with a mizzenmast stepped forward of the rudder and smaller than its foremast

leeward – the direction away from the wind; the opposite of 'windward'

mast spreader – a spreader is a spar on a sailboat used to deflect the shrouds to allow them to better support the mast

pooped – to have a large wave break over the stern of a vessel and onto the deck

port – left

reaching – sailing across the wind

rigs – the combination of masts, sails and spars

scuppers – an opening cut through the bulwarks (side-rails) of a vessel so that water falling on the deck may flow overboard

schooner – a sailboat with two or more masts where the forward mast is shorter than the main mast

sea room – the amount of distance between the vessel and the shore

sloop – a single-masted sailing ship usually carrying a mainsail and a single jib or headsail

starboard – right

tiller – a steering arm attached to the head of the rudder which turns the rudder

Venturi effect – the velocity of the wind increases due to the influence of surrounding land formations

windward – directly upwind

winged – injured/damaged; also, where a yacht runs directly downwind with the headsail set on one side and the mainsail on the other

yawl – a yawl is a two-masted sailing craft similar to a sloop or cutter but with an additional mast located well aft of the main mast, often right on the transom

SYDNEY HOBART YACHT RACE
WINNERS 1945–2018

Year	Overall Winner	Fleet	Line Honours	Elapsed Time
1945	RANI, Capt John Illingworth, UK	9	*RANI, Capt John Illingworth, UK	6:14:22:00
1946	CHRISTINA, J.R.Bull, NSW	19	*MORNA, Claude Plowman, NSW	5:02:53:33
1947	WESTWARD, G.D.Gibson, Tas	28	MORNA, Claude Plowman, NSW	5:03:03:54
1948	WESTWARD, G.D.Gibson, Tas	18	*MORNA, Claude Plowman, NSW	4:05:01:21
1949	TRADEWINDS, Merv Davey, NSW	15	WALTZING MATILDA, Phil Davenport, NSW	5:10:33:10
1950	NERIDA, Colin Haselgrove, SA	16	MARGARET RINTOUL, A.W.Edwards, NSW	5:05:28:35
1951	STRUEN MARIE, Tom Williamson, NSW	14	*MARGARET RINTOUL, A.W.Edwards, NSW	4:02:29:01
1952	INGRID, J.S.Taylor, SA	17	NOCTURNE, J.R.Bull, NSW	6:02:34:47
1953	RIPPLE, Ron Hobson, NSW	24	^SOLVEIG, Trygve & Magnus Halvorsen, NSW^	5:07:12:50
1954	SOLVEIG, Trygve & Magnus Halvorsen, NSW	17	KURREWA IV, F.& J.Livingston, NSW/Vic	5:06:09:47
1955	MOONBI, H.S.Evans, NSW	17	EVEN, F.J.Palmer, NSW	4:18:13:14
1956	SOLO, Vic Meyer, NSW	28	KURREWA IV, F.& J.Livingston, NSW/Vic	4:04:31:44
1957	ANITRA V, Trygve & Magnus Halvorsen, NSW	20	*KURREWA IV, F.& J.Livingston, NSW/Vic	3:18:30:39
1958	SIANDRA, Graham Newland, NSW	22	SOLO, Vic Meyer, NSW	5:02:32:52
1959	CHERANA, Russ Williams, NSW	30	SOLO, Vic Meyer, NSW	4:13:33:12
1960	SIANDRA, Graham Newland, NSW	32	KURREWA IV, F.& J.Livingston, NSW/Vic	4:08:11:15
1961	RIVAL, Alby Burgin & N. Rundle, NSW	35	ASTOR, Peter Warner, NSW	4:04:42:11
1962	SOLO, Vic Meyer, NSW	42	*ONDINE, S.A. ('Huey') Long, USA	3:03:46:16
1963	FREYA, Trygve & Magnus Halvorsen, NSW	44	ASTOR, Peter Warner, NSW	4:10:53:00
1964	FREYA, Trygve & Magnus Halvorsen, NSW	38	ASTOR, Peter Warner, NSW	3:20:05:05
1965	FREYA, Trygve & Magnus Halvorsen, NSW	53	STORMVOGEL,C.Brynzeel, South Africa	3:20:30:09
1966	CADENCE, H.S.Mason, NSW	46	FIDELIS, J.V.Davern, New Zealand	4:08:39:43
1967	RAINBOW II, Chris Bouzaid, New Zealand	67	PEN DUICK III, Eric Tabarly, France	4:04:10:31
1968	KOOMOOLOO, Denis O'Neil, NSW	67	ONDINE II, S.A.('Huey') Long, USA	4:03:20:02
1969	MORNING CLOUD, Edward Heath, UK	79	CRUSADE, Sir Max Aitken, UK	3:15:07:40
1970	PACHA, Sir Robert Crichton-Brown, NSW	61	BUCCANEER, Tom Clark, NZL	3:14:06:12
1971	PATHFINDER, Brin Wilson, NZ	79	KIALOA II, Jim Kilroy, USA	3:12:46:21
1972	AMERICAN EAGLE, Ted Turner, USA	79	AMERICAN EAGLE, Ted Turner, USA	3:04:42:39
1973	CEIL III, Bill Turnbull, Hong Kong	92	*HELSAL, Tony Fisher, NSW	3:01:32:09
1974	LOVE & WAR, Peter Kurts, NSW	63	ONDINE III, S.A.("Huey') Long, USA	3:13:51:56
1975	RAMPAGE, Peter Packer, WA	102	*KIALOA III, Jim Kilroy, USA	2:14:36:56
1976	PICCOLO, John Pickles, NSW	85	BALLYHOO, Jack Rooklyn, NSW	3:07:59:26
1977	KIALOA III, Jim Kilroy, USA	131	KIALOA III, Jim Kilroy, USA	3:10:14:09
1978	LOVE & WAR, Peter Kurts, NSW	97	APOLLO, Jack Rooklyn, NSW	4:02:23:24
1979	SCREW LOOSE, Bob Cumming, Tas	147	BUMBLEBEE 4, John Kahlbetzer, NSW	3:01:45:52
1980	NEW ZEALAND, NZ Round the World Cmte, NZL	102	NEW ZEALAND, NZ Round the World Cmtee, NZL	2:18:45:41
1981	ZEUS II, Jim Dunstan, NSW	159	VENGEANCE, Bernard Lewis, NSW	3:22:30:00
1982	SCALLYWAG, Ray Johnston, NSW	118	CONDOR OF BERMUDA, Bob Bell, Bermuda	3:00:59:17
1983	CHALLENGE, Lou Abrahams, Vic	173	CONDOR, Bob Bell, Bermuda	3:00:50:29
1984	INDIAN PACIFIC, John Eyles/Gunter Heuchmer,NSW	151	NEW ZEALAND, NZ Round the World Cmtee, NZL	3:11:31:21
1985	#SAGACIOUS, Gary Appleby, NSW	179	APOLLO, Jack Rooklyn, NSW	3:04:32:28
1986	EX TENSION, Tony Dunn, NSW	123	CONDOR, Bob Bell, Bermuda	2:23:26:25
1987	SOVEREIGN, Bernard Lewis, NSW	154	SOVEREIGN, Bernard Lewis, NSW	2:21:58:08
1988	ILLUSION, Gino Knezic, Vic	119	RAGAMUFFIN, Syd Fischer, NSW	3:15:29:07
1989	ULTIMATE CHALLENGE, Lou Abrahams, Vic	126	DRUMBEAT, Alan Bond, WA	3:06:21:34
1990	SAGACIOUS V, Gary Appleby, NSW	105	RAGAMUFFIN, Syd Fischer, NSW	2:21:05:33

Year	Overall Winner	Fleet	Line Honours	Elapsed Time
1991	IOR: ATARA, Harold Cudmore/John Storey, Ireland IMS: SHE'S APPLES, David Strong, NSW	99	BRINDABELLA, George Snow, ACT	3:01:14:19
1992	IOR: RAGAMUFFIN, Syd Fischer, NSW IMS: ASSASSIN, Robin Crawford, NSW	110	NZ ENDEAVOUR, Grant Dalton, NZL	2:19:19:18
1993	IOR: WILD OATS, Roger Hickman/Bruce Foye,NSW IMS: CUCKOOS NEST, Nigel Holman, NSW	104	NINETY SEVEN, Andrew Strachan, NSW	4:00:54:11
1994	RAPTOR, A.Eichenauer, Germany	371	TASMANIA, Robert Clifford, Tas	2:16:48:04
1995	TERRA FIRMA, Scott Carlile/Dean Wilson, Vic	98	SAYONARA, Larry Ellison, USA	3:00:53:35
1996	AUSMAID, Georgio Gjergja, Vic	95	*MORNING GLORY, Hasso Plattner, Germany	2:14:07:10
1997	BEAU GESTE, Karl Kwok, Hong Kong/China	114	BRINDABELLA, George Snow, ACT	2:23:37:12
1998	AFR MIDNIGHT RAMBLER, Ed Psaltis/Bob Thomas, NSW	115	SAYONARA, Larry Ellison, USA	2:19:03:32
1999	YENDYS, Geoff Ross, NSW	79	*NOKIA, Stefan Myralf/Michael Spies, Denmark	1:19:48:02
2000	SAP AUSMAID, Kevan Pearce, SA	82	NICORETTE, Ludde Ingvall, Sweden	2:14:02:09
2001	BUMBLEBEE 5, John Kahlbetzer/Iain Murray,NSW	75	ASSA ABLOY, Neal McDonald, Sweden	2:20:46:43
2002	QUEST, Bob Steel, NSW	57	ALFA ROMEO II, Neville Crichton, NZL	2:04:58:52
2003	FIRST NATIONAL REAL ESTATE, Michael Spies/Peter Johnston, NSW	56	SKANDIA, Grant Wharington, Victoria	2:15:14:06
2004	AERA, Nicholas Lykiardopulo, UK	116	NICORETTE, Ludde Ingvall, NSW	2.16:00.04
2005	WILD OATS XI, Bob Oatley/Mark Richards, NSW	85	*WILD OATS XI, Bob Oatley/Mark Richards, NSW	1:18:40:10
2006	LOVE & WAR, Simon Kurts/Lindsay May, NSW	78	WILD OATS XI, Bob Oatley/Mark Richards, NSW	2:08:52:33
2007	ROSEBUD, Roger Sturgeon, USA	82	WILD OATS XI, Bob Oatley/Mark Richards, NSW	1:21:24:32
2008	QUEST, Bob Steel, NSW	100	WILD OATS XI, Bob Oatley/Mark Richards, NSW	1:20:34:14
2009	TWO TRUE, Andrew Saies, SA	100	ALFA ROMEO II, Neville Crichton, NZL/Aus	2:09:02:10
2010	SECRET MENS BUSINESS 3.5, Geoff Boettcher, SA	87	WILD OATS XI, Bob Oatley/Mark Richards, NSW	02:07:37:20
2011	LOKI, Stephen Ainsworth, NSW	88	INVESTEC LOYAL, Anthony Bell, NSW	02:06:14:18
2012	WILD OATS XI, Bob Oatley/Mark Richards, NSW	76	*WILD OATS XI, Bob Oatley/Mark Richards, NSW	01:18:23:12
2013	VICTOIRE, Darryl Hodgkinson, NSW	94	WILD OATS XI, Bob Oatley/Mark Richards, NSW	02:06:07:27
2014	WILD ROSE, Roger Hickman, NSW	117	WILD OATS XI, Bob Oatley/Mark Richards, NSW	02:02:03:26
2015	BALANCE, Paul Clitheroe, NSW	108	COMANCHE, Jim and Kristy Clark, USA	02:08:58:30
2016	GIACOMO, Jim Delegat, NZL	88	*PERPETUAL LOYAL, Anthony Bell, NSW	01:13:31:20
2017	ICHI BAN, Matt Allen, NSW	102	*LDV COMANCHE, Jim Cooney/Samantha Grant, NSW	01:09:15:24
2018	ALIVE, Phillip Turner, TAS	85	WILD OATS XI, the Oatley Family, NSW	1.19.07.21

* New Race Record

\# The rules did not provide for a first place following the penalising of Drake's Prayer which had provisionally been first prior to a protest. Nor did it allow for lower placed yachts to move up a place when other yachts were penalised. Because there was no 1st place, Sagacious officially was recorded as second but as the overall winner.

^ In 1953, Wild Wave took line honours but was unable to retain the title. Josephine and Nimbus lodged protests against Wild Wave. After a marathon five hours, the protest against Jock Muir's Wild Wave was upheld for two reasons. Firstly, Wild Wave was the windward yacht that had converged onto Josephine, and then failed to keep clear. Secondly, Wild Wave had failed to keep clear of and collided with Nimbus; therefore, she was disqualified and Solveig IV was declared the line honours winner.

SPECIAL NOTE: The following yachts were faster than the line honours boat but for various reasons were not counted:
1978: SISKA II, Rolly Tasker, WA (owner/designer) 03:06:19:00. Ruled ineligible to compete because did not have valid rating certificate. Sailed to Hobart independently, not as competitor.
1983: NIRVANA, Marvin Green, USA (designer David Pedrick, USA) 03:00:48:13. Disqualified for failing to give Condor enough shore room during a gybing duel up the Derwent River to the finish.
1990: ROTHMANS, Lawrie Smith (designer Rob Humphreys, UK) 02:19:07:02. Disqualified from receiving line honours award and penalised 10% of overall corrected time placings for breaching Rule 26 (advertising)
2017: WILD OATS XI, Mark Richards (designer Reichel/Pugh, USA). Wild Oats XI provisionally claimed its ninth line honours crown and third race record time when it finished in 01:08:48:50. Subsequently penalised one hour and relegated to second place after an international jury upheld a protest from LDV Comanche (Jim Cooney, NSW) over a right-of-way incident soon after the start. Line honours and race record awarded to LDV Comanche.

132 yachtsmen and yachtswomen have competed in 25 or more Sydney Hobarts, with 4 reaching the 50 races milestone and a further 10 reaching the 40 races milestone.

Each person has their name engraved on the beautiful Huon Pine map of Tasmania that celebrates reaching the 25 Hobart milestone – it hangs in the CYCA clubhouse.

The list of 'Hobart Heroes' up to and including 2018 Rolex Sydney Hobart Yacht Race is:

- Tony Cable (NSW) – 52 since 1961 (1 overall win, 2 line honours)
- Tony Ellis (NSW) – 51 since 1963 (1 overall win, 2 line honours)
- Bill Ratcliff (NSW) – 50 since 1963
- Colin Wildman (NSW) – 50 since 1963 (1 overall win, 1 line honours)
- Syd Fischer (NSW) – 47 since 1962 (1 overall win, 2 line honours)
- Bruce Gould (NSW) – 46 since 1963 (2 overall wins, 2 line honours)
- Lindsay May (NSW) – 46 since 1973 (3 overall wins, 1 line honours)
- David Kellett (NSW) – 45 since 1968 (1 overall win, 2 line honours)
- John 'The Fish' Bennetto (TAS, dec) – 44 since 1947 (1 overall win, 1 line honours)
- Lou Abrahams (VIC, dec) – 44 since 1963 (2 overall wins)
- Michael Spies (NSW) – 42 since 1976 (1 overall win, 1 line honours)
- Richard 'Sightie' Hammond (NSW, dec) – 40 since 1952 (2 overall wins, 2 line honours)
- Bernie Case (VIC) – 40 since 1962 (1 line honours)
- Mike Green (NSW) – 40 since 1977 (3 overall wins, 1 line honours)
- Roger Hickman (NSW, dec) – 39 since 1974 – (3 overall wins)
- Bruce Taylor (VIC) – 38 since 1980
- Ed Psaltis (NSW) – 37 since 1979 (1 overall win)
- Kingsley Piesse (VIC) – 36 since 1983
- Phil Eadie (NSW) – 35 since 1972 (3 overall wins, 2 line honours)
- Peter Green (NSW, dec) – 35 races since 1947 (1 overall win)
- Richard Norman (NSW) – 35 since 1955 (2 overall wins)
- Fraser Johnston (NSW) – 35 since 1963 (2 overall wins)
- Colin Tipney (NSW) – 35 since 1979 (1 overall win, 2 line honours)
- Ralph Carlier (NSW) – 35 since 1973
- Jack Goluzd (NSW) – 35 since 1978 (2 overall wins, 3 line honours)
- Colin Anderson (VIC) – 34 since 1973 (2 overall wins)

- Don Mickleborough (NSW, dec) – 34 since 1958 (1 line honours)
- Colin Betts (NSW) – 34 since 1955 (3 overall wins, 2 line honours)
- Tony Kirby (NSW) – 34 since 1983
- Robert Case (NSW) – 34 since 1985 (1 overall win)
- Geoff Rouvray (NSW) – 33 since 1967
- Roger Howlett (TAS) – 33 since 1969
- David Lawson (NSW, dec) – 33 since 1961 (1 line honours)
- Kim Jaggar (NSW) – 33 since 1977
- Tony Hearder (NSW) – 33 since 1975 (3 line honours)
- Carl Crafoord (NSW) – 33 since 1980 (4 overall wins)
- Larry Jamieson (NSW) – 33 since 1983 (2 overall wins, 1 line honours)
- Maurice Cameron (NSW) – 32 since 1974
- Don Lang (VIC, dec) – 32 races since 1952 (1 overall win)
- Noel Drennan – 32 since 1980 (2 overall wins, 3 line honours)
- Adam Brown (NSW) – 32 since 1985 (3 overall wins, 1 line honours)
- Peter Fletcher (VIC) – 32 since 1987
- Gavin Gourlay (VIC) – 32 since 1984
- James Permezel – 32 since 1985
- John Woodford (NSW) – 32 since 1979 (1 overall win, 1 line honours)
- Alby Burgin (NSW, dec) – 31 since 1955 (1 overall win)
- Peter Shipway (NSW) – 31 since 1968 (2 overall wins, 5 line honours)
- John Harris (NSW) – 31 since 1971 (2 overall wins, 2 line honours)
- Peter Inchbold (NSW) – 31 since 1980 (1 overall win)
- Steve Jarvin (NSW) – 31 since 1981 (2 overall wins, 14 line honours)
- Ian (Barney) Walker (VIC) – 31 since 1983 (3 overall wins, 3 line honours)
- Damian Parkes (NSW) – 31 since 1976 (1 line honours)
- Max Crafoord (NSW, dec) – 30 races since 1953 (3 line honours)
- Albert Mitchell (NSW) – 30 since 1954 (2 overall wins)
- Peter Kurts (NSW, dec) – 30 races since 1964 (2 overall wins)
- Magnus Halvorsen (NSW, dec) – 30 since 1946 (5 overall wins, 3 line honours)
- Lester Nibbs (TAS) – 30 since 1960
- Rod Jackman (TAS) – 30 since 1971
- Geoff Barter (NSW) – 30 since 1974
- Ian Potter (NSW) – 30 since 1976 (1 line honours)
- David Blanchfield – 30 since 1985 (1 overall win)
- Michael Coxon (NSW) – 30 since 1979 (1 overall win, 5 line honours)
- Julian Freeman – 30 since 1982 (2 overall wins, 2 line honours)
- Bill Sykes – 30 since 1981 (1 overall win)
- Robbie Burns (NSW) – 29 since 1974 (1 overall win, 1 line honours)
- Bruce Jackson (NSW) – 29 since 1952
- Peter Duffield (NSW) – 29 since 1968
- Graeme Fraser (NSW, dec) – 29 since 1973
- Robert Moore (NSW) – 29 since 1985
- John Solomon (TAS) – 29 since 1967
- David Ellis (NSW) – 29 since 1977 (2 overall wins, 3 line honours)
- Richard Grimes – 29 since 1983
- Peter Messenger (NSW) – 29 since 1980 (4 overall wins)

- Matt Allen (NSW) – 29 since 1980 (2 overall wins)
- Bob Fraser (NSW) – 28 since 1973 (1 overall win, 2 line honours)
- T W (Bill) Thompson (NSW, dec) – 28 since 1956 (2 line honours)
- Hugh Treharne (NSW) – 28 since 1968 (2 overall wins)
- Erik Adriaanse – 28 since 1986 (1 overall win, 2 line honours)
- David Hodgson (NSW) – 28 since 1981 (5 line honours)
- Hugh Brodie (NSW) – 28 since 1982 (1 overall win)
- Steve Grellis – 28 since 1987
- Greg Johnson (NSW) – 28 since 1980 (1 overall win, 1 line honours)
- Sean Langman (NSW) – 28 since 1982
- Phil Molony – 28 since 1975
- Greg Prescott (TAS) – 28 since 1980
- Sven Runow (NSW) – 28 since 1985 (4 overall wins, 7 line honours)
- Stan Darling (NSW, dec) – 27 since 1947 (5 overall wins, 2 line honours)
- Des O'Connell (NSW, dec) – 27 since 1947
- Rolfe Mische (NSW, dec) – 27 races since 1963 (1 line honours)
- Josko Grubic (SA, dec) – 27 since 1966
- Richard Bearman (NSW) – 27 since 1969
- Peter Joubert (VIC, dec) – 27 since 1968
- John Mooney (VIC) – 27 since 1969
- Simon Firth (TAS) – 27 since 1973 (1 overall win)
- Graeme Freeman (TAS/NSW, dec) – 27 since 1970 (4 line honours)
- Lew Carter (NSW) – 27 since 1973
- Mike Hesse (NSW) – 27 since 1965 (2 overall wins, 1 line honours)
- Michael Bellingham – 27 since 1976 (1 overall win)
- Adrienne Cahalan (NSW) – 27 since 1984 (2 overall wins, 6 line honours)
- Bruce Clarke (NSW) – 27 since 1986 (2 overall wins, 4 line honours)
- Ian Davis – 27 since 1977 (2 overall wins)
- Brad Kellett (NSW) – 27 since 1992 (1 overall win, 1 line honours)
- Peter Sheldrick – 27 since 1987 (1 overall win, 1 line honours)
- Andrew Taylor – 27 since 1986
- Bob Thomas – 27 since 1988 (1 overall win)
- Warren Anderson (NSW) – 26 since 1970
- Alan Butler (VIC, dec) – 26 since 1946 (3 overall wins, 1 line honours)
- Jim Dunstan (NSW) – 26 since 1972 (1 overall win)
- Michael Formosa (NSW) – 26 since 1981
- Peter Hopkins (TAS) – 26 since 1982
- Colin O'Connor – 26 since 1974
- Darren Senogles (NSW) – 26 since 1987 (2 overall wins, 2 line honours)
- Grant Wharrington (VIC) – 26 since 1982 (1 line honours)
- Bill Watson (TAS, dec) – 26 since 1973 (3 line honours)
- John Williams – 26 since 1975
- Jeremy Rae – 26 since 1992 (1 overall win, 1 line honours)
- Graeme Ainley – 25 since 1975
- Bill Riley (NSW) – 25 since 1976
- Russell Evans (VIC, dec) – 25 since 1958
- Toby Richardson (TAS) – 25 since 1973 (3 overall wins, 3 line honours)

- Ian Treharne (NSW) – 25 since 1967
- Tony Poole (NSW) – 25 since 1977
- Hugh O'Neill (NSW) – 25 since 1981
- George Snow (NSW) – 25 since 1975 (1 overall win, 2 line honours)
- John Walker (NSW, dec) – 25 since 1981
- Robert Green (VIC) – 25 since 1965
- Jim Holley (NSW, dec) – 25 since 1986
- Hugo van Kretschmar (NSW) – 25 since 1976 (3 line honours)
- Iain Murray (NSW) – 25 since 1977 (3 overall wins, 9 line honours)
- John Whitfeld – 25 since 1990 (1 overall win)
- Jim Nixon – 25 since 1992
- Sam Hunt (NSW) – 25 since 1993 (2 overall wins, 1 line honours)

Leading Yachtswomen

Yachtswomen have been sailing in the Sydney Hobart since the very early days of the bluewater classic, with one (Adrienne Cahalan) already past the 25 race milestone.

Eighteen women have competed in 10 or more, but fewer than 25, races:

- Felicity Nelson (NSW) – 23 since 1987
- Vanessa Dudley (NSW) – 23 since 1984
- Gail Harland (NSW) – 22 since 1990 (1 overall win)
- Mary Holley (NSW) – 16 since 1997
- Sue Crafer (NSW) – 16 since 1990
- Sally Gordon (NSW, dec) – 15 since 1994 (1 overall win)
- Jan Howard (NSW) – 14 since 1978
- Louise Stevenson (NSW) – 13 since 1994
- Annie Lawrence – 13 since 2005
- Amanda Wilmot (NSW) – 12 since 1987
- Audrey Brown (NSW) – 12 since 1987
- Julie Hodder (NSW) – 12 since 1984
- Wendy Tuck (NSW) – 12 since 2006
- Stacey Jackson – 12 since 2001 (1 line honours)
- Cathy Josling (NSW) – 11 since 1992
- Dinah Eagle (NSW) – 11 since 2002
- Lee Meyer (NSW) – 10 since 1992
- Kerry Goudge (NSW) – 10 since 1985

AUTHOR'S NOTE

'Oh how mighty oaks from little acorns grow' – or more fittingly, 'Oh how from a casual dinner and drinks does a mighty sporting icon grow'.

The casual get-together happened in Sydney in 1945, and today, 75-years on, we are celebrating the outcome of that gathering – a nationally and internationally acclaimed annual event, the Sydney Hobart Yacht Race.

Ironically, when the guests were welcomed to the dinner that evening, no thought had been given to racing yachts offshore. After all, the host organisation, the Cruising Yacht Club of Australia, had been formed only months earlier by a small group of sailing enthusiasts whose primary interest was coastal cruising in company.

It took only a few fateful words from an Englishman to change all that.

Six months later, what was originally planned to be a cruise south from Sydney by two yachts with family and friends as crew, burst into the public domain via media interest. In December 1945 the acorn of an idea for a cruise became the root for the mighty Sydney Hobart Yacht Race.

It is no doubt because of my family's maritime heritage that I still vividly remember when, in the early 1950s, my father pointed out to me a photograph published in Sydney's *Daily Telegraph* of the start of the Hobart race the previous day. It showed the large, leading yachts rounding South Head, at the entrance to Sydney Harbour, ploughing their way towards the open sea.

It must have excited me as, soon after, I was making my own backyard sailboat out of wooden packing cases, a broomstick and one of my mother's old curtains. My crew were my two brothers, Dennis and Bruce, and the family cat, and we 'sailed the world' together.

Years later, when I left school as a 16-year-old competitive sailor and started my career in journalism as a copy/messenger boy with the *Daily Mirror* in Sydney, covering the start of the Hobart race was one of my first outdoor assignments.

Since then, the Hobart race has been in my blood. Today, decades later, I'm a 50-year member of the CYCA, I am still covering the Hobart race, and am directly associated with it as media manager for the Oatley family's supermaxi, *Wild Oats XI*.

Little wonder then, after having written thousands of words on the Hobart race and done countless hours of television coverage, I jumped at the opportunity to be the author of the official CYCA book celebrating the remarkable 75-year history of the Hobart classic.

This is my eighteenth book and of all of them, it has been one of the most challenging, due to the extraordinary number of yachts and sailors that collectively have forged the classic's illustrious and lengthy history. To this end, I am indebted to the following for their assistance:

- CYCA Commodore Paul Billingham and his Board members:
- Vice Commodore – Noel Cornish
- Rear Commodore – Janey Treleaven
- Rear Commodore – Dr Sam Haynes
- Treasurer – Arthur Lane

- Directors – Leander Klohs, Justin Atkinson, David Jacobs, Bradshaw Kellett
- Chief Executive Officer - Eddie Moore
- CYCA archivist/historian, Bradshaw Kellett
- CYCA long-time members, Peter Shipway, David Kellett and Tony Cable for proofreading and research assistance
- CYCA staff
- Australian National Maritime Museum – in particular, David Payne
- Carl Ryves
- Kay Cottee AO
- Duncan van Woerden (dec'd)
- Bill Barry-Cotter
- Journalists: Bob Fisher (UK), Malcolm McKeag (UK), Bob Ross (Aust), Peter Campbell (Aust)
- Ant Crichton-Brown (UK), Harold Cudmore (UK), Bruce Mundle (USA), Butch Dalrymple-Smith (France), Campbell R Middleton (Aust)

My research material included:

- Alan Payne's biography – by Adrian Herbert. Published in *Wooden Boat* magazine
- Jack Earl – *The Life and Art of a Sailor* – by Bruce Stannard (1991)
- *From Ratbags to Respectability* – a history of the Cruising Yacht Club of Australia – by David Colfelt (2008)
- *Man of Iron – Ship of Steel – the story of Vic Meyer and Solo –* by Kevin Bourke (2014)

- *The Sydney to Hobart Yacht Race* – by Michael Ludeke – 4th edition (2014)
- *Ragamuffin Man – The World of Syd Fischer* – by David Salter (2017)
- *Being with Benny* – by Bob Ross (2018)
- And, my own book, *Fatal Storm,* (1999/2008)

Additional research material was obtained via Google and Wikipedia.

In completing this historic undertaking I must salute the wonderfully professional crew of dedicated book-lovers at the ABC Books division of HarperCollins Publishers. In particular, I must again thank my always enthusiastic and encouraging publisher, Helen Littleton, who has been an inspiration and a rudder for the majority of books I have written relating to Australian maritime history. Special mention must also be made of copy editor, Mark Evans, who did a superb job within a very tight timeframe; and senior editor, Lachlan McLaine, who was a calm and solid guiding light; and the designer of the impressive cover Mark Campbell. Not to be forgotten are the sales and publicity teams at HCP, and the hard-working typesetter, Graeme Jones, who has set all my maritime history books.

Beyond the publishing house, I must also thank the booksellers who have been wonderfully supportive of my books for many years. On a personal note, my grateful thanks goes again to my wonderful PA, Liz Christmas, who has been ever reliable and a tower of strength for twelve of my eighteen books. She is always 'on deck' when needed.

Most importantly, I must salute my first mate and partner, Chrissie Power, who has stood by me throughout this very demanding project and always come up smiling.

Finally, there is my ever expanding national and international crew – my readers – whom I must recognise and thank for their loyalty and encouragement.

Once again, I have been left in no doubt that while writing is often a solo profession, with such a crew around me I am never alone.

Thank you all

Rob Mundle